# THE WISE MEN

## *of the* WEST

# VOLUME II: THE EAST

VOLUME II: THE EAST

# THE
# WISE MEN
*of the* WEST

*Successful*

A SEARCH FOR THE PROMISED ONE

IN THE LATTER DAYS

*a novel by*

## JAY TYSON

ISBN 13: 978-1-7324511-7-9

Library of Congress Control Number: 2020935116

Printed in the United States of America
Second Printing: 2021
18 17 16 15 14          5 4 3 2 1
Edited by Mark Heinz
Illustrations by Heather Bousquet
Cover and Interior design by Glen Edelstein

SOMETHING
OR **OTHER**
PUBLISHING

Info@SOOPLLC.com
For bulk orders, e-mail: Orders@SOOPLLC.com

*If in the uttermost corners of the East*
*the sweet savors of God be wafted,*
*he will assuredly recognize*
*and inhale their fragrance,*
*even though he be dwelling*
*in the uttermost ends of the West.*

From "Tablet of a True Seeker" in *The Book of Certitude*

*On this journey the traveler abideth in every land*
*and dwelleth in every region.*
*In every face, he seeketh the beauty of the Friend;*
*in every country he looketh for the Beloved.*
*He joineth every company,*
*and seeketh fellowship with every soul,*
*that haply in some mind he may uncover the secret of the Friend,*
*or in some face he may behold the beauty of the Loved One.*

From "The Valley of Search," the first of *The Seven Valleys*

To everyone who has humbly hoped to see,
or prayed to witness,
the coming of the Promised One
and to those who have longed to be
among the first generation of His followers
this book is dedicated.

## A NOTE OF CAUTION:
## PLEASE READ "VOLUME I: THE WEST" FIRST

MOST READERS OF THIS current volume will have already read Volume I. For anyone else, who might be inclined to start with Volume II, the author highly recommends you instead begin by reading Volume I.

As noted in the introduction to that volume, this story is more than a novel. It is a spiritual exploration, and explorations are perilous. So, like all good explorers, we must choose our route carefully. Lessons learned at the early stages of this journey become vital foundations and sure footholds, enabling us to continue the journey and understand further lessons at its later stages.

A long journey gives travelers the benefit of time to think and reflect on what they have learned so far, before moving on to the next challenge.

So read and reflect on Volume I first. Then return to this volume, well-prepared for further spiritual adventures.

There are no shortcuts.

# Contents

## VOLUME II: THE EAST

# CONTENTS

# MAP

# A Few Notes for the Reader

OCCASIONAL NOTES OF GENERAL INTEREST have been added at the bottom of the page on which they occur. Additionally, for those readers interested in a more complete understanding of the historical facts upon which the story is based, please note that when the names of historical events or people first appear in the text, I have placed these names in italics. Details about them can usually be found in an online encyclopedia under the name thus provided. In cases where further sources of information might be helpful, I have provided an endnote leading to additional information and a bibliography at the back of the book. As to the cities, towns, and historic places mentioned, all of them are real, although a few might have changed names since 1843. The map provided at the beginning of Chapter 1 will help the reader follow along.

Quotations from the Bible are taken almost entirely from the King James Version; direct quotes from Scripture are in italics. This was, by far, the most widely accepted English version of the Bible in the 1840s and remains one of the most widely used. In addition, when referring to a specific biblical quote, the narrative often provides only the chapter, not the verse. Anyone who is inclined to look up the quote is thereby encouraged to read the whole chapter and thus to understand the quote in greater context.

Similarly, quotes from the Quran, also in italics, are generally taken from George Sale's version, translated in 1734. This was the first version to be translated directly from the Arabic into English and one of only two English versions available in the 1840s. It remains one of the few versions that attempt to translate every word into English rather that leaving several transliterated Arabic words in place. It also provides a wealth of explanatory notes helpful to the Western reader.

I have striven to the best of my ability to provide an accurate description of the times, places, and people. I trust that the scholar who focuses on the particular details of the history of any of these places will indulge occasional inaccuracies I might have inadvertently included. This is, necessarily, my own individual understanding of history. As such, it can never be authoritative nor is it intended to be. Although many of the ideas are rooted in the teachings of the Baha'i Faith, some of my own extrapolations may also be found. I hope the reader will take all of them as an opportunity for reflection and discussion, and as a doorway to a more detailed study of the history of these times, rather than as an end in themselves.

Many first names in the Middle Eastern world are simply Arabic versions of biblical names. Where this occurs, I have typically added the Western version in parentheses upon the introduction of the character to assist the Western reader.

The reader will note that I have adopted the convention that pronouns that refer to any of the Messengers of God will normally be capitalized out of respect and also as a way to distinguish references to Him from references to others. Two exceptions to this rule are noted: (a) pronouns among the words or thoughts of someone who does not recognize the validity of the Messenger are not capitalized and (b) when discussing the messenger in relation to God, his pronouns are not capitalized as he exists in the state of utmost humility in that relationship.

As in most historical fiction, I have refrained wherever possible from introducing direct interactions between historical characters and fictional characters. In the few instances where this necessarily occurs, I have made every effort to keep these interactions as historically plausible as possible.

# List of Fictional Characters

| | Name | Relationship/Role | 1st Ref |
|---|---|---|---|
| 1 | Zach Thompson | Main character—a true seeker | Introduction |
| 2 | Gabriel Robinson | Nephew of Zach | Chapter 14 |
| 3 | Sarah Thompson Robinson | Sister of Zach/Mother of Gabriel | Chapter 14 |
| 4 | Isaiah Robinson | Husband of Sarah/Father of Gabriel | Chapter 14 |
| 5 | Josiah Thompson | Father of Zach | Chapter 7 |
| 6 | Daniel Thompson | Brother of Zach | Chapter 14 |
| 7 | Clara Thompson | Wife of Daniel | Chapter 14 |
| 8 | Jeremy | Zach's assistant & traveling companion | Chapter 7 |
| 9 | Elijah Goodman | A follower of William Miller in England | Chapter 7 |
| 10 | James Lawrence | Orientalist, traveling companion | Introduction |
| 11 | Father Timothy | Catholic Priest | Chapter 12 |
| 12 | Shaykh Hakim | Muslim Shaykh from Akka | Chapter 2 |
| | James Lawrence | Orientalist & traveling companion | Chapter 7 |
| 13 | Siyyid Youssef | Traveling companion — Akka to Jerusalem to Tiberias | Chapter 1 |
| 14 | Moshe | Jewish keeper of the Cave of Elijah | Chapter 11 |
| 15 | Suleiman | Host in Jerusalem | Chapter 2 |
| 16 | Musa | Guide —Tiberias to Karbila | Chapter 1 |
| 17 | Da'ud | Kelek captain on the Euphrates | Chapter 2 |
| 18 | Ayyub | Guide going into Karbila | Chapter 3 |

| 19 | Hasan | Traveling companion—Karbila to Persia | Chapter 3 |
|----|-------|----------------------------------------|-----------|
| 20 | Arjan Singh | Sikh traveler on the Silk Road | Chapter 4 |
| 21 | Shapur | Zoroastrian traveler to Saveh | Chapter 5 |
| 22 | Ardeshir | Zoroastrian elder in Saveh | Chapter 5 |
| 23 | Mustafa | A follower of Shaykh Ahmad, who has heard of a child with innate knowledge | Chapter 8 |
| 24 | Hajji Yacob | Owner of inn in Mohammerah | Chapter 8 |
| 25 | Jibril | Bookkeeper at inn in Basra | Chapter 10 |
| 26 | Harun | Friend of Hasan's in Najaf | Chapter 10 |
| 27 | Harold Matthews | Caretaker of James's home in London | Chapter 12 |

Historic (non-fictional) characters: There are many figures from the nineteenth century (or earlier) who appear in the book. They are introduced in *italics* in the text to distinguish them from the fictional characters listed above.

# THE WISE MEN

## *of the* WEST

### VOLUME II: THE EAST

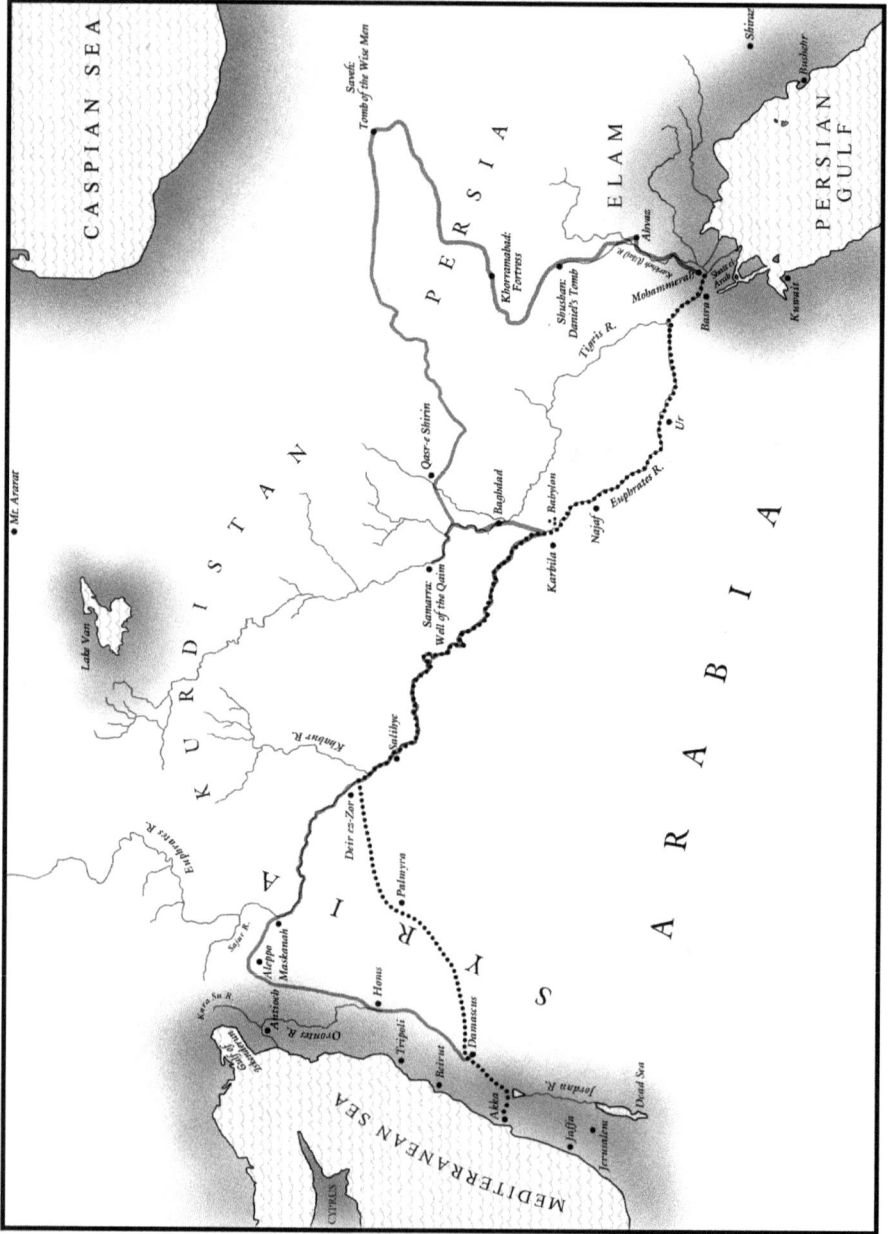

The Journey to the East

# Introduction

ZACH THOMPSON'S STEADFAST BELIEF that Christ would return in 1844, inspired as it was by Adventist *William Miller's* teachings—together with his late father's dying wish that Zach should travel to the Holy Land, seeking reports of a Child with innate knowledge—had led him to start this search, as described in the previous volume. Along the way, he found James Lawrence of London, who shared his understanding and whose familiarity with Arabic and life in the Holy Land made him an invaluable traveling companion. But two months of searching through the lands where Jesus had lived failed to turn up any signs of the One they sought.

Nevertheless, they discovered two critical things: firstly that Christians were not the only ones expecting a Promised One. Thousands of Jewish people from communities around the world had already migrated to the Holy Land during the previous three decades in expectation of their Messiah. This had been sparked not only by the frequent Old Testament references to the return of the Jewish people to the Holy Land but more specifically by a prophecy that the "gates of wisdom on high and the wellsprings of lower wisdom" would start to open in the Jewish year 5600 (1839–40 AD), as indicated in passages of the Jewish mystical book, the Zohar. Beyond this, and contrary to all of Zach's expectations, they were amazed to learn that the Shiite Muslims were also expecting their Promised One to return in the Muslim year 1260 AH, which was exactly the same as the year 1844 AD. Although the Shiite Muslims had arrived at this date by an entirely different means from what is found in both the Book of Daniel and the Book of Revelation, Zach was astounded by this connection, linking Islam directly to the mysterious references to "1260" in two of the most prophetic books in the Bible.

Secondly, they discovered several indications from Christian, Jewish, and Muslim sources that all pointed their attention to the East and, in several cases, specifically to the land of Persia. So now, their immediate goal was to find the great teacher of Islamic expectations, Siyyid Kazim, who had reached many of the same conclusions that Zach and James had reached concerning the nature of the Promised One's appearance. He was apparently teaching in Karbila, a Shiite holy city on the lower reaches of the Euphrates River, not far from Persia.

Near the shores of the Sea of Galilee, they had met Musa, a trustworthy Shiite with an interest in Siyyid Kazim's teachings, who had agreed to serve as a guide in their travels beyond the Holy Land.

# Chapter 1

# TOWARD ALEPPO AND
# THE EUPHRATES

THE JOURNEY FROM DAMASCUS would be first northwest and upward to reach the Bekaa Valley and then northeast along the valley through Baalbek to reach Homs and Aleppo. The western bend of the Euphrates River was just two days' journey east of Aleppo.

On the first day, as the caravan was following a river up the Wadi Barada, cutting through the hills, Zach found himself pondering an earlier question regarding how God's Messengers could be different and yet, in some sense, all be a single Messenger. He asked Musa what he thought about this.

Musa responded, "Sometimes a thing may appear in two different ways, depending on your perspective." When Zach inquired further, Musa said he would show him when the caravan stopped for a break.

At the midday stop, they asked James to watch and water the animals while Zach and Musa retired to a quiet place further upstream. Musa spread two prayer rugs in the shade of a tree and invited Zach to join him in midday prayers.

After the prayers, Musa offered his thoughts. "Let us consider the dawn," he started. "If I were to ask you whether it is an event or an eternal condition, what would you say?"

"Why, it is an event of course," responded Zach. "We witness the event every morning."

"That is undeniably true," Musa replied. "But close your eyes for a moment to help us consider this truth from another perspective."

3

Zach complied.

"Imagine yourself rising above the earth, as high as the eagles fly," he said slowly. "Now imagine yourself even higher, above the highest of the clouds."

The air seemed to be cooler as Zach imagined himself at that height.

"Now imagine yourself high above the clouds so that the horizon of the earth is no longer a straight line but the curve of a very large circle.... And now...imagine yourself so high up that you can see the entire globe in one glance.... And finally, imagine that the earth is so far away that it looks no bigger than your fist at arm's length."

Zach had never thought like this before. He felt immensely distant from home.

Musa continued, "Can you see the sun at your right?"

"Yes."

"And the earth at your left? And do you see the earth, mostly illumined by the sun but partly in its own shadow?"

"Yes, of course."

"And the earth is slowly turning so that the part of the dark side you see is moving into the light?" Zach nodded. Musa continued, "So where is the dawn?

"Well, I suppose that the dawn is that half-circle line," replied Zach, "where the dark side is moving into the light. And the other half of the circle—where the light side is moving into darkness—that is the dusk."

"True indeed. And how long have they existed—the light side of the earth, the dark side, and the half-circle lines in between them?"

"Why, they have existed ever since the day that God created the sun and the earth!" replied Zach.

"So, from your *current* perspective, dawn is not an event but rather it is a continuous condition that will exist as long as the sun shines and the earth exists."

"Why, yes! This is true!" Zach was pleased to learn this point.

"And in this realm," Musa asked, "is there yesterday, today, and tomorrow?"

Zach felt a sense of constancy realizing that the shining sun and the spinning earth seemed to be continuing in their own ways indefinitely. "From here," he said, "one's sense of time in entirely different."

"Well said," replied Musa. "Now that you have learned this, you can come home."

Zach felt himself landing on the earth almost with a thud as he opened his eyes. "I can see what you mean now when you say that reality can appear quite differently depending on one's perspective. I'll be careful not to insist that my own perspective on reality is necessarily the only one possible.

"Now I think I understand how the appearance of God's Messenger is, on the one hand, a historical event with the particulars of time and place, much like the appearance of dawn from where I stand on the earth. But there is an aspect of His appearance that is unchanging and eternal so that we can truly say that there is only one Messenger of God, although He has appeared in many separate places and was given a different name each time."

Musa smiled. "Now you are beginning to understand. Perchance this may aid you when you go to explain some of the Holy Writings, which are written from the eternal perspective."

Zach pondered the implications of that understanding for the rest of the day as they rode on.

*       *       *

THE EVENING FIRE FELT good in the chilly air of late November at this elevation. But the cooler weather made the daytime journey pleasant as they moved northeast along the inter-mountain valley of Al Zabadani. They then descended via another wadi to the Bekaa Valley—essentially an upper extension of the Jordan Valley. From here, the road would remain nearly level all the way to Homs and Aleppo.

As they traveled northward out of Baalbek, Zach mentioned that he had been reading some of the Quran during their evening caravanserai rests, but he found it a little difficult to follow.

"That's because you are used to the Bible," James ventured, "especially the New Testament, in which so many of the teachings of Jesus are embedded in the story of His travels and the people whom He meets. The Quran, on the other hand, is purely God's revelation to Muhammad. The chapters

5

are not in chronological order, but rather, they are in order by length, from longest to shortest, similar to the order of the letters of Paul in the Bible."

"Perhaps," Musa added, "you need to know a bit more about the story of Muhammad's life to understand the context of the various chapters."

Zach agreed that this would be helpful, so Musa commenced a long explanation.

He started at the beginning, with Abraham and His first son, Ishmael. Zach knew the story from Genesis of how Abraham had sent Ishmael and his mother, Hagar, into the wilderness due to the jealousy of Sarah, Abraham's wife. "I remember how God protected them by showing Hagar a well when their water had run out and how Ishmael eventually grew up in Paran, south of the Holy Land, married, and had twelve sons."[1]

James added, "During our travels with Youssef, we learned how Paran was the old name for the western part of Arabia."

"Exactly," replied Musa, "and the well that God showed them is known as the well of Zamzam.

"Later, Abraham came to visit and, with Ishmael, built the House of God there in the shape of a cube, which is the *Kaaba*, toward which we all face in prayer even today. He commanded the people to make a pilgrimage to it. The oasis of Mecca grew up around it, and the people—descendants of Ishmael—believed in one God, just as his father, Abraham, had taught. Even the descendants of Isaac would occasionally visit.

"But alas, over the generations, other influences came in, and the people lost their understanding of the importance of worshipping the one true God. The pilgrimage had become a cause of much commerce. Perhaps some felt that allowing the inclusion of various idols from other groups would increase the size of the pilgrimage and help their businesses flourish. In any case, the central role of adherence to God's teachings was displaced by other interests. Thus, part of Muhammad's mission was to cleanse this sanctuary, even as Jesus had done in Jerusalem."

"An interesting comparison," Zach noted. "Now when I read the chapter entitled 'Pilgrimage,' I'll understand it better."

Musa continued with some background on the birth of Muhammad—how His father had died before He was born and thus He was raised by

His mother and an uncle. "He was well known for His wisdom and justice in resolving disputes. He married Khadijah, an established businesswoman several years older than He. He, too, worked in the caravan trade, leading caravans up and down the Hejaz. He also liked to spend time in a cave in nearby Mount Hira, outside of Mecca, to pray and meditate.

"Although several people noticed signs that there was something special about Him, the revelations did not begin until His fortieth year. When the angel Gabriel first appeared to Him, He was terrified. He came home and hid Himself, thinking perhaps that He was going mad."

"Interesting," said Zach to James. "I've always tended to give more credence to those who do not *want* to be a prophet. Would any reasonable person seek out such a calling?" It reminded him of the reluctance that Mr. Miller had for his own assignment.

"His wife reassured Him and then went to tell her cousin, Waraka. Although old and blind, he recognized immediately that Muhammad was the One who had been foretold. She brought this encouraging news back to Him. Together, she and Waraka were the first to believe in His message. Gradually, as the revelations became more regular," Musa continued, "He came to accept the idea, although the experience of revelation was always very draining."

"Yes," James recalled, "Youssef taught us about Waraka as one who recognized Muhammad early on as a result of Christian prophecies."

"Indeed. The Prophet had some early success in attracting followers. But this also attracted early resistance and persecution from those who felt threatened by His teaching that the idols were powerless.

"For twelve years, the revelations continued, and the numbers of His followers gradually grew. Most of the chapters of the Quran were revealed during this period, but many of the longer ones were revealed after Muhammad and His followers were forced to flee Mecca. So if you wish to read the earliest part of the revelation first, start with the shorter chapters, which are at the end.

"During these years, the resistance and threats also grew. Muhammad's followers tended to be the simpler people, while those who threatened them were often the wealthy and powerful clan chiefs. Initially, they would not dare to attack Muhammad directly, for He was protected by His uncle, who was one of the chiefs of the clan. But they showed no such restraint against many of Muhammad's followers, who did not have such family ties for protection. These chiefs feared the loss of their influence, not only among their own clans but also the loss of trade with the pilgrims, who had been coming from all over Arabia to Mecca for generations in order to worship their idols in the Kaaba.

"So as the news of His claim started to spread outward to the surrounding tribes, and as some of those people became believers, it appeared that the worst fears of His enemies were being realized. Additional persecutions followed, but Muhammad somehow knew that His followers would be welcomed by the Christian king of Abyssinia (Ethiopia). Therefore, He sent forth the first emigrants carrying Islam to the continent of Africa. And indeed, the king welcomed and protected them there.

"It was also during this period that the miracle of Muhammad's 'Night Journey' to Jerusalem and to heaven and back took place."

"Yes, Youssef told us of that," mentioned James. "I believe there is some controversy regarding whether this physically occurred or was a spiritual vision."

"Yes indeed. It is something that I wish to hear about directly from Siyyid Kazim when we reach Karbila," said Musa.

Continuing the story, he added, "Muhammad's reputation for fairness and for justice in settling disputes eventually reached the ears of the people of the nearby town of Yathrib—later known as Medina, the City of the Prophet. These people invited Muhammad and His followers to leave Mecca and to settle in their city instead. Many of His followers did. Muhammad remained in Mecca for a little while, until a day when the angel Gabriel appeared and warned Him of how a group of people from all of the clans of Mecca was planning to kill Him that very night. He quietly slipped past them and left the city and, after taking a circuitous route, arrived two weeks later safely in Medina. Thus, the main 'emigration' was completed, and the Islamic calendar began as of that date."

"It was in 622 of the Christian Era," James added, "and from thence dates the year 1260, which begins a mere seven weeks from now," he said with a note of solemnity.

"But that doesn't add to 1844," Zach objected.

"Remember," James explained, "it is a lunar calendar, which has shorter years. It takes 103 lunar years to make 100 solar years. So you'd have to subtract..." he paused to do a quick calculation, "38 of the 1260 lunar years, making 1,222 solar years. Add that to 622 AD and you arrive at next year's date in the West—1844."

Musa resumed, "The people of Medina accepted Muhammad's claim to Prophethood, and they became known as 'the Helpers.' Together with 'the Emigrants' or 'the Companions' from Mecca, they formed the first community of Islam and applied the laws that Muhammad had revealed to guide the life of their community. Prior to this, the Prophet had been the spiritual guide and teacher to a group of followers, much like Jesus. But although God taught us much about *personal sacrifice* through the sacrifice of Jesus at that time, He also taught us much by enabling Muhammad to live and to become both an effective *governor* of a city and its *chief protector*, with all the duties these tasks entailed.

"Constructive as this period was, all knew that the leaders of Mecca still despised them and saw them as a threat that should be uprooted while they were still few in number. Fighting between the various tribes and towns was commonplace in those days. Meccan raiders stole cattle and camels from the people of Medina, further aggravating the losses of property the Companions previously suffered when forced to leave Mecca. Scouting parties kept a watchful eye on the developments of the neighboring tribes and occasionally clashed. One such clash resulted in the death of a Meccan. Some of the Meccans, looking for any excuse to raise a cry for assembling an army against the people of Medina, used the news of this loss to their advantage.

"Muhammad sought a peaceful solution, but the Meccans outnumbered their opponents three to one, and they were better equipped. They saw this as an opportunity to eliminate Muhammad and his band of followers once and for all, so their leaders were in no mood for peace when their forces met at the wells of *Badr*. However, God guided Muhammad and His followers in the battle, and when it ended, they had lost only 14 men, while the Meccans had lost five times as many, including some of the most outspoken opponents of Muhammad, with even more taken as prisoners. The Meccans were stunned.

"News of the victory convinced some of the towns along the Red Sea route to ally themselves with Muhammad. This further threatened the trade routes for the Meccans, who now had to find longer, more difficult alternatives. Within two years, Meccan animosity had again built up, and they assembled a much larger force. Although the ranks of Muhammad's followers had also grown, when the *Battle of Uhud* loomed, they were outnumbered seven to one. Muhammad strategically placed His men for the battle, and He instructed those who would control critical positions not to leave their posts under any condition. At first, the battle seemed to be going in Muhammad's favor. But some of His followers, forgetting His instructions, left their posts in order to collect some of the spoils. The resulting hole in their defenses was exploited by the Meccans, which resulted in a reversal for Muhammad and His followers—and the learning of a critical lesson about the importance of following *exactly* what the Prophet asks His followers to do. In the confusion of battle, some of the Meccans thought Muhammad had been killed. Although the Meccans killed a tenth of Muhammad's followers, it was not a complete rout, and both groups returned to their respective cities.

"The third of the three main battles with the Meccans was known as the *'Battle of the Trench.'* Yet it was hardly a battle at all. After another two years, the Meccans, this time encouraged by some of the Jewish leaders, made agreements with several of the surrounding tribes to unite to defeat Muhammad. Together, they assembled a force of over 10,000 men—far superior to the forces of Medina. But now, a new strategy for defense was suggested by Salman the Persian."

"Oh yes," recalled Zach, "Youssef spoke of him. He was the Zoroastrian-Christian who followed Christian prophecies to find Muhammad."

"Exactly so," replied Musa, "and Salman described a defensive measure that he knew from his homeland—digging a trench that neither the camels nor the horses could easily cross. Nor could they afford to stop near it, for they would be in easy range of the archers on the other side. Muhammad adopted this approach, and the trench, protecting Medina's exposed northern side, was completed shortly before the massive army arrived outside of the city. The Meccans had never seen such a defense, and while they spent days arguing about how to overcome it, the supplies of this large army dwindled. After two weeks, it was clear that the large numbers of men and animals remaining in one place could be as much of a hindrance as an asset. The stand-off continued with no serious fighting as several days of cold, wet weather made conditions in the camp of the besieging Meccans even worse. Then a violent storm came up with winds so severe as to blow down every tent and extinguish every fire. The besiegers, hungry and cold, gave up and returned to the towns from which they had come.

"In the course of these events, one of the Jewish tribes of the area, which had sworn a covenant of mutual protection with Muhammad, treacherously violated its covenant, thereby exposing the entire community of Medina to attack from the south. This was the third such tribe of the Jews to violate their pact. The punishment of exile for the first two tribes was apparently too merciful as it failed to dissuade the third tribe from such treachery. The men of this tribe understood that justice in the violation of their oath called for their deaths. After the conclusion of the Battle of the Trench, the Prophet directed His forces southward to surround the traitors. He appointed an arbitrator from a neighboring tribe, who heard the case and, following the Jewish law, pronounced a verdict. Recognizing their own guilt in this matter, the men accepted their execution without a fight."[2]

"My goodness!" exclaimed Zach. "This sounds more like some of the stories from the Old Testament."

Musa replied, "In some regards, the conditions in those days were more similar to the conditions during Old Testament times than they were to the time of Jesus.

"But the outcome of all of this is that the Meccans never again tried attacking Muhammad. Other tribes tried, but it always ended in defeat for them and the enlargement of the dominion of Islam. The Muslims saw the hand of God helping them, and the Prophet's description of the reality of the next world gave His followers the assurance of a wonderful future, whether they lived or died on the battlefield.

"The following year, Muhammad had a dream that inspired Him to travel to Mecca as a pilgrim. He traveled with 1,600 other unarmed men, dressed in pilgrim's garb. The Meccans, fearing that He had other intentions, blocked His entry into the city. After much discussion between the two sides, the truce of *Hudaybiyah* resulted, which postponed the pilgrimage for a year, permitted Meccans to become Muslims without fear of reprisals, and initiated a pact in which both sides agreed to refrain from attacks for ten years. Although His followers felt humbled by having to return to Medina without having completed their pilgrimage, the Quran called it a 'conspicuous victory,' and indeed, it turned out to be so. From that date, Islam was firmly established. There would be no turning back."

"Yes," replied James, "I recall hearing of the importance of that date—628 in our calendar—when I was in Egypt. It seemed to be an acknowledgement by the Meccans, the largest force in the area, that Muhammad and His teachings were here to stay."

"Affairs remained peaceful between Mecca and Medina for the next two years while a small community of believers in Mecca started to grow. Muhammad and 2,000 followers came from Medina on pilgrimage at the end of the first year as planned and without incident. But by the end of the second year, some of the Meccans became angry and arose to kill twenty of the Muslims—a clear violation of the truce that could not be ignored. Therefore, Muhammad assembled His followers to march on Mecca. As they did, several of the Bedouin tribes, which had come to support Muhammad, joined in the march so that by the time He reached Mecca, this army numbered more than 10,000.

"As they encamped in the hills outside of Mecca, Muhammad asked them to spread out and each to light a campfire. The size of the army, clearly visible at night for all the Meccans to see, must have struck fear in their hearts because they did not make any attempt on the following day to resist His entrance into the city. Though they feared a slaughter, the Prophet stopped to thank God for the bloodless victory they had been given. He did not destroy the people of Mecca, nor force any conversions, nor plunder the city, but He did go to the Kaaba to destroy all 360 of the idols there. His example of showing forgiveness and forbearance to a surrendered city would set a pattern that served His followers well during the centuries of Islamic expansion that followed.

"A few other tribes attempted attacks in these latter years, but none had sufficient strength or success to overcome Muhammad's forces. As more and more people recognized the truth of the Prophet, their historic allegiance to family and clan gave way to a wider allegiance—an allegiance to the one God and to the teachings of His most recent Prophet."

"That is an amazing story of triumph against overwhelming odds," said Zach.

"Surely God tipped the balance in favor of Muhammad," replied Musa. "As the news spread, more and more of the Arabian tribes sent representatives to either announce their allegiance to the new Prophet or at least to investigate His claims, which invariably led to their acceptance.

"The Prophet led one final expedition north into a territory of Christian tribes in Tabuk. Again the city accepted His leadership without a battle. Some became followers. Those who chose to remain Christians or Jews were only required to pay a modest tax for the protective service that Islam provided. Thus, again, the Prophet set an example that was followed for centuries, allowing for the expansion of the domain of Islam without any forced conversions.

"After a final pilgrimage to Mecca, Muhammad's spirit returned to the realm of God," Musa concluded.

Zach and James continued learning more details about the life of Muhammad until at length they reached the city of Homs, where the caravan rested for a few days of trade.

\*     \*     \*

AS THEY DEPARTED FROM Homs the following morning, Musa had more to add.

"I realized last night that my story of the beginnings of Islam, focused as it was on the trials and successes of Muhammad and His community, failed to include a larger dimension of its success."

"And what would that be?" asked James.

"That would include the story of His outreach to the wider world for He contacted the rulers of His day, and they responded in various ways."

"Yes, I recall Youssef mentioning that," said Zach, "but tell us the details."

"The first was the *Najashi*, the righteous leader of the Christian kingdom of Ethiopia. As I mentioned yesterday, a few years before His main group moved to Medina, the Prophet sent a group of His followers to the king there. They were welcomed, and when some of His enemies pursued the group and tried to dissuade the king from accepting them, he inquired about what the Quran stated regarding Jesus. He was quite impressed with its parallels to Christian belief. Thus he defended the Muslim community and sent their enemies away empty-handed. Although he did not become a Muslim, friendly relations with the Muslim community were established.

"During the Medina period, Muhammad sent a message to the *Muqawqis*, the Christian vicegerent of Egypt in Alexandria. The Muqawqis acknowledged that a Prophet was expected but said he thought that He was to arise in Syria. Nevertheless, he responded respectfully and sent the Prophet several gifts, including two female servants, one of whom, *Mariah* (Mary), the Prophet married as a way of cementing a strong bond between their families. A decade later, when the Islamic army reached Alexandria, internal conflict between the various Christian groups there, together with the good relations that Muhammad had previously established, induced the Muqawqis at that time to accept Islamic rulership without a fight."

"Yes," noted James, "I've heard that it was common practice in those days for leaders to accept women from other leaders as wives in order to cement the bonds between the leaders."

"This is true," replied Musa, "and Muhammad was no exception in that regard. In the latter part of His earthly life, after His first wife, Khadija, had passed away and He became the governor of Medina, He took additional wives under His care. In almost all cases, these were either women who served as a marriage bond with other communities or they were widows of martyrs from the battles. The only exception was when Abu Bakr, one of His strongest supporters, gave his young daughter in marriage to Muhammad.* He provided care and sustenance to them all.

"But to return to the story of His contacts with surrounding kingdoms," Musa continued, "the Prophet also dictated a letter to the governor of

---

* Being a part of Muhammad's family from a young age, she lived long after the original generation had passed away. Thus she was able to provide firsthand memories and valuable guidance to the evolving Islamic community during most of its formative years.

Bahrain, *Munzir, son of Sawa Al Tamimi*, who ruled over much of the eastern side of Arabia, on behalf of the Sasanian empire in Persia. He responded in the affirmative, thus bringing a large area of Arabia peacefully into the Islamic fold.

"He also sent a letter to *Heraclius*, the emperor of Byzantium."

"Ah yes," added James, "Heraclius—emperor of the new Rome, or Rum as some call it, for the last emperor of the old Rome in the West had died in 476. The unity of Western Europe was shattered and still remains shattered to this day. Byzantium in the east, on the other hand, had become the main Christian civilization."

"True," replied Musa, "but the emperor had nearly exhausted himself and his forces in two decades of war with the Persian Zoroastrians just prior to Muhammad's arrival. Then something most remarkable occurred in this very city of Homs during those days, which came to my mind as we rested there last night."

"And what was that?" Zach inquired.

"While Heraclius was visiting Jerusalem after his forces had taken it back from the Persians, he had a vivid dream that indicated that the period of Byzantine sovereignty over the Holy Land and Syria would soon give way to 'the victorious kingdom of a circumcised man.' In the morning, he started to make inquiries due to the dream. This led to his learning through a Bedouin from Arabia of the appearance of the new Prophet. He was amazed to discover that these Arabs had retained the practice of circumcision from the time of Abraham. It was shortly thereafter that he received a letter from the Prophet that confirmed even more what he had come to believe. To make sure, he summarized all that he had learned and sent it to his wisest adviser in Constantinople, who replied, 'He is the Prophet whom we expect. There is no doubt of it. Therefore, follow Him and believe in Him.'[3]

"Heraclius received that reply while he was right here in Homs. He invited all of the chief Byzantines of the city to gather in a room of his palace and asked them to pledge allegiance to the new Prophet. They all refused. Seeing their refusal and knowing that forcing them was useless, he made light of his earlier statement, claiming he was just testing their faith."

15

"That is indeed an amazing story," offered James. "I have not come across it in any Western histories that I have read. But," he paused, "then again, I suppose that the Christian community would not think it worthy of recording."

"Understandable," Musa replied. "It is also said that his dream had convinced him of the folly of trying to block the expansion of Islam northward into Syria and that when he left, he looked back and said, 'O land of Syria, for the last time, I bid thee farewell.' And so it was. Within a year of his departure, the leaders of Islam had defeated the remaining Byzantine forces there and occupied the rest of Syria."

"It is impossible for me to imagine," added Zach, "how much different history might have been had those Byzantine leaders accepted Heraclius' request and had Christian civilization peacefully merged with the teachings of Muhammad."

"Perhaps God looked favorably on the openness of Heraclius," said James, "for Asia Minor remained in Byzantine hands for the next four centuries after Syria came under Muslim control, and the European parts of the Byzantine Empire continued for another four centuries beyond that."

"An interesting thought," acknowledged Musa, "especially when contrasted with the experience of the Sasanian Empire of the Zoroastrian East for the Prophet wrote to their leader too. *Khosrow II* responded arrogantly by tearing up the letter. When the Prophet heard this, He said, 'Even so, O Lord, tear from him his kingdom.'[4] Shortly thereafter, one of Khosrow's sons, *Kavadh II*, killed him and usurped the throne from his brother.

"And sure enough, disunity wracked the Sasanian leadership for several years—a disunity that provoked them to fight against the Muslim forces that arrived in Mesopotamia a few years later. In battle after battle, the Persians suffered a surprising string of defeats and retreated until the whole of the Persian Empire came under the control of Islam."

"Yes, we heard some of that story from Youssef," said Zach. "Now I understand much more about how Islam expanded rapidly to the north, to the west, and to the east of its birthplace."

"Yes, and it expanded even more quickly to the south, where Yemen was controlled by the Persian Empire. Khosrow, worried about the things he had already heard about the rise of the Prophet, instructed his viceroy there, *Badhan*, to investigate. Badhan sent emissaries to the Prophet, and they returned to Yemen with a strange message, asking the viceroy to enter Islam and noting that the angel Gabriel told Him that the king of Persia had been killed on that very day. When, shortly thereafter, a messenger arrived from the Persian capital announcing the death of Khosrow, Badhan recognized that only a true Prophet could have known this in advance, and so he gave his allegiance to Muhammad instead of to the new Persian king. Thus, Yemen became the first kingdom to enter Islam.

"So we can see that although success came in different manners, the Prophet's outreach to the southwest, west, north, east, southeast, and south laid the foundation for a vast expansion of the realm of Islam.

"But let me return to the beginning for a moment. Do you remember in the Book of Genesis, when God promised to Ishmael that He would make of him a great nation?"

"Yes," replied Zach, "chapter 17, as I recall."

"Well, when you understand that Muhammad and almost all of the early Muslims were descendants of Ishmael and how the spiritual 'nation,' which is Islam, spread over much of the known world, you come to understand just how fully God's ancient promise to Ishmael was fulfilled. Even if you think of a 'nation' as only the people who speak a single language, the Arabic nation became one of the largest ever known. Six centuries after the nation of Isaac and his descendants had been dissolved by the Romans, the nation of Ishmael and his descendants arose and became vastly larger than the nation of Isaac's descendants had ever been."

"That's another fascinating observation that I had never considered before," offered Zach. He was beginning to appreciate the new perspectives and insights that his travels afforded.

Their conversation continued over the course of the remaining days on the way to Aleppo, with Musa filling in as many of the details of Muhammad's life as he could remember. He explained that these 'hadith'—the traditional stories and sayings of Muhammad—were not direct revelation from God and therefore would not be found in the Quran itself. While many were quite believable, some were more doubtful. Musa explained that they were not written down at first but just circulated orally. Some people were prone to embellishment, and when they were finally written down a couple of centuries after Muhammad's earthly life, the chain of transmitters was also recorded in the hope of identifying those who were most likely to be accurate.

"On several occasions, particular circumstances recorded in the stories led to the revelation of specific verses of the Quran. And thus," he concluded, "it can be very helpful to understand the stories behind many of the verses of the Holy Book."

At length, they reached Aleppo, a rather desolate city that had been in both economic and physical decline for more than a century due to changes in trade, attacks from surrounding villagers, and famine. The city had lost three quarters of its population as a result of an earthquake in 1822 and cholera and plague that struck in the subsequent years. It had suffered again in 1831 when the Egyptians took over Syria and yet again in 1840 as the Ottomans took it back. Thus, the travelers found little reason to remain there, other than to restock their supplies for the upcoming journey on the Euphrates.

# Chapter 2

## LEARNING FROM A NEW HOLY BOOK ON AN ANCIENT RIVER

THE CARAVAN JOURNEY FROM Aleppo to Maskanah on the shore of the Euphrates was two days' travel over flat land, making this leg of the journey easy.

During this time, Musa recalled some of the achievements of Islamic civilization. He cited not only the gathering of all knowledge in Baghdad, as James had mentioned earlier, but advances in several particular fields.

"It was Islamic civilization," Musa noted, "that picked up the usage of ten numerals from India and carried it westward. A young man named Gerbert from France, educated in Islamic Spain, learned the advantages of this 'Arabic' numeral system. He became *Pope Sylvester II* at the end of the Christian 10th century and decreed that Arabic numerals should be used and the cumbersome system of Roman numerals should be abandoned."

"Yes," James confirmed, "Europe learned much of advanced mathematics from Islamic civilization, including what we call 'algebra,' which came from the Arabic word, 'Al-jabr.' Similarly, the ancient knowledge of chemistry was passed to the West with the Arabic name 'Al-kimiya,' which we have called 'alchemy.' Its study led to advances in medicines and the refinement of metals, porcelain, and colored glass."

Musa added, "Yes, the ability to produce glass of various colors advanced greatly during that period so that mosques could be decorated with beautiful windows."

"Indeed, our cathedrals in Europe owe a debt of thanks to the Islamic chemists who developed the techniques for making the colored glass they used," acknowledged James.

Musa resumed: "Muslims also learned the knowledge of paper-making—so essential for the recording of knowledge—from the Chinese, who had carefully guarded its secret for many centuries. Its production outside of China started in Muslim lands eleven centuries ago, greatly facilitating the collection of knowledge by the Abbasids in Baghdad, who rose to power at the same time. Paper production spread westward through the Muslim world, eventually into Muslim Spain, but it would not be produced in Christian lands for more than 400 years after the Muslims had mastered the process."

James acknowledged that this was consistent with what he had heard from other sources concerning the development of European civilization after Islamic civilization had led the way in past centuries.

A kelek on the Euphrates

As they got their first glimpse of the Euphrates, Musa explained that it would be necessary to sell their animals in town. The flow of the river was low at this time of year, and no boats large enough to carry the animals would be found. So, the following day, while James and Zach took their animals to the market for sale, Musa went in search of a boat heading all the way to Karbila. Selling the animals was not difficult, but they had to wait a few days along the shore before finding a suitable craft—a kelek.

A kelek was a small riverboat, or perhaps more accurately a kind of large raft, made of bundles of reeds from the river marshes held together with poplar planks and buoyed up with a couple hundred inflated goatskins. Zach looked at it doubtfully, especially when he realized that it had no sail and would move downriver mostly by the current, with the help of the captain and his assistant to steer the craft to the best part of the river.

After hailing a mostly empty one that was passing, Musa noticed Zach's apprehensive expression. "Don't worry," he said. "These people have been using keleks for centuries to move people and goods downstream."

After some negotiations, he introduced Zach and James to Da'ud (David), who was the owner and captain of the craft.

The kelek had a modest hut, which would be their abode for the next month. One corner of the craft had a small clay fireplace for cooking food. They settled in and were soon underway, but before long, a thought occurred to Zach.

"There are no sails on this craft and no tow paths along the riverbank, so how does a kelek get back upstream?" he asked.

"It doesn't," replied Musa calmly. "Once they reach their destination downstream, the craft is disassembled, and the pieces are sold off. The captain and the oarsman are also camel drivers, so they join a caravan for the trip home. Then they build a new kelek for their next downstream journey."

Zach mused on what seemed to him like an odd approach to shipping. But being in a foreign land, he knew that he still had much to learn. Then it occurred to him that this arrangement would affect their own travel plans: While going downstream to Karbila by riverboat would be relatively easy, the return trip would have to be overland by caravan.

It was December 24, and Zach again thought back to life in Perth Amboy, trying to imagine the Christmas preparations that must have been going on there. It all felt so very far away. Here, the river moved along slowly while much of its headwaters lay sleeping as snow in the mountains on the Anatolian plateau to the north. The river meandered greatly, and the oarsman was continually busy watching for shoals and guiding the craft toward the deepest channel. They landed their craft in the evenings, when it became too dark to see the shoals clearly, generally anchoring along mid-river islands, relatively safe from bandit tribesmen who could be lurking on the main shores.

"So this is the mighty Euphrates," said James admiringly, "backbone of the Fertile Crescent!" They looked out at the nearby fields and orchards irrigated by the river.

"It is also one of the four rivers mentioned as early as the second chapter of the Book of Genesis," Zach added, "all of which flowed out of the Garden of Eden. I must admit, though, that whenever I've looked on a map, I could not find a place from which any four rivers diverged. Rivers normally merge together on their way to the sea—they don't usually diverge."

"I have wondered about that myself," replied James. "But I've also wondered whether those were really meant to be normal rivers at all."

"How to you mean?"

"Well, rivers, particularly in this arid part of the world, are symbols of life. Wherever the freshwater is, there will be fields, orchards, gardens, animals, and people. In the same way, spiritual life is delivered by the teachings of God. These teaching emerge from a single unknown divine Source and spread out in all four directions to infuse this material world with spiritual life. We speak of Judaism, Christianity, Zoroastrianism, and now Islam. These are like four mighty rivers of life flowing into our parched world."

Musa, who had been listening, now added, "Yes, it is very much like that in the Quran. How often the Prophet describes the garden of paradise in the world of the spirit! And when He does, He almost always refers to the blessed waters flowing through this garden and giving life to it. I take these waters to mean all of the wondrous truths that enliven our souls."

"A similar scene is provided to the Christian world in the last chapter of the Bible," Zach noted.

"For my part, I am very much looking forward to some quiet time here on the boat, allowing us to study the translation of the Quran we found in Jerusalem," James said.

Life on the kelek was much easier than in the caravan as they simply floated downstream without any effort on their part. With time available to them, Zach and James started their study of the Quran, sharing in reading it aloud, aiming to cover at least 21 pages each day so they would finish it, along with the author's long introduction, by the end of their 30-day voyage.

As Musa had suggested, they decided to start with the chapters that had been revealed during the Mecca period—the earliest period of Islam, when Muhammad had a small band of followers, similar to the period of Jesus' ministry. These chapters were often shorter and dealt mostly with man's relationship with God. The later period, known as the Medina period, was one in which Muhammad was both a spiritual leader of His followers *and* a governor who was responsible for the welfare and protection of the city He had been invited to govern.

"You may find some teachings that apply to governing a whole district to be new since Jesus never lived in such circumstances," explained Musa.

As they started their reading, Zach was surprised to learn that a substantial portion of the Quran was a retelling of many of the stories in the Bible—from both the Old and New Testaments.

Zach was aware that even among Christian groups, there were some disputes about the details of some of the biblical stories, with questions of how accurately they had been conveyed and recorded in ages long ago. Muslims, on the other hand, understood the Quran to be a revelation from God via the angel Gabriel, which had been carefully preserved, word-for-word, over the last twelve-and-a-half centuries. Its words were written down by scribes shortly after they were revealed and then read back to Muhammad for Him to confirm. Thus Muslims regard its version of biblical stories as a more accurate history of the events than even the Bible itself.

James and Zach read chapters on Noah and Abraham and the story of Joseph in Egypt. There was also the story of Jonah and an entire chapter devoted to Mary. The Quran affirmed the Christian beliefs about her, recognizing that she was a virtuous woman throughout her life and a virgin at the time of Jesus' birth. One chapter was devoted to the "Family of Imran," which, though not mentioned in the Bible, was the maternal grandfather of

Jesus and great uncle of John the Baptist. The book included several stories of the members of the Holy Family. Some of the miracles attributed to Jesus seemed even more remarkable than anything that Christian leaders claimed about Him, including a quotation of the words He spoke while He was still an infant.

"'We...gave evident miracles to Jesus the son of Mary, and strengthened Him with the Holy Spirit,'[5] read Zach. "It surely does not sound like Muhammad denied the truth of Jesus."

Even in the chapters that were not named after a biblical character, they often found new stories of various figures of the Old and New Testaments, shedding interesting insights on their lives and teachings. And not only the good characters. The evils of Satan and of Gog and Magog were also clearly cited.

They noted also how dramatically the Quran warned the people of those days of the extreme perils of hell for those who refused to believe and how wondrous was the promise of heaven for those who believed and did good works, especially in chapters 55 and 56. Additional warnings were given with the force of history, particularly in chapter 11, which cited the many cases of peoples in the past, whose disobedience to the Divine command led to their destruction. James and Zach were familiar, of course, with the stories of Noah and that of Abraham and Lot at Sodom and Gomorrah, as well as the story of Moses and the Egyptians. But here, they also learned of similar stories of a prophet named *Hud*, another named *Saleh*, and a third known as *Shoaib*. All provided God's teaching to the peoples around them. Most of the recipients were heedless and thus suffered plagues or destruction. Muhammad often spoke of His chief role as being a "warner" in the hope that His hearers would not ignore God's teachings.

"Yes," said James, "although one finds the monotheistic Christian world to the west in Egypt and the monotheistic Zoroastrian world to the east, most of the people in the in-between lands of western Arabia had refused to accept the monotheism that both faiths offered. The tribe that occupied Mecca and controlled access to the Kaaba there gained enormous wealth from the worship of the many idol-gods inside it and the resulting pilgrimage trade. Teaching people to accept new beliefs was one thing; teaching them to change their livelihood was a wholly different matter. I suppose that the early fierce resistance to Muhammad's teachings came, more than anything else, from their attachment to their ways of earning money from the traveling pilgrims."

"Not so different from Jesus," added Zach, "when He drove the money changers away from the Temple area—it seemed to be the beginning of the troubles that the religious leaders were able to exploit to turn the people against Him."

James thought about it and then said, "Indeed—I suppose it is also not so different from many of the Christian leaders during Muhammad's time, whose love of their positions of power and their money turned them away from considering His teachings."

"But it seems that during the days of Muhammad, at least the people of the Hejaz ultimately heeded His warnings," Zach noted.

"Yes," said Musa, "large numbers became followers during His lifetime, and it was spread throughout Arabia within the following ten years."

Musa noted that James and Zach were reading their English version of the Quran.

"If it is a good translation, I'm sure it will explain many marvelous things in your own language," he told them. "But I don't think it could possibly be translated in such a manner as to also convey the power and poetic beauty of the original words. Indeed, that was one of the mightiest miracles of the Prophet's revelation. Words with such power and poetic beauty, if they could be written at all, normally were worked out gradually by skilled poets over a long time. In the case of the passages of the Quran, they came without stopping from the Prophet."

"Did Muhammad have any training as a poet?" Zach asked.

"None whatsoever. More importantly, He made no claim to be the source of these passages. Instead, He insisted that He was only reciting that which the angel Gabriel had revealed to Him.

"And when people challenged His claim that these were the words of God, He replied that if these were simply the words of a man, then surely there were other men among the Arabs who could produce chapters of their own with similar power, meaning, and poetic beauty. But no one was able to submit anything that was comparable."

Musa then recited a few of the shorter chapters, which he had memorized. The language was in the highest form of Arabic, but having read the English now, both James and Zach were able to understand the Arabic, and they, too, marveled at the power and beauty of the poetic words.

"When the Promised Qaim appears," Musa commented, "I have no doubt that the words He reveals will be similar in character to those of Muhammad. Indeed, I suppose that we would find that such power and poetic beauty characterized the original words of all of the Prophets of the past if we could but hear them in Their native tongue."

The river flowed on eastward, passing many villages with their irrigated farms on flat terrain, until it reached the confined channel through the Jebel Bishri plateau, which towered some 400 feet above the river. Passing through this strategic stretch, they soon passed an abandoned fortress on the right bank.

"The fortress of *Zenobia*, queen of the Palmyrene Empire," offered Musa.

"What was that?" asked Zach.

"It was a part of the Roman Empire in the Third Century AD," explained James, "that temporarily broke away from Rome and was led by a rare queen—Zenobia—who expanded her dominion until it reached from Egypt to Persia. Alas, although she led brilliantly and inspired many with the tolerant intellectual environment she promoted, the overwhelming numbers of the Romans eventually led to her capture after a long siege at Palmyra."

"You seem to know a lot about the subject," suggested Zach.

"Well, as you may have noticed, we in Britain have had a tradition of rulership by queens, in addition to our kings, going back for a few centuries now."

"Ah, yes," Zach replied, "and even today with Queen Victoria."

*　　*　　*

"WHAT DAY IS IT?" inquired James, for the unvarying daily routine had caused him to lose track.

Zach reached for his diary. "It is Monday, January 1."

"Then we have entered the holy year—1844."

"Yes, on the Christian calendar," replied Zach, "but we still have three more weeks before we enter the year 1260 AH."

They asked Da'ud if they would reach Karbila by that date. "By the will of God," he replied. Indeed, thought Zach, when you have no sails or oars, you have almost no control over your speed; then your arrival time will surely depend on the will of God.

After a stop in Deir ez Zor to restock their supplies, they returned to their studies. They were reading the 44th chapter of the Quran, entitled "Smoke," which speaks of "the day when the heavens shall produce a visible smoke which shall cover mankind." James and Zach had noticed that the Quran contained many references to the dramatic things that would occur at the time of the end of the age and how it reminded them of passages in the Bible that spoke of the sun being darkened and the moon turning to blood.

"There seem to be many such references," commented Zach.

Musa was listening. "Do you understand them literally or spiritually?"

"We believe these have spiritual meanings—that they refer to the loss of true spiritual guidance from the leaders of religion in the days prior to the coming of God's next Messenger. How could the real sun be darkened and the moon turn to blood?"

Musa paused to consider for a moment and then said, "No doubt they have true spiritual meanings. But could they also have a literal meaning? Would a thick smoke darken the sun? Might it turn the moonlight to the color of blood red?"

"Well, possibly," replied Zach, "but how could such a thing happen?"

"I will tell you," Musa replied. "When I was a young lad, about ten years old, we all saw, for a long time, a haze in the air that seemed to darken the sun, made the moon appear red, and also created brilliant red sunrises and sunsets. So much haze was in the air that it felt cooler for much of the year."

Zach paused and then asked, "What year was that?"

"It was in 1231."

Zach did a quick calculation. "1816 in our calendar. And yes! I remember that year very well—a year when we all went hungry because frost in the summer killed most of the crops in New York and New England, while a severe drought killed much in the South. The farmers had almost nothing to sell. In early June in our area, the temperature was below freezing. And when, a couple of days later, we witnessed a total eclipse of the moon, an ominous feeling about the fate of the world gripped many."

James nodded in agreement. "In England, we called it *'the year without a summer'* because there were so many cold days and days with torrential rain and flooding. Most of the crops failed, and many people came close to starvation, not only in my country but also in others across Europe. And it continued into the winter and the following spring. So that same smoke that ruined our harvests affected you as well?"

"I believe it affected the whole world," replied Musa, "*and* I think I can tell you where it came from."

James and Zach, curious as ever, asked him to proceed.

"Of course, during that year, we wondered whether this might be one of the signs of the end of the world, of which the Quran had spoken. There was much wonder and talk, and it inspired many people to start searching. After things returned to normal, some of that interest waned, but it remained on the minds of many people. A few years later, my father asked me to accompany him on his pilgrimage to Mecca. I was honored to make this journey with him. While there, we heard another pilgrim who had made the long journey from the far-off island of Java, at the eastern end of the great ocean. He told us that almost a year before we saw anything in the Galilee, an entire island had exploded east of Java. He said that although people in his country had seen volcanoes erupt before, no one could remember seeing anything remotely close to this in size. It continued for ten days, with smaller explosions continuing for three months. So loud was the blast that his relatives in Sumatra, 1,500 miles from the site, had heard it. Neighboring islands were wiped out. He said that tens of thousands of his countrymen had died, and those who survived were only able to do so by finding a way to escape the smothering dust. Large numbers of people, both there and here, understood it to be a sign of the end.[†]

---

† The explosion of Mt. Tambora in Indonesia in 1815 was, by far, the largest explosion in recorded history. It took about a year for the sulfuric acid aerosol particles to migrate through the upper atmosphere to the northern hemisphere, deflecting sunlight and causing famine due to crop failure in what became known as the 'Year without a Summer' of 1816.

"If you would read the beginning of chapter 69, 'The Inevitable,' you will understand why so many in that part of the world saw it as the fulfillment of Quranic prophecy."

Zach reached for the translation of the Quran and read about the inevitable coming of the Day of Judgment: "When the earth shall be shaken with a violent shock and the mountains shall be dashed to pieces, and shall become as dust scattered abroad..."

"Interesting indeed," said James.

Zach sat back and thought for a moment before saying, "You know, that is *very* interesting. So many people were affected, and so many were motivated to think of the fulfillment of God's prophecies. As I recall, Mr. Miller had said that the turning point in his religious life occurred in September of 1816, which would have been at the end of that frigid summer. Also, for the young Joseph Smith, I read that it was the crop failure of 1816 that motivated his parents to move the family to Palmyra, where, during those years, religious revivalism was experiencing a rebirth, due in no small part, I suppose, to these 'signs of the heavens.'"

James agreed. "It is certainly possible that some of these prophecies may have their fulfillment both in spiritual terms and in physical ones.

"It also aligns with Jesus' teaching from Matthew 24:14—that the end would come once the gospel had been preached 'as a witness to all nations.' You may recall that Madagascar was finally opened to our *London Missionary Society* in 1818—often regarded as the final nation to be opened to His teachings."

Zach added, "If, as some of His teachings suggest, the same generation that witnesses these things will also witness His return, then the time is surely now for a generation is about thirty years, and almost twenty-nine years have elapsed since that great explosion."

They pondered the significance of all of these things as the craft continued down the river.

\*     \*     \*

A FEW DAYS LATER, as James was gazing wistfully out at the river, he said, "I'm not the first Englishman who has come this way. I recall reading, about seven years ago, the news of our attempt to find a better sailing route from India to the Mediterranean. Since the seasonal winds of the Red Sea can make sailing very difficult there, it was proposed that we might sail from the Persian Gulf up the Euphrates. From the upper Euphrates, it is but a short overland trek west to reach rivers that lead into the Mediterranean Sea, so the *'Euphrates Expedition'* was organized and all of the pieces of two paddlewheel steamers were hauled up from the Mediterranean and assembled on the upper reaches of the river, with the goal of sailing to the Persian Gulf."[6]

"That's fascinating," replied Zach. "Did they have any luck?"

"Alas, mostly bad luck. The riverbed does not seem to lend itself to easy navigation for large vessels. And although the river seems calm now, fierce storms can come up in the month of May and create large waves on some segments of the river. One such storm capsized one of the two ships. Several crew members drowned, and the survivors crowded aboard the other ship for the rest of the journey. These and other difficulties led them to conclude that in spite of the contrary winds, the Red Sea route and the overland portage from Suez to Port Said was the better passage."

Later that day, after passing the village of Salihye, they saw the hull of the *Tigris*—the ship that had been lost—still half buried and half emerging from one of the shoals. James paused for a prayer in honor of his twenty countrymen and fellow explorers who had lost their lives there.

*       *       *

AS THEY CONTINUED THEIR study of the Quran, they came across the various passages that had been cited to them from Shaykh Hakim in Akka, from Suleiman in Jerusalem, and from their traveling companions, Youssef and now Musa. Zach felt like many of the pieces in his knowledge of Islam were starting to fit together.

In chapter 61, they came upon Muhammad's reference to being Ahmad (in Arabic)—that is, the Illustrious (in English)—and "the Periclyte" (in Greek), noting how similar this was to the Greek "pereclete," which, in John

14, 15, and 16, was translated as the Comforter. Fortunately, the translator, George Sale, had explained this in his copious notes.

Some things were new too. Zach read from chapter 10: "Unto every nation hath an apostle been sent."

"Does that mean," he asked Musa, "that there are more Messengers than the ones listed in the Bible and the Quran?"

"Yes indeed," answered Musa. "We know of the scriptures of some, but God's teachings were given to others as well, which may not have been written down and have thus been lost to history. Still, wherever you travel, you find that people have the concept of having a Creator and some knowledge of the virtue of being good. God has not withheld His teaching from any people. But people all too often have chosen to turn away from Him."

"One theme that I've noticed in reading the Quran," Zach said, "is the frequency of their mention of the 'Day of Judgment' or the 'Last Day.' Muhammad seems to be continually warning His people of it. But I was thinking, even if we did not live in this current age of fulfillment, each of us will have our own 'last day' and, as we enter into the next world, our own 'day of judgment.' It is certainly 'the day which none can put back,' as the Quran says. And no one can deny that this kind of 'Last Day' is coming for each of us."

"True," replied James, "but it is also true that the Last Day at the End will be different. If God's Messenger returns without the outwardly obvious miracles, then we are called upon to carefully exercise our own judgment about the teachings and assertions of anyone who claims this lofty position. You recall how Jesus, in Matthew 24 and 25, describes that we must remain spiritually awake in order to make our judgment at that time. After that, God will judge us on how well we did. So we, as students, must first make our judgments while we undergo the test. Then the Teacher will judge us."

"Another thing I have noticed," added Musa, "is references to the 'gathering' of the peoples of the world, which the Prophet mentions on several occasions. This seems to be something that is a special aspect of our age. But I confess that I'm not certain what it means and if it is something that happens in this world."

31

Zach replied, "Jesus also spoke of a time of the gathering of all of the different folds of God's sheep, in John 10. And I suppose it is conceivable nowadays that a few people from places all over the world could sail on ships to some central point. Maybe each would carry His message back to his own people."

"Possibly so," James commented. "And possibly this suggests that the means of travel will improve in the future. Perhaps the steamboats of the rivers will be outfitted for traveling across the oceans and messages will move with them on a regularly scheduled basis."

"It's hard to imagine how messages could move more rapidly than on the clipper ships that have recently been built in America and Britain," noted Zach with some pride. "Some of them will fly along at 20 miles per hour if the winds are good."

Generally, they all agreed that the "gatherings" referred to in both the Bible and the Quran were much more possible now than they had ever been in the past.

They were nearing the end of their reading and the end of their journey on the river. Zach commented that some of the laws he had read in the Quran seemed rather harsh.

"They were revealed to my ancestors," replied Musa "who were a harsh and undisciplined people, living in what we call 'the days of ignorance.' As you may have noted from your reading, God had sent earlier prophets— Hud, Saleh, and Shoaib—to other Arabian tribes. They were totally rejected by those people. No one followed Them. But God did not forget us. Nay, He revealed what was needed to shake us into wakefulness for we were a people in deep slumber."

"I have sometimes reflected on the harshness of the laws of the Old Testament," noted James, "and how similar they were in some ways to the teachings of the Quran. Both were revealed to peoples of the desert, who were often nomadic and living in harsh conditions. Jesus was able to build on the established monotheism and moral principles of Judaism. Muhammad did not have such a foundation upon which to build, since most of the people were lost in idolatry at the time He appeared."

"Good points," replied Zach, "but praying five times a day seems like a lot to me."

"Perhaps it is necessary to enable us to keep God always near to our thoughts and hearts," Musa replied.

"In any case," added James, "it seems to have worked. The people of Arabia were wholly transformed by the Quran's teachings, and its civilization arose to lead the way during the ages when Europe slumbered in darkness."

"Thirty days of fasting also seems like a lot," Zach noted, "even if it is only in the daytime."

"You may recall," James said, "that Christians formerly fasted during the daylight hours for forty days. And at night they refrained from eating meat or eggs. That was the original Lenten season. But over the centuries, the practice has waned."

Zach had not been aware that Christian fasting had such a history.

"Many of the details of the laws of Islam," Musa offered, "were not specifically laid out in the Quran but have been added either by hadith or by later Muslim leaders. You need not worry too much about them. When the Promised One appears, I believe He will scatter the mountains of old laws and doctrines into dust and provide new ones for the new age."

While completing their study of the Quran, including the long chapters that were revealed later in Medina, they came across verses that Youssef had mentioned back in the Galilee—one that prohibited aggression but encouraged fighting to defend Islamic lands (2:190), one that prohibited violence and contention in religion (2:256), and, finally, one that clearly recognized the legitimacy of the Sources of both Judaism and Christianity (2:136):

> *We believe in God, and that which hath been sent down unto us and that which hath been sent down unto Abraham, and Ishmael, and Isaac, and Jacob, and the tribes, and that which was delivered unto Moses, and Jesus, and that which was delivered unto the prophets from their Lord: We make no distinction between any one of them, and to God are we resigned.*

Both James and Zach reflected on how much they had learned and how the actual teachings of the Quran were much greater than the limited and often pejorative descriptions they had heard from many preachers in the West. They felt they were now ready to meet and learn from the famed Siyyid Kazim, whom they had heard stories of ever since their arrival in Akka. But they were not ready for the tragic news they were about to receive.

# Chapter 3

# COMMOTION IN KARBILA

It was the 25th day of January when the kelek reached the Karbila area. By this time, their beards were fully grown, and their faces and hands had been darkened by much exposure to the strong sunlight. Zach was reasonably fluent in Arabic, although his accent tended to echo James', which came from his early years in Egypt. Wearing the typical robes and turbans and with their brown eyes, they could pass as Muslims, although their accents would indicate that they were not local.

Zach was thinking about how his eastward travels were also steps backward in time—from London to Rome, then to the Holy Land, and now back to the places where much of the Book of Genesis had reportedly occurred. Abraham had come from Ur, somewhere southeast of here; Noah's ark had come to rest at the top of Mt. Ararat, some distance to the north. He mentioned these thoughts to James.

James replied, "Yes, we have now entered the Tigris–Euphrates plain. The Tigris River—or Hiddekel as it is known in Genesis 2—is only about twenty miles to the east now. The original Garden of Eden may have been located somewhere in this vicinity. As you had noted, both rivers are mentioned in the description of the Garden."

At a bend in the river, where a tributary diverged, Da'ud drew the kelek ashore. He bid them to wait there while he found a local friend who had a smaller boat that could carry them up this smaller branch of the river.

"Ayyub (Job) will take you to the heart of Karbila," said Da'ud as soon as he returned. "He's a trustworthy friend." A price was negotiated, their belongings were transferred, and they bid farewell to Da'ud before spending the rest of the day on the journey into Karbila.

Most of the people here were Shiite, including Ayyub, so Musa ventured to explain that his friends were hoping to meet with *Siyyid Kazim*.

"I'm afraid that will be impossible," said Ayyub solemnly.

"Impossible? Why do you say that?" Musa replied abruptly.

"I am sorry to tell you," answered Ayyub with a saddened face, "that the noble Kazim has died—just about three weeks ago."

"What?!" James almost yelled. Zach gasped as if he had been hit hard in the chest. They were crestfallen at the idea that they had made this very long journey only to be thwarted by the untimely death of the very man they were seeking. Musa, too, was downcast. Siyyid Kazim seemed to be the man who held the keys that could lead them to the goal of their quest. How could they possibly proceed now that he was gone?

"Do not be too worried," offered Ayyub with encouragement. "I have also heard that Kazim's foremost disciple, *Mulla Husayn*, who has traveled far and wide at Kazim's request, returned from his distant travels in eastern Persia just a few days ago. I understand that he is planning to address his fellow disciples tomorrow evening. You can hear him then." Ayyub was able to describe the location of Siyyid Kazim's home, where he and his followers usually met.

Toward the end of the day, the little boat reached the center of Karbila, where the river's bank was covered in steps to facilitate an easy dismount from the boats bringing the thousands of pilgrims who flocked to this site each year. Climbing up the stream bank, they immediately noticed the tall minarets and the golden-domed shrine of Husayn, together with a similar shrine for his half-brother, Abbas, both of whom were martyred at the Battle of Karbila in 680 AD. The city was crowded with pilgrims, who, Musa explained, were gathering here for Ashura, the annual commemoration of the martyrdom of Husayn. They had arrived on the fourth day of the Islamic year 1260, and the commemoration would take place on the tenth day. Finding a room in a caravanserai was not easy amid all the incoming pilgrims, but at last one was secured, and they settled in.

The following day, they found their way to Siyyid Kazim's home and were welcomed, along with a large crowd of others, by his widow, whose face, head, and body were totally covered by the dark chador and veil commonly worn by all women in public in this region. Though grieved by his passing, she was a strong supporter of his work. Zach noted a curtain that separated off a section of the room.

"The women's section," said a young Persian man who had been watching them.

"The Shaykhis have women among their followers?" asked James, knowing how rare it was in this part of the world for women to be involved in discussions of religious matters.

"Several," replied the young man, who introduced himself as Hasan. He explained that he had been a close follower of Siyyid Kazim and had been among the group of followers who accompanied the Siyyid on his last journey a few months earlier.

"Let me tell you a fascinating story about our recent travels," he continued.

"Siyyid Kazim was neither ill nor was he particularly old, and yet he often spoke of how his own teacher, the late Shaykh Ahmad, had told him that he would not live to see the coming of the Promised One. He knew that the promised year was fast approaching."

Hasan introduced them to *Mulla Aliy-i-Bastami*, another disciple of Siyyid Kazim who had also been with him on this journey north to the shrine of the two Kazims—the seventh and ninth of the twelve Imams of Shiah Islam—a little north of Baghdad.

Hasan continued, "About two months ago, we were part of the group that accompanied him on his annual visit to Kazimayn. While traveling, after we had stopped for the midday prayer, an Arab shepherd approached him and told him of a powerful dream he had recently had, in which the Prophet Muhammad appeared and asked him to await Siyyid Kazim's arrival here, at this very spot, describing him by name. Muhammad then told the shepherd to tell Siyyid Kazim, 'Rejoice, for the hour of your departure is at hand.' He then predicted the exact day—five weeks later—on which Siyyid Kazim would depart from this world.

"We were amazed but saddened to hear of this dream, but even more amazing was Siyyid Kazim's response. Rather than being distraught or downcast, Siyyid Kazim was overjoyed at receiving this news and assured the shepherd that his dream was certainly true. He encouraged us to rejoice, and he reminded us that his passing was an essential condition before the Promised One would appear.

"Then, exactly as foretold in the dream, he completed his visit to the Kazimayn shrine and returned here to Karbila. On that day, he fell ill. He died a few days later, on the *Day of Arafah*—the holiest day in the year and the exact day that Muhammad had described in the shepherd's dream. That was just 27 days ago."

They were amazed to hear the story. Zach thought for a moment and then looked up in wonderment, saying, "That was the very last day of 1843 in the West. And in the East, the year 1260 has begun just a few days ago. It is almost as if an old age was closing and with this year—1844 AD or 1260 AH—a whole new age is opening before us."

Zach and James proceeded to explain their background to Hasan and how their search for the return of Jesus had led them first to the Holy Land and now to an awareness that there was so much more to the story, which they had been hoping to learn from Siyyid Kazim.

Hasan welcomed them and assured them that they could learn all of what the Siyyid had taught by listening to his immediate disciples. Their teacher's departure at this time, far from being a catastrophe, was in fact a sign that things were moving forward as both Shaykh Ahmad and Siyyid Kazim had revealed.

Hasan explained that Mulla Husayn, a young follower from northeastern Persia, was the foremost disciple of Siyyid Kazim and that the Siyyid had sent him on a mission to gain the support of some of the highly regarded Shiites who had shown an inclination to accept the teachings of Shaykh Ahmad. This mission had taken him to Isfahan in western Persia and then to Mashhad in the far northeastern corner of the country. His success in Isfahan had won much public praise from Siyyid Kazim. Mulla Husayn was returning from Mashhad when the Siyyid passed away.

"It is interesting that Siyyid Kazim passed away on a day that is significant to you in the West," Hasan ventured, "as well as to us here in the East. I also found it interesting that Mulla Husayn, returning from his travels just four days ago, arrived here on the very first day of this auspicious year—the year we have been looking forward to for the past one thousand years."

There was growing discussion and excitement in the room until suddenly everyone hushed themselves as they noticed Mulla Husayn enter. He was a younger man than they, only about thirty years old, but recognized by all as being the most learned of Siyyid Kazim's disciples.

In speaking to the group, the young man acknowledged that many of the followers of Siyyid Kazim were talking about who should be the leader of the Shaykhi school now. Several had suggested that Mulla Husayn himself should take that role.

But in ringing tones, Mulla Husayn reminded them that the foremost teaching of Siyyid Kazim was that now was *not* the time for continued schooling and discussion. Now was the time for *action!* He emphasized that the promised year had now arrived. He reminded them their late master had taught them that now was the time to disperse and start their search throughout Persia to find the One foretold in the Quran and the hadith and, more specifically, by both Shaykh Ahmad and Siyyid Kazim.

One of the students spoke up, saying to Mulla Husayn, "Surely our next leader must be one who knows of, and follows, all of the teachings of Shaykh Ahmad and Siyyid Kazim. So he must be one of their former students. And is there anyone among his former students better suited than you?"

But Mulla Husayn silenced him abruptly, insisting that the Promised One whom they sought would never be a student. Indeed, He had no need for education of any kind, for His knowledge was directly from God. He pointed out that neither Muhammad nor Jesus had been religious scholars. He warned them not to allow the veil of scholarship to become a barrier between themselves and the One they hoped to find.

Zach and James had already learned how Shiah Islam was, like Protestant Christianity, divided into many branches, schools of thought, or denominations. They had various leaders competing with each other—sometimes drastically—for followers, influence, and the wealth it brought. Unlike their

American counterparts, though, they were also competing for governmental favor—in this case, the favors of the Shah, the king of Shiite Persia. As with Christianity, the large majority of Shiah authorities were strongly attached to the literal understanding of the fulfillment of their religion's prophecies. They were so attached to the idea that the Twelfth Imam's return would be a physical body arising from the cave into which he had disappeared 1,000 years earlier that they despised any interpretation to the contrary.

During the ensuing weeks, Zach and James not only confirmed what they had learned earlier in Akka and the Holy Land but also learned much about the details of the teachings of both Shaykh Ahmad and Siyyid Kazim. The idea that Muhammad's visit to heaven during His "Night Journey" was through His spirit rather than His body or that the prophecies of the "Last Day" could be fulfilled spiritually rather than materially—these were so revolutionary that they probably would not have survived had they not found favor with the Shah back in 1817. The passing of the Shaykh in 1826 and the Shah in 1834 gave Siyyid Kazim's opponents the opportunity to denounce the Shaykh's teachings. But Mulla Husayn's recent travels had successfully reinvigorated the faith of those who had initially been favorable toward these teachings. Now the passing of Siyyid Kazim was seen by many as another opportunity for his opponents to openly denounce these teachings once again.

Thus, they realized that they would have to be cautious when speaking and traveling. But they also discovered that there were many among the followers of Shaykh Ahmad who had grown so accustomed to discussing his teachings that they did not want to do anything so bold as traveling from town to town to conduct a serious search for the promised Twelfth Imam. They preferred to stay home and to discuss theological points.

"It reminds me," said Zach to James, "of the story at the end of Luke 9, regarding the young man who said he wanted to follow Jesus but needed to bury his own father first. Jesus made it clear that he must put all other things behind him and not look back."

During a later talk, Mulla Husayn repeated his plea by reading directly from Siyyid Kazim's instructions saying, "*O my beloved companions! Beware,*

*beware, lest after me the world's fleeting vanities beguile you. Beware lest you wax haughty and forgetful of God. It is incumbent upon you to renounce all comfort, all earthly possessions and kindred, in your quest of Him who is the Desire of your hearts and of mine. Scatter far and wide, detach yourselves from all earthly things, and humbly and prayerfully beseech your Lord to sustain and guide you. Never relax in your determination to seek and find Him who is concealed behind the veils of glory...."*

He then repeated a theme that Zach and James had heard ever since their meeting with Shaykh Hakim back in Akka regarding the two Messengers: *"'Verily I say, after the Qaim the Qayyum‡ will be made manifest. For when the star of the Former has set, the sun of the beauty of Husayn will rise and illuminate the whole world. Then will be unfolded in all its glory the 'mystery' and the 'secret' spoken of by Shaykh Ahmad.... 'To have attained unto that Day of days is to have attained unto the crowning glory of past generations, and one goodly deed performed in that age is equal to the pious worship of countless centuries.'"*[7]

During the course of these meetings, they met many of the students of Siyyid Kazim. Most were from various towns or cities in Persia. But they were interested to note that there was one, *Sa'id Hindi*, who had been drawn from the city of Multan, in the Punjab province of far off Hindustan. Although Zach had thought that he and James had traveled a long distance overland from Akka, he soon realized that Sa'id Hindi had traveled more than twice as far overland as they had. Although he spoke the Hindi language, he was not a Hindu. Musa explained that a large part of the population of Hindustan, especially in the north, was Muslim, and about a quarter of them were Shiite, so it should not be so surprising that the news of Shaykh Ahmad and Siyyid Kazim's teachings should have reached them, as it had reached Musa's own Shiite community in Tiberias.

Zach and James continued to learn more over the course of their time in Karbila. Regarding the exact timing of the Return within the year 1260, there was no certainty. However, they noted that the exact beginning of 1,000 years after the death of the 11th Imam and the disappearance of the

---

‡ Qaim ("He who ariseth") and Qayyum (the "Self-Subsisting")

12th would fall on March 28. And they knew that exactly 2,300 years after the edict that Daniel had cited was the first day of spring—that is, March 21, 1844. Any time after those dates, it seemed that the Christian, Persian, and Muslim calendars and prophecies would all be in alignment.

Regularly attending the talks that were given by various disciples of Siyyid Kazim, they learned more details of what he had been teaching. They learned that the promised Qaim would be, like all of the previous Imams, a "siyyid," that is, a descendant of Muhammad. As such, He would be permitted to wear the green turban as a sign of His lineage. As they already expected, He would possess innate knowledge. But also, He would be young in age—in His twenties—medium in height, abstinent in smoking, and free of bodily deficiencies. These conditions, Zach and James agreed, greatly narrowed down the number of possibilities but, alas, did nothing to narrow the geographic range.

As they got to know Hasan, they confided in him their intention to search in Persia and to visit the resting place of the Wise Men in Saveh and possibly the shrine of the prophet Daniel. They recognized that a knowledge of basic Persian would be essential in these travels and asked Hasan to give them lessons in the language.

On the seventh day of their stay, James and Zach were awakened by loud shrieks of weeping and, looking through the gate of the caravanserai, were amazed to see many men in blood-stained robes marching through the street with swords, knives, and chains. At first, they thought that the city was under attack, until they noticed that each man was striking himself rather than striking those around him.

Musa explained, "Today is *Ashura*, the day on which we commemorate the tragic martyrdom of the third Imam, Husayn, grandson of the Prophet, who willingly came here at the invitation of the residents, although he knew that betrayal might await him. The believers here failed to keep their promise to defend him. And thus, he was killed in the most tragic of circumstances. The name 'Husayn' has become synonymous with a person who is willing to make the ultimate sacrifice for God. While many Shiites expect Him to return from the sky, Shaykh Ahmad taught us instead to expect One who was willing to sacrifice Himself—someone who represents the return of the self-same spiritual qualities as the original Husayn.

"Today, the people punish themselves on behalf of our ancestors and as a reminder to never allow such a thing to happen again."

But as Zach thought about what he had learned of some of the extreme denunciations that Shaykh Ahmad and Siyyid Kazim had received, he wondered whether such extremism was compatible with their desire to avoid repeating this great mistake of the past, when the Promised One would appear yet again.

\*     \*     \*

AFTER EXHORTING THE OTHER disciples, during the whole month of Muharram, to prepare for active search, Mulla Husayn and two of his relatives decided to travel south two days' journey to the holy mosque in Kufa near the shrine of Ali in the city of Najaf and to start a 40-day vigil of prayer and fasting there, beseeching God to guide them. Zach and James were reminded of the forty days of prayer and fasting that Jesus had undertaken at the start of His mission, and they marveled at his dedication.

Shortly after that, Mulla Aliy-i-Bastami left also with a larger group of companions, again heading toward Kufa. Among them were Sa'id Hindi and *Mirza Muhammad Ali*.

The latter was a brother-in-law of a Persian poetess name *Qurratu'l-Ayn*. She had a passion for learning of religious matters—rare among her gender. And rarer still, she had parents who encouraged her learning. She became a staunch supporter of the teachings of Siyyid Kazim and was frequently in correspondence with him. Like Mulla Husayn, she had been traveling to Karbila at the end of the year, and like him, she was gravely disappointed to hear of his death, which happened a few days prior to her arrival. She told her brother-in-law that she had seen the face of the Promised One in a dream, and thus she wrote a letter declaring her allegiance to Him, asking her brother-in-law to deliver it to Him since she was confident that his search for Him would be successful.

Indeed, Qurratu'l-Ayn would have loved to have joined in such a search, but the widow of Siyyid Kazim implored Qurratu'l-Ayn to remain with her, where she could assist in sharing his teachings with any others who were seeking answers in Karbila.

As the searching men departed, Qurratu'l-Ayn's role in giving the talks at Siyyid Kazim's library concerning the true teachings of Islam expanded. Zach, James, Musa, and Hasan were among the many students who remained for a few more weeks of learning and discussion. Although they could not see through the curtain that separated the men from the women in the room, it sounded as if the women attending now perhaps outnumbered the men. Musa and Hasan were particularly amazed at how much the poetess knew of the Quran, the many hadith, the teachings of all of the Imams, and the famous poets of Islamic and Persian history. She often taught with beautiful poetic verse in a voice that was enchanting to all who listened.

In mid-March, Musa approached James and Zach with a sorrowful face.

"I would love to continue with you on your search into Persia," said Musa. "However, my knowledge of Arabic and Arab ways will be of little use to you among the Persians. Both my family and my farm are expecting my return in season, and I fear that an extended absence may create havoc with both. I have learned much, and I have much to report back in Tiberias.

"But I will not leave you without assistance. I have asked Hasan if he would take my place as your guide through Persia, and he has agreed. As a native of that land, he will provide you with much better service than I could hope to offer. He was planning to start by returning north to the Kazimayn shrine, which is on the route to Saveh. You could continue your Persian lessons with him as you travel. So, begging your pardon, I humbly request that you grant me permission to take my leave."

Zach and James thanked Musa profusely for all that he had done for them and granted his request. Before departing, Musa helped them find two camels and a donkey for their upcoming travels, while Zach provided him with the funds he would need to make the return trip overland. He assured Musa that they would visit him in Tiberias, upon their own return trip, to share any news of discoveries from Persia. Thus, they parted as steadfast friends.

Zach and James started preparations for their own departure but remained for a couple of days to commemorate with Hasan the feast of *Naw Ruz*—the Persian New Year—on the spring equinox.

The two had learned much about the teachings of Shaykh Ahmad and Siyyid Kazim during their nearly two-month stay in Karbila. Of all that they had learned, the most persistent theme was one that Zach had also learned from his father: The Holy Books are rich in spiritual insights, but one must pray and meditate on their inner spiritual meanings rather that becoming attached to an outward interpretation. He knew this to be true with the Bible. These two teachers of Karbila also made it clear that it was equally true with the Quran and the many traditional stories of Muhammad's life.

"Today," Zach said wistfully, "is exactly 2,300 years after the decree of Artaxerxes, which was the starting point of Daniel's amazing prophecy. Any day between now and December 31 will meet the expectations of the 2300, 1844, and 1260 found in the Jewish, Christian, and Islamic prophecies." On the following morning, all three men set out on their search together.

*　　*　　*

IT WAS AN EASY three-day journey from Karbila to Baghdad through the lush farms of the Tigris and Euphrates River plain. The air was pleasant, and although a morning shower wetted them on the second day, everything had dried out by the late afternoon.

Hasan had not previously known an American and decided to take this opportunity to ask Zach about life there. He was particularly interested to know more of the native peoples of America.

Zach noted that his firsthand knowledge of them was limited. "But from what I've heard, they are both brave and noble. I'm told that part of my country's form of government—allowing states to rule their internal affairs while confining the national government to rule only on issues *between* the states—was copied from the federation of the Iroquois tribes that once ruled over much of the northern inland regions. And they learned this from a Prophet who was called *The Great Peacemaker*."

"Interesting," Hasan replied, "especially in light of the Quran's teaching that God has sent Messengers to all of the people of the world."

Later, as they approached the city's gate, Hasan announced, "Welcome to Baghdad—the Madinat al-Salaam, or City of Peace, for so it was named by its founder, al-Mansur, who established the Abbasid Caliphate here almost 1,100 years ago." Though peaceful within, it was still a walled city whose gates were closed at night to ward off thieves and highwaymen.

"Yes," added James, "as I recall, the Abbasids ruled most of the Islamic world from here for 500 years, during what is called the 'golden age of Islam.'"

"Indeed," continued Hasan. "Herein was established the first House of Wisdom, whose purpose was to gather knowledge from all over the known world in an open atmosphere of inquiry. Scholars from as far as India and China in the east and Europe and Africa in the west came here to share their knowledge and to learn from each other and from the innumerable written works that were all being translated here into the Arabic language."

After the city's destruction by the Mongols in 1258, however, it had suffered three centuries of capture by various powers. And during the last three centuries, the Turkish-speaking Ottoman Empire had ruled over it. Zach could see that it had not retained the splendor of its earlier days.

A few days' rest in Baghdad enabled James to visit the British Residency there—established by the East India Company to facilitate communications along the route to India. He wrote to his university to advise them that his return would be delayed for a semester at least. Zach again posted a letter to his family, then went with Hasan to the jewelry market to convert some of the gems hidden in his clothes into Persian qiran for the trip eastward.

Northward out of Baghdad, Hasan pointed out the field in which Siyyid Kazim had met the Arab shepherd and heard of his dream just a few months before. They continued to the Kazimayn shrines, one of the most sacred sites for Shiah Islam. James and Zach were impressed by its size and the beauty of its twin gilded domes, the four minarets, and the colorful glazed tile and mirror mosaics. Verses from the Quran decorated much of the structure. Here they remained for several days to meditate on all that they had learned and to pray for God's guidance.

Heading farther north, James said that he would like to see the burial site of the 10th and 11th Imams, which was also the site from whence, according to many Shiites, the 12th Imam should arise after 1,000 years. It was about two days' journey off the road to Persia, following the Tigris River upstream. James said that since they had visited the Mount of Olives, where Christians expected Jesus to return, they should also visit the place where the Muslims—at least the Shiites—expected their Promised One to return.

Shrine of the 10th and 11th Imams on the right
with the Mosque of the Occultation on the left

The Askari shrine in Samarra was almost as large as the Kazimayn mosque, and it also had two domes, although not matching ones. One dome was for the tombs of the 10th and 11th Imams. Hasan explained that like many of their predecessors, after the teachings and location of these Imams became known, they were poisoned by agents of the Caliph, who would not tolerate any other claims to authority in Islam. To minimize their risk, they sometimes remained incognito and communicated with their followers through an intermediary, who was known as a "gate."

The other dome covered the "Chamber of the Occultation" and the "Well of the Occultation," where the 12th Imam is said to have disappeared, or become hidden or "occulted." So complete was this occultation that no agent of the Caliph was ever able to find him. Many Shiites believed that since his disappearance in 260 AH, the thousand-year "day of separation" was nearly ended, and therefore, during the present year, he would arise from this place. Thus, he was called the Arising One (Qaim) as well as the Guided One (Mahdi).

The chamber area was a room adjacent to the well, where the faithful could come to pray for the Imam's return. And during this special year, it was quite full, making it easier for James and Zach to enter with Hasan. Wearing the common robes and turbans and approaching with bowed heads, they aroused no suspicions.

Although they didn't believe that the Promised One would physically arise from that spot, all three of them took the opportunity to pray there for God's guidance in their quest. Zach, in particular, was acutely aware that they were about to leave the Ottoman realms, through which they had been traveling ever since their arrival in Akka. They were also about to leave the Arabic-speaking world. He and James were only gradually gaining knowledge of the Persian language, and thus they would be quite dependent on Hasan's translations for a while.

After leaving the site, Zach, being of a practical inclination, asked, "If the religious leaders are so certain that the Qaim is down at the bottom of the well, why don't they simply yell down to him—or perhaps climb down to find him?"

Hasan rolled his eyes at this suggestion. "All would regard it as an act of blasphemy!" he explained. "Anyone attempting it would probably be killed for trying. Moreover, most of the followers believe that the well is connected to long passageways that lead to the distant jeweled cities of Jabulsa and Jabulqa, where the Qaim lives. Some believe these to be real places, according to their understanding of the sayings of the Prophet and the various legends that have arisen since then. A few people long ago even claimed to have traveled to these cities. But none of these claims could ever be substantiated. In any case, Shaykh Ahmad has taught us that these were always intended to suggest spiritual places, not physical ones. And thus the Qaim will arise, not from a well in the mosque but in the same manner that all of the other Messengers of God have arisen."

Hasan paused for a moment to consider further Zach's question and then said, "Answer me this: If a Christian could harness enough birds to carry him through the sky, would he use such a flock in the hope of finding Jesus in the heavens?"

Zach and James both chuckled at the notion. But as they thought about some of their countrymen, they were not quite sure how to answer this question.

# Chapter 4:

# TRAVELS ALONG THE SILK ROAD

Heading northeast now toward the Zagros Mountains of Persia, Zach commented that many holy places—Karbila, Najaf, Kazimayn, and Samarra—all seemed to be located in this small region.

"The four shrine cities, the Atabat (the Thresholds), as we call it," commented Hasan. "But that's only a part of it. A little farther south of Najaf lies Ur, the original home of Abraham. To the southeast lies Shushan, with the tomb of the prophet Daniel. To the northeast of us lies Saveh, where the Magi of Jesus' day are said to be buried. Some say that the original home of Zoroaster lies in Urmia, northwest of there. And a couple of weeks' journey north of our present location, beyond the mountains of Sulaymaniyah," he nodded toward the mountains on the northern horizon, "lies Mount Ararat, where Noah's ark came to rest."

"Yes," acknowledged James, "although much of the spiritual history of the West is anchored in the Holy Land, much of the most ancient history of the Bible, as well as Zoroastrian history and much of Shiah Muslim history, seems to be anchored right here."

\*     \*     \*

They had been traveling in the caravan for a few days when a well-dressed young man in a tightly wound turban and a trimmed black beard came alongside and said in perfect English, "Good day, gentlemen. I trust you are finding the journey satisfactory?"

51

Zach and James were surprised to hear someone speaking in their native language so clearly, with only a slight Indian accent. Inquiring, they found that this was Arjan Singh, a merchant of Sikh background who was returning to his home near the Hindu Kush, in the city of Peshawar, where he had grown up ever since the Sikh Empire had taken control of the city in 1818.

"Your command of the English language is excellent," commented James. "How did you come to learn it so well?"

"We merchants find it advantageous to learn the language of the people with whom we trade," Arjan explained, "and we have been trading regularly with the British East India Company since before I was born. You are no doubt aware that the spread of the Company's sphere of influence from Calcutta and up the Ganges Plain has continued for the past two centuries, so of course, it is most fitting and proper for us to learn your language."

James was impressed. "But tell me, what is it that brings you to Iraq and Persia?" he said.

"Good sir!" Arjan exclaimed. "Do you know nothing of the road upon which you travel?"

"Of course," replied James, "this is the road from Baghdad to Tehran."

"Yes indeed," replied Arjan, "but it is so much more than that! You are traveling upon the ancient Silk Road, the greatest trade route the world has ever known. For millennia we traveling merchants have lived by moving goods from the great Eastern civilizations of Hindustan and China to the great Western civilizations of Persia, the Ottomans, Egypt, and Europe. Through the ages, many a city and, indeed, many a kingdom have grown rich off of the trade that has flowed along this route.

"Until recent times, travel by sea was regarded by most merchants as far too risky for sending high-quality silks and expensive spices and other precious materials. All possible land routes are funneled here, between the Caspian Sea to the north and the Persian Gulf to the south. The Zagros Mountains, which run between these seas, place even more limits on the east–west routes, so this very route upon which we travel has become the most important trade route in the region and, indeed, in all of the world.

And I myself have traveled it from Constantinople to Calcutta and from Jerusalem to Tibet."

"That's interesting to learn," commented Zach, not knowing the details of the larger Asian geography particularly well. The extent of his own overland travels suddenly seemed rather small by comparison.

"Upon this route," Arjan added proudly, "people of all religions and most nationalities have moved. The trade and travel passing along it have laid the foundation for the mixing of peoples, the growth of knowledge, and the broadening of understanding between East and West. Christian and Jew, Muslim and Zoroastrian, Buddhist, Hindu, and we Sikhs, as well as many others, have traveled together, talked together, and learned broadly, generally without strife. For while we merchants are sufficiently mindful of our religious obligations, we are also mindful of our obligations to deliver and sell the loads we carry."

He paused for a minute to consider this picture before moving on to more practical matters, adding, "But do tell me, what brings *you* to this part of the world? Do you have goods to sell in Tehran? Perhaps some fine jewels?" He could see that their animals were not heavily laden.

Zach explained about their background and how their quest for the Promised One of Christianity and Judaism had led them to some new understandings of Islam and how its expectations of a Promised One had some strange parallels to their own. He further explained how they were now seeking to learn more about the prophecies of the ancient Persian religion of Zoroaster in Saveh since they felt that the success of the Magi in finding Jesus demonstrated that Zoroaster, too, must have been a true Prophet.

"Ah, yes," replied the Sikh gentleman. "But if you hold that Zoroaster was truly a Prophet, then you must also recognize the divine origin of the Hindu religion as well."

"And why should that be so?" inquired James.

"Because, while Zoroaster revealed many new teachings, He was also building upon, and correcting, the ancient religion of his ancestors, which had regressed into polytheism. But the religion of his ancestors and the religion of the Hindus both have their earliest roots in the same ancient Vedic teachings."

"An interesting lesson," said James, mulling it over, "perhaps not so different from Muhammad's relation to Judaism. We have learned that although most of the tribes of western Arabia were polytheistic prior to His coming, those around Mecca were descendants of Ishmael and thus had roots in the ancient monotheistic religion of their forefather, Abraham. So the teachings of Islam are similarly built on ancient Jewish foundations, in addition to Jesus' teachings."

"Indeed," continued Arjan. "These great religions of mankind have originated in three great nests: Moses, Jesus, and Muhammad in the West—that is, Egypt, Palestine, and the Hejaz; Noah, Abraham, and Zoroaster in the central nest of the Tigris–Euphrates and Persia; and Buddha and Krishna, and others of India's distant past, in the East, on the plains of the Ganges and Indus Rivers. When you travel in all three areas, you will come to discover that while they differ in many details, the essence of their message is much the same."

"Yes, indeed, we are learning this to be so," said James. "And what of your religion? From whence did the Sikh religion come?"

"*Guru Nanak* was from the Punjab—the northern reaches of the Indus River in the north part of Hindustan. He lived amidst the conflict between the Hindus and the Muslims about 300 years ago. He studied both religions. He also traveled far and wide over all of these lands," said Arjan as he nodded and glanced toward the east and the west. "It is said that he traveled westward as far as Mecca and eastward through the Hindu realms and even into China.

"He proclaimed that Hinduism and Islam were as two brothers, and their common Father is God."

"Interesting," replied James, "but I have always thought of Hinduism as a polytheistic religion, while Islam is strictly monotheistic."

"And what of Christianity?" replied Arjan. "Monotheistic or not?"

"Why, monotheistic of course!" James answered, rather surprised at the question.

"Yet the Christians pray to statues and paintings, just like the Hindus."

"Well, not exactly," James answered. "Protestants like myself do not pray to statues at all. And even the Catholics and the Orthodox pray to ask assistance from a saint or angel who is in the next world but who can influence events in our world. They only use a statue or a painting to help remind them of a particular saint or angel and thus to focus the attention of their prayers."

Arjan explained, "Many of the Hindus also pray to the spirits of former saints or holy men, whose statues and images serve as a reminder. You may call them 'gods' if you prefer to make them sound foreign, but in reality, are they so different from the saints of Christianity?"

Neither James nor Zach had encountered such an explanation before.

"Also, according to the more advanced *Brahmin* teachers, many of those supposed gods are, in reality, the various qualities of the one God. Some say that Hinduism has only three gods: *Brahma*, the Creator; *Vishnu*, the Sustainer; and *Shiva*, the Transformer or Destroyer. Yet the most advanced of the Brahmin religious leaders tell me that even these three are simply three aspects of one central God of the universe."

"I'll confess that I do not have much knowledge of Hinduism," replied James as Zach listened to the exchange. "And, like most people, I have never actually visited the next world, so I cannot speak of firsthand experience regarding exactly Who may be listening to our prayers. I can tell you what I believe, but who can tell of the next world for certain? All we can do is merely echo what others have said before us."

After a moment of thought, Zach inquired, "What I would like to know is whether your prophet, Guru Nanak, taught anything about the coming of the next Messenger."

"Guru Nanak was not a prophet," explained Arjan. "He was a *guru*, or wise teacher—the first in a line of ten such gurus. He learned much from reading the teachings of the past, from traveling and talking with people of many places, and, most of all, from praying and meditating on what he had discovered. Living amongst the contending Hindus and Muslims, he prayed and meditated on what he had learned and shared his realizations with the people. He taught of how an aspect of God dwells within each person; he taught of equality, kindness, and virtue. Many found that these teachings resolved their dilemmas, and so they followed him. But he did not claim to be a prophet like Moses or Muhammad. Thus, he did not make prophecies of the future."

"I see," replied Zach with a note of disappointment, still hoping to find additional clues to help them with their search. "What then of Hinduism? Do they have prophecies of a coming Messenger?"

"The last of the ten gurus of our religion, *Gobind Singh*, translated one of the passages from Hinduism, saying this:

> *When there is incest, adultery, atheism, hatred of religion, no more dharma (when the right way or the true path is lost), and sin everywhere, the impossible Iron Age has come; in what way the world will be saved? For the helpless, the Lord himself will manifest as the Supreme Purusha (Spirit). He will be called the Kalki incarnation and will be glorious like a lion coming down from heaven.*[8]

Arjan added, "*Kalki* will ride a white horse, carry a sword, and sound a trumpet as He destroys the wicked. He will bring an end to the current age, which has lasted many thousand years, and usher in the Golden Age. He will reign on the earth for a thousand years."

"That's very interesting!" declared Zach. "In almost every way, it sounds like the description that John provided of Christ's return, in chapters 19 and 20 of the Book of Revelation."

"In my travels," Arjan continued, "I have had opportunities to discuss Hindu teachings at length with several of the followers of that religion as we travel the road together. One explained to me that Kalki would be the last of the 10 avatars, or spiritual guides, mentioned in the Hindu scripture. He is to appear at the end of the eon. He is the destroyer of evil.

"I remember a few lines from the *Bhagavad-Gita*, in which Lord Krishna explains the pattern to His companion, Arjuna, saying:

> *When goodness grows weak,*
> *When evil increases,*
> *I make myself a body.*
> *In every age I come back,*
> *To deliver the holy,*
> *To destroy the sin of the sinner,*
> *To establish righteousness.*"[9]

56

"Yes!" shouted Zach. "Yes, that is it exactly!" He paused thoughtfully and then added, "In all that I have read from any of the scriptures, I have never heard the promise of the Lord's return described as clearly and as directly as Krishna has given it here. Here, at last, is a clear description of the *manner* of His coming. Not from the sky as my Christian brothers expect nor arising from out of the ground as many of the Muslims imagine. He simply creates another body for Himself and is reborn in the new age. Ah, if my fellow Christians could understand this one point alone, their understanding of the return of Jesus would be so much easier!" Zach pulled out his diary to write this down.

"I do not disagree," replied James. "And from this I can see that we may need to expand our list of true revelations. But we would still like to know whether they had any guidance about the exact time and place of His next appearance."

Arjan Singh explained that there were many schools of thought in Hinduism and many ideas about the future. Some say that the *Kali Yuga*— the age of vice—is close to its end. They said that it was to last 4,800 years after Lord Krishna left this mortal world, and it is about that time now."[10]

"Exactly how long ago did Lord Krishna pass away?" asked Zach.

"Alas," replied Arjan, "I have heard several different dates from different Hindu teachers. They have few detailed records as you keep in the West. They seem more inclined to look for the spiritual conditions described in their scriptures—conditions similar to the passage that Gobind Singh translated. From what I've seen, those conditions are near at hand, if they are not here already."

"Do the Hindu teachers give any indication of the place from which Kalki will come?" asked James.

"Again, there are many schools of thought. Several suggest that it will be from somewhere outside of Hindustan. In particular, the *Kalki Purana*, that is, the book of prophecies about Kalki, suggests that He would come from *Shambhala*."

"Where is that?" asked Zach.

"No one knows. Some say it is simply a mythical place. Others say it means a place outside of the lands of the Vedas. Still others say it refers to Purshottam, as found in that same book."

"And where is Purshottam?" James inquired.

"It is often understood simply as 'the land,' but I am told that it is the ancient Sanskrit name for Parsatham, or the Land of the Parsis."[11]

"The Parsis are the Persians," noted James. "So in addition to the clue from Muhammad's comment about Salman, we have another prophecy pointing toward Persia."

"That is very good to know, but does it mention a city?" asked Zach.

"I have not heard of the mention of a specific town or city."

Zach was frustrated by this. Then Arjan added, "I do recall hearing the prophecy of *Surdas*, a blind saint who lived in the 1500s, about the same time as Guru Nanak. This saint stated that an event would occur in the year 1900, which would initiate a cycle of Truth that would last for a thousand years."[12]

"He said it would not happen until 1900 AD?" asked Zach, disappointed.

"No, this prophecy was about 1,900 years on the *Vikram Samvat* calendar," Arjan explained.

"Was that a solar calendar? And when did it begin?"

"Yes, it was a solar calendar, and it started 56 to 57 years before the Western calendar began."

"So that means..." Zach paused to do some subtraction in his head, "why, that means the year Sudras spoke of was none other than this very year we are in today—1844!"

"Yes," said Arjan, "that thought has indeed crossed my mind too."

"And it matches with the Christian teachings of the thousand-year reign of Christ that begins with His return, as noted in chapter 20 of the Book of Revelation," added James.

They traveled along quietly for a while, each thinking about how amazing it was that the peoples of Judaism, Christianity, Islam, and Hinduism—separated by nation, culture, and vast distances—could have prophecies that each picked out the same exact year, centuries or millennia later. Coincidence on this scale was simply impossible.

*     *     *

THE FOLLOWING DAY, AS they were approaching Qasr-e-Shirin at the border of the Ottoman Empire, they again struck up a conversation with their Sikh friend, eager to learn more from him before they parted ways.

"So from what I have heard about Hinduism," James said, "there are 10 avatars. Krishna was the ninth, and Kalki will be the tenth."

"Actually," responded Arjan, "most Hindus regard Krishna as the eighth. The Buddha was the ninth."

"Buddha? Really?" James said incredulously. "I thought Buddhism was a separate religion that had broken away from Hinduism."

"And so it was," replied Arjan, "until about a thousand years ago, when several of the writers of the Hindu puranas, or lore, began to acknowledge the spiritual significance of the Buddha, yet without becoming His direct followers. Gradually, more and more of the Hindu writers came to accept this view, although not all. But most of them see Buddha as the ninth avatar of Hinduism and the coming Kalki as the tenth."

"So tell me, then, what do you understand of the Buddha and his religion?" asked James.

"The Buddha was another founder of a great religion and was no doubt inspired by what He heard from the realm of the spirit, even as Christ was," replied Arjan. "He arose in northern Hindustan, where the Hindu religion was practiced, much as Christ arose in the Jewish part of the world. Once during my travels through the high mountains of Tibet, an early winter blizzard forced me to take refuge in a monastery with a group of Buddhist monks. During the months while I awaited the spring snowmelt, I learned something of their teachings."

"I have heard that they do not believe in God," remarked Zach cautiously.

"The Buddha spoke of the Absolute, the Uncreated—a spiritual reality beyond our understanding. Perhaps...," Arjan added with a wry smile, "a more advanced concept of God than is normally found in the West?"

Zach remembered Jesus' statement from John 4:24 that "God is a spirit" and acknowledged the similarity.

"In any case," Arjan continued, "the religion of the Hindus had developed so many gods, it is not surprising that the Buddha did not speak of God as a great Person. Otherwise, the people would surely have just added Buddha and His god to the pantheon of Hindu deities and holy men.

"Instead, He generally put aside the theological and philosophical questions with which religious leaders often busy themselves, in order to focus on alleviating the suffering of the people all around Him. Recognizing the impermanence of all things in this world and recognizing that these things are ultimately illusory in nature, He wisely taught the people to let go and be detached from such things that they might avoid suffering. Through a practice of detachment, prayer and meditation, they would then gradually attain enlightenment about the true reality of things, both in this world and in the spiritual realms.

"Whatever He taught, it must have struck a chord with many people because His teachings spread widely. Within about two centuries the great king, Emperor Ashoka, adopted Buddhism as his religion, and it soon spread throughout all of Hindustan. The emperor sent out his missionaries, including some to the neighboring empire to the west, the Greek empire of Alexander, which had extended itself to the borders of Hindustan at that time. It also spread to Ceylon and to Siam and north into central Asia and from thence eastward into China and Japan."

"Did he speak of any connection with the religions of the past?" asked Zach.

"The monks told me that in the current eon, there had been three Buddhas prior to Gautama Buddha, so He was thus the fourth. Although He gave a different name for each of these three, many regard them as identical to the sixth, seventh, and eighth avatars of Hinduism—*Manu* (or *Parashurama* as He was sometimes known), *Rama*, and *Krishna*. The other five earlier avatars are from an earlier eon, of which Gautama Buddha did not speak. Thus the Buddhists expect the *fifth* Buddha, while the Hindus expect the *tenth* avatar. But both are focused on a final One who is still to come.

"So," said James in a pondering tone, "like the Muslims, Christians, Jews, and Zoroastrians, the Buddhists and the Hindus have a clear concept that a new Prophet, Teacher, or Savior will appear in the future to guide the people."

"Indeed," replied Arjan.

"And what of that future?" asked Zach.

"The monks taught me that the fifth Buddha would arise at a time when most aspects of the original Buddhism had disappeared and the people were again lost in their understanding. When I heard of it, it sounded very much like the Kali age that Lord Krishna described—the time when He would again step forth into the world.

"These monks said He would be called the Buddha Maitreya—the Fully Awakened One." Arjan paused for a moment as he summoned a memory then added, "The monks taught me part of the 'Sermon of the Great Passing,' given by the Buddha near the end of His life. In it, He said:

> *I am not the first Buddha who came upon earth, nor shall I be the last.*
>
> *In due time another Buddha will rise in the world, a Holy One, a supreme enlightened One, endowed with wisdom in conduct, auspicious, knowing the universe, an incomparable leader of men, a master of angels and mortals.*
>
> *He will reveal to you the same eternal truths which I have taught you.*
>
> *He will preach his religion glorious at the goal, in the spirit and in the letter.*
>
> *He will proclaim a religious life, wholly perfect and pure, such as I now proclaim.*
>
> *His disciples will number many thousand, while mine number many hundred.*
>
> *He will be known as Maitreya, which means 'he whose name is kindness.'* [13]

"That sounds very similar to what we have heard of the other religions," said Zach. "Whether He is described as the return of the past Messenger or as the coming of One who is very similar to the original Messenger, it seems that all of the religions have an expectation that someone will come again in the future."

"Aside from describing the conditions of the times when He would return, did He describe the date or the place?" inquired James.

"As to the time," Arjan replied, "when I stayed with them five years ago, several had expressed a sense of excitement because they held that He would appear sometime within the final century of their calendar. And that century began," Arjan paused to work it out, "in the middle of last year in the Christian calendar."

"So," Zach pondered, "the Buddhists, too, believe that we have entered an age of the fulfillment of their religious prophecies. And it will take place between mid-1843 and mid-1943."[14]

"So it would seem," replied Arjan.

They all rode in silence for some time, contemplating the amazing confluence of the prophecies from all of the prophetic religions.

After a while, James said, "It is fascinating for us that his century was picked out of all 24 preceding centuries since the Buddha's lifetime. And it is certainly a confirmation that these prophecies must be coming from the same Source as ours in the West. But," he paused, "alas, they are still not specific enough to add to what we already know."

"And what about the place? From where will the Buddha Maitrya come?" asked Zach.

"Even among the Buddhists that I've met, the answer is not entirely clear," replied Arjan. "Some have no answer at all. But the monks in Tibet and many others describe the future Buddha as 'Amitabha,' which means 'the Buddha of unbounded glory.' They say He will not come alone. Rather, there is one who will come before Him and one who will come after Him. Together, they are called the 'Three Saints of the West.'[15] It is said that They will come from the 'Pure Land.'"

"Of the West?" asked Zach. "And where is the 'Pure Land'?"

"Some say the Pure Land is the next world," explained Arjan, "but some simply say it is Sukhavati—the Western Paradise.'"

"The West?" asked Zach with surprise. "That is the opposite of what we in the West hear. The Bible—both the Old and New Testaments—seems to indicate that we should look to the East. We always tend to think of the East as the source of religion."

"Indeed," said James, "that would seem to be contradictory. Unless..." He paused for a moment. "Unless each of these Messengers was speaking from the perspective of the general location of His future followers. In that case, the Bible is telling us in the West to look toward the East, and the Buddha is telling His followers in the East to look to the West. Then, taken together, we would have to conclude that we should look in the place that is halfway between the two."

Zach's face broke into a broad smile. "And that would be Persia— exactly where we are headed!"

"You are certainly headed in the right direction," commented Arjan, "but it is a very large country."

"God willing," said James, "we will find some Zoroastrians whose prophecies may deliver us to the correct place."

"Yes," Zach added, "their Magi were successful in following their prophecies to find Jesus when He was born. Perhaps they will know more about the exact place in their country where the Promised One will appear in this age."

At length they reached the town of Qasr-e-Shirin, or Castle of Shirin, the boundary of the Ottoman and Persian Empires. The hills of Mesopotamia were behind them now, while the Zagros Mountains lay ahead. Zach was pleased to think of the original Magi who, coming down from these mountains, had almost certainly trod upon the very same path that he and his companions were now traveling.

Arjan Singh said he would remain in the markets here for several days while trading some of his goods. James and Zach were happy to have had the opportunity to speak in their native tongue once again and thankful to have learned so much from this friend. But their growing anticipation of what they might find in Persia drove them to press onward.

"Our blessings be upon you," said James, "for all that you have taught us and upon your religion, which has recognized the truth of the many Prophets of the past. It is even as the morning star, which has arisen during the darkest hours of the night to guide us wayfarers until the dawn."

"In truth," said Arjan, "I have learned much from you as well."

And so they parted as friends. James and Zach took some time to translate everything they had learned into Arabic for Hasan.

After passing the border, Zach asked James, "What do you make of the prophecy of 'Three Saints of the West?'"

"That is a good question," he replied. "The other religions have spoken of two—a forerunner, like John the Baptist, and Jesus. But a third one—one who would come after? That's certainly different."

"True," said Zach as they traveled onward. "There was also one other thing that I found fascinating. It was Arjan's understanding of religion as coming from three great sources—an eastern one in the plains of north India, a central one here in western Persia and eastern Mesopotamia, and a western one in Palestine, Egypt, and the Hejaz of western Arabia. It answers one question that I had."

"And what was that?" asked James.

"Do you recall, from our reading of chapter 24 in the Quran, the prophecy that God's lamp would be lighted by the oil of the 'blessed tree, an olive neither of the east nor of the west?' Now I can understand this as one more clue pointing us to this central nest of the Prophets—neither in the Indus–Ganges area in the east nor in the Palestine–Hejaz area in the west but instead right here in the Mesopotamian–Persian center."

"Yes," agreed James. "Jesus said that we should look to the east of where He was for the place of His return; Buddha suggested we should look to the west of His homeland for the Pure Land of the fifth Buddha. And the Quran said we should look to the center and suggested Persia. Hindu sources also suggest Persia. These all agree only if we are here in this central region—the land of the Wise Men, which is just ahead." He nodded toward the east, where the mountains of Persia loomed on the horizon.

# Chapter 5

# INTO THE LAND OF
# THE WISE MEN

JAMES AND ZACH CONTINUED to inquire in the caravansaries, coffeehouses, and bazaars where they stopped as to whether anyone had heard of any stories of a child who seemed to have innate knowledge. But the response was always no—sometimes accompanied by stares of disbelief.

They rested in Hamadan for a few days and obtained provisions for the next leg of their journey. They had not traveled far from Hamadan when Hasan noticed a new traveler who had joined the caravan. He traveled on a mule instead of a horse and wore a turban that was twisted instead of being folded. His shoes had broad, up-turned toes, and all of his clothes were either dull brown, gray, or yellow. By each of these means, Hasan recognized immediately that this man was a Zoroastrian for Persian society required these and other less obvious distinctions so that the "infidel Zoroastrians" could be easily spotted. He kept to himself and generally tried to stay out of the way of any Muslims, as Zoroastrians were required to do.

Hasan explained this to Zach and James. They were surprised to see that a people who seemed to have been greatly respected by Muhammad were now being treated by His followers in such a disrespectful way. Zach and James were aware of the praises that Old Testament prophets Isaiah and Ezra had both heaped on the Persian-Zoroastrian king Cyrus. Moreover, they were keenly aware of the accuracy of Zoroaster's prophecy concerning the appearance of Jesus.

To Zach and James, it seemed a blessing to have this man in their midst for their next destination was Saveh, where they hoped to meet with some of the native Zoroastrians to learn more about their prophecies and to see if there was anything useful they might learn about the original Wise Men, who, according to Marco Polo at least, had come from there and been buried there. Although the man was initially wary, Hasan was able to strike up a conversation, assuring the man that he had no ill will toward the man's religion nor his community. His name was Shapur, and he was returning to Saveh after attending to some family matters in Hamadan.

After getting to know Shapur a bit and feeling that he could be trusted, Hasan ventured to explain that he was traveling with two Westerners who were scholars and were interested in learning more about the Zoroastrian religion. He explained that they wanted to visit the burial place of the magi who had returned to Saveh after finding the infant Jesus. He inquired as to whether there might be anyone in Saveh who might be able to assist them in their quest.

Shapur thought for a moment and then answered cautiously, "If you can wait a little in Saveh when we get there, I will inquire and let you know."

Hasan thanked him, and their journey continued. That evening, as they rested at the caravanserai in the village of Famenin, he introduced Shapur to Zach and James and assisted in translating. Shapur was interested to meet people from so far away and was especially interested to hear of their tales of their journey from those distant lands in the West.

Shapur also provided them with an introduction to ancient Persia. "We have recently left Hamadan," he noted, "formerly known as Ecbatana. It was one of the five great capitals of the ancient Persian Empire."

"The Persian Empire had five capital cities?" asked Zach, astonished by the notion.

"Yes, and you have already traveled through two of them. In addition to Ecbatana in the north, we had Ctesiphon, a little southeast of where Bagdad currently stands. Both served as summer residences for the Royal House. In the winter months, though, they could retire to Persepolis or to Pasargadae, both near the city of Shiraz. Or they could go to Shushan, in the southwest of our country."

"Yes, Shushan—we plan to visit that city too. It is a holy city for us as it was the place where the prophet Daniel saw the vision and heard the prophecy that brings us here."

They discussed the majesty of Cyrus and his dynasty, its positive interactions with the Jewish people, and Daniel's prophecies. By the time they reached Saveh, they had gotten to know each other fairly well, in spite of the language barrier. While Zach, James, and Hasan spent the following day restocking their provisions, Shapur set out to speak to some of the members of the Zoroastrian community. At the end of the day, he returned with the news that one of the older members of the community, who had studied Zoroastrian scriptures and commentaries for many years, was willing to meet with them at his home the following day. His name was Ardeshir.

They arrived the next morning at the door of a low-level house. By law, the Zoroastrians were not allowed to build houses higher than about seven feet. The front door had white paint splashed around it—another requirement so that Muslims could avoid contact with those who were now called infidels.

Ardeshir welcomed Zach and James into the small house. He was intrigued to have visitors from so far away, although he was a bit apprehensive when seeing that Hasan was with them. But a translator was needed since the Westerners were still learning the Persian language. Ardeshir decided that he would just need to be cautious in Hasan's presence.

After introductions and some tea, James explained that they were searching for any knowledge of the Promised One and, in particular, any knowledge that the Zoroastrian scriptures might offer. He acknowledged that they knew very little about the Zoroastrian faith, but they knew that it must have contained some prophecies about at least one Messenger because, almost 2,000 years ago, some Zoroastrian magi, motivated by those prophecies, set out on their thousand-mile journey from Saveh and found the new Messiah in Bethlehem. He added that they wanted to know more about that ancient prophecy and to learn if there were any others about the current age.

Ardeshir sat and thought for a long moment. Finally, he said, "You will not understand my answer unless you first understand some of the history of our religion. It is an ancient religion, stretching far into the distant past. Yet our land, being located in the middle of the world, has seen much destruction over the centuries as empires from every direction have invaded our cities and destroyed many of our people and many of the sacred texts that Zoroaster revealed."

And with that, he began an explanation of the coming of Zoroaster and the history of His followers. He explained that like Moses' teachings, Zoroaster's revelation brought new understandings and insights that reinvigorated and built upon some of the existing religious understanding of that age—the ancient religion of the Aryan peoples that was akin, in some respects, to the ancient religion of the people of Hindustan. But it had devolved into polytheism during the centuries prior to Zoroaster's appearance. Therefore, Zoroaster's main teaching was that there was a single God, whom He called "the Lord of Light and Wisdom" (*Ahura Mazda*) in addition to other spiritual beings who could influence our lives, for better or for worse.

Ardeshir explained, "Zoroaster was a prodigy as a child, who seemed to know many things without ever having received that knowledge from others. He was extraordinarily kind toward others, especially the poor and needy, while unconcerned about acquiring things for Himself. He was deeply devoted to God. As a youth, He left his home and spent several years in the wilderness, communing with God and asking Him for guidance. At about age 30, the 'angel of the good mind' appeared to Him and led His soul to the presence of God."

"This seems similar in many respects to the life of Jesus," thought Zach.

"In the beginning, His polytheistic countrymen did not want to listen to His teachings," Ardeshir added.

"Like Muhammad," mentioned Hasan.

"After several years, his cousin became his first follower. He suggested that they leave their homeland and travel northeast to Bactria, whose king was reported to be very good and wise. When Zoroaster taught there, *King Vishtaspa* became His follower as well. From there, other converts came in. He continued to reveal teachings for over 40 years."

"Like Moses," said Zach.

"Yes, except that after all of His efforts to establish the new religion, He sacrificed Himself while defending against an attack on one of the temples led by a group that sought to overthrow His new teachings."

"Somewhat like Jesus," noted James, "who died in order that His message might live."

Ardeshir resumed, "His teaching placed emphasis on how right thoughts can help us choose the right words and how right words can lead us to right actions. He brought us many teachings about good and evil and the nature of man.

"The teachings had spread for some centuries when *Cyrus the Great* arose to unite the Medes of the north and the Persians of the south, thus establishing the great Persian Empire. He was half Median and half Persian; his mother was from the north and his father from the south. In applying the teachings of Zoroaster, King Cyrus treated his subjects, and all the peoples of the lands he captured, with justice, which attracted the support and blessings of many of them.

"Thus, when he conquered Babylon, his empire was extended over the Jewish people who had been taken from Jerusalem into captivity by the Babylonians. Then the two monotheistic religions of the world came into direct contact for the first time.

"Zoroaster taught plainly about life after death, well before such a teaching appeared in Jewish or Christian scripture. He taught that there is both a heaven and a hell as well as an in-between state and that these are spiritual conditions rather than physical places, although they are described in physical terms. He spoke of how we would be judged by God upon our death according to our thoughts, words, and deeds. He also taught us of angels and evil spirits that can affect us in this world, including a primary evil spirit, whom the Jews, Christians, and Muslims now call 'Satan.'

"Zoroaster also spoke of the Holy Spirit, which revealed God's message to Him.

"And He spoke of the coming of future Messengers, or *Saoshyants*, from God, how they would appear about every thousand years, and how great tribulations would occur at the time of their appearance—even the

69

end of the world—as a result of people's failure to listen to their teachings. He spoke of how the dead would be resurrected at that time to witness the coming of the new Messenger."

"All of these teachings we also find in the New Testament," commented Zach.

"And in the Old Testament," added James.

"And in the Quran," added Hasan.

"It is not surprising," replied Ardeshir, "that the later prophets of Judaism as well as the writers of the New Testament and Muhammad should have picked up these ideas. Persia was the largest empire ever known in this part of the world at that time. In some periods, it extended to Jerusalem and as far west as Egypt. So its religious teachings—the teachings of Zoroaster—were well known during the formative ages of each of the Western religions."

Zach offered a more inclusive perspective: "Or perhaps that same Holy Spirit, which spoke to Zoroaster, also spoke to those prophets of the Old Testament and to Jesus and Muhammad? Perhaps it continued to speak about a single spiritual reality?"

"Perhaps," offered Ardeshir with a note of doubt. He was, of course, reluctant to concede that these more recent Messengers might be, in some way, legitimate.

He continued, "For many centuries, much of the scripture of Zoroaster was preserved orally, as was the custom in those days, by carefully learning each of the verses and reciting them so they would be preserved in their pure form. Some were written down, but few copies were made. The oral history was considered more pure and virtuous—you had to really know the scripture. Knowledge of writing was the province of few, and some regarded it as wicked and suited only for mundane financial affairs—whereas the spoken word was accessible to all.

"But they never anticipated the coming of the Accursed Alexander a few centuries later," he continued with a note of sadness in his voice.

"Do you mean *Alexander the Great*?" asked Zach.

"We *never* refer to him as 'great,'" muttered Ardeshir.

"Yes," acknowledged James while casting a scolding glance at Zach. "I suppose Zach hasn't considered this from the Persian perspective before."

"He was a polytheist and the destroyer of the noble truths of Zoroaster. He destroyed so much of our priestly class, the magi, and extinguished the sacred flames that had been burning in the fire temples for centuries," Ardeshir said with disgust. "His warriors killed many who were the living memories of the sacred verses and destroyed much of the few written scriptures that we had. Although some were able to be saved secretly, very much was lost.

"But eventually those Greeks were overrun by the *Parthians*, who came to us from the northeast. They were also followers of Zoroaster, but they were generally more tolerant of foreign religions."

"Yes," James added, "and, as I recall, they were in power in Persia when the Magi came to find the infant Jesus."

"Indeed. The followers of Zoroaster remained in power through the Parthian period and through the *Sassanid* period, which lasted until the coming of Islam. Although great efforts were made to restore the scriptures during those periods, the Muslim conquest was another disaster for us, and later invasions by the Turks, the Mongols, and Tamerlane only added to our difficulties.

"So as you can see, we who live midway between the East and the West have a long history that is fraught with much loss and suffering from the west, the north, and the east. Most of the original words of Zoroaster have been lost over time, or they were replaced with partly remembered fragments from a later period. We know the generality of His teachings, and we venerate those verses that we still have, but for many specifics, we are unable to go back to the original words of Zoroaster.

"Now you have come to inquire about the verses from the Avesta that led the Magi of the Christian Bible to find Jesus at the time of His birth. This much I can say: No one knows for certain. It seems likely that Zoroaster lived perhaps ten or eleven centuries before Jesus. He spoke of future Saoshyants, who would return after about a thousand years for each of the next three thousand years. So it is understandable that the priests, or magi as we call them, would have been expecting to find a Messenger in the years leading up to the birth of Jesus."

"What led them to Jerusalem?" asked Zach.

"I am not certain, but we do have a verse that says, *'On the night when the King will be born, a token will come to the earth—a shower of stars will rain from the sky.'* And again, *'At thirty years of age, He will come to a conference with Me, the Lord of Wisdom.'*[16]

Zach looked at James, and James looked back.

"That certainly sounds like Jesus," said James. "He was about thirty years old when His mission began with 40 days of prayer to God and meditation while in the wilderness, which could certainly be described as a 'conference' with God."

"And," Zach added, "that would explain why they came seeking 'the king' of the Jews. They had told King Herod that they had seen His star while they were in the east. Perhaps they were referring to this shower of stars."

"Or," added James, "perhaps they saw a great comet, which also brought with it a shower of meteors."

Turning to Ardeshir, Zach said, "Surely it must have been wonderful news for the other magi to discover that Zoroaster's prophecy was accurately fulfilled after a thousand years or so. They must have all been very excited by that!"

"I don't know," Ardeshir replied. "If the magi who found Jesus had any success in convincing other magi upon their return concerning the truth of their findings, it is not known to history. Perhaps most of their fellow magi felt that the promised Messenger must come from Persia, or He must at least be a follower of Zoroaster. Perhaps they felt that the magi who traveled westward to Jerusalem went too far. Or perhaps it was impossible for them to believe that the Messenger could have come to a family that was not from the royal or warrior class, as Zoroaster had been, but rather of the family of a lowly carpenter. And to have been born in a stable, where animals feed! How could this have been a true Messenger of God with such a lowly place in life?

"And in any case, most believed that the Saoshyant would be born of a virgin, who had bathed in the holy Lake Kasaoya in southeastern Persia."

"But Jesus *was* born of a virgin," offered Zach, "and perhaps the reference to the lake was allegorical. Or it was a reference to the great lake of Galilee, just east of Nazareth."

James asked, "What would most of the other magi have thought about the coming of a new Prophet? They were, as I understand it, the intellectual leaders of their time. They were highly respected and knowledgeable, and as such, most were wealthy as well. Would they have realized that the fulfillment of the prophecy might change everything, including their positions in society?"

"Hmm... It is possible," acknowledged Ardeshir slowly. "They may have found the news to be less positive than what the magi who found Jesus had expected."

James replied, "It sounds like many of these other magi were perhaps not much better than the Jewish scribes and Pharisees, whose love for their positions and power prevented them from recognizing Jesus."

"Perhaps," Ardeshir responded defensively, "or perhaps they just felt that it was more prudent to wait and see. Perhaps they heard, a few decades later, that Jesus had not succeeded in convincing the king of the truth of His message—as Zoroaster had been able to do—and so perhaps they felt that he could not have been the Saoshyant. When they heard that this Jesus had been crucified and that he had very few followers, perhaps they rightly concluded that the magi of Bethlehem were mistaken. Or at least that it would be good to wait to see if a better candidate for the Saoshyant would soon appear."

"And so they waited," James suggested with a pause. "And they kept waiting until they died. And the next generation had grown accustomed to waiting, so they waited too. And after a couple of generations, their expectations were locked onto certain interpretations that their fathers or grandfathers had believed so that accepting any other interpretation became impossible because they clung so tenaciously to the views that their fathers had taught them."

"Well," replied Ardeshir grudgingly, "I suppose that is one possible perspective. But what makes you think it was actually so?"

"It is a pattern," explained James. "I can see it in the expectations of the Jews during the time of Jesus. I now also see it in the expectation of the Jews and the Christians at the time of Muhammad. And I can even begin to see it in my own people in their expectations today. Unwilling to acknowledge the possibility of their own fallibility and unwilling to open their minds to a variety of plausible understandings of ways in which the prophecies might be fulfilled, the religious leaders develop a single interpretation in their own minds then refuse to consider anything that doesn't fit the mold that they themselves have created. They become locked onto it, as if they themselves were the All-Knowing One, and so they refuse to accept the possibility that other valid understandings might exist."

"In any case," Ardeshir resumed, "I can simply assure you that we have no written records of any magi returning from Bethlehem with news of the birth of a new Prophet nor of any return to Jerusalem 30 years later to learn what Jesus had to teach as a grown man. A few Persians may have remembered the story of the magi who found Jesus, for when the first Christian teachers arrived here several decades later, it appears that they were able to find this site here in Saveh, where the remains of these magi had been buried. Eventually, when their community grew, they built a church over the spot. Centuries later, after the Muslim invasion, the Muslims, aware of its significance from the Christian Bible, apparently took over the church and built a mosque over it. And the mosque is still here."[17]

"But did the early church grow here as a result of the other Zoroastrians following the same line of reasoning of the Christ-searching Magi?" asked Zach.

Ardeshir shrugged. "Over the first few centuries of the Christian times, a few Persians became Christians but not many. It was not like the Armenians to the northwest. The Christian community grew more quickly there, amongst the Roman and Greek pagans but also among the Zoroastrians there."

"Yes," added James, "I also have read about the early Armenian churches. Their followers spread throughout Armenia, including that part that is now northwestern Persia, not too far from here, in the first century AD. Christian communities there gradually grew during the next two centuries, as they did elsewhere in the Roman Empire. But they still constituted a relatively small percentage of the population when something miraculous happened that caused the king of Armenia, *Tiridates the Great*, to become a Christian.

"I don't recall all the details of the story, but I remember hearing that he became a Christian in 301 AD—several years *before* the conversion of Constantine in Rome—and that as a result, Armenia was actually the first nation to adopt Christianity. If the Magi had left any favorable impression of Christianity amongst the Zoroastrians of Persia, it apparently did not reach the ears of the shah in those years, for the Persian king of the Sasanian dynasty, *Shapur II*, did not seem to regard the new Christian leaders of Rome and Armenia any more favorably than he had regarded the former pagan Roman leaders, with whom Persia had been fighting for several centuries."

Ardeshir acknowledged that this was true. It seemed that the force of historical precedence or the desire of religious leaders to maintain their positions had blinded the political leaders on both sides to the religious similarities that then existed between the new Christian religion and the ancient Zoroastrian one.

"It changed briefly," Ardeshir resumed, "about a hundred years later, when the 14th Sasanian king, *Yazdegerd I*, came to power. He favored religious tolerance toward Christians and Jews. He married a Jewish woman, who became the queen of the realm. Christianity was recognized as an acceptable religion throughout his empire in 410 AD. Some say he even considered converting to Christianity. He had peaceful relations with the Eastern Roman Empire. In fact, his relations with the Roman emperor, *Arcadius*, were so positive that upon Arcadius's death, it was discovered that Arcadius had written that he entrusted the training of his only son—the future Byzantine Emperor—to Yazdegerd."

"One can only wonder," Zach said to James wistfully, "how history might have been different if Yazdegerd had followed the example of Tiridates and become Christian. The ancient conflict between the Persian East and the Greco-Roman West would have been buried by a common recognition of Christianity as the natural successor not only to Judaism but also to Zoroastrianism."

"Yes," James agreed, "they both would have avoided the more than 200 years of intermittent warfare between their empires that followed Yazdegerd's reign, and Christian civilization would have been greatly strengthened throughout the East."

Ardeshir added, "Our magi class, which still had great influence, would never have allowed it. They had too much at stake in their own positions."

"Alas! A thousand times alas for these attachments!" groaned Zach. "If they could simply have followed the example of the humble Magi who found Jesus, consider what mutual destruction could have been avoided!"

"Yes indeed," agreed James. "It seems as if it is easier for leaders to motivate their followers with fear of others than to create a motivation based on the mutual respect and understanding that comes from a recognition of their common roots. Why was it that the Christian leaders of that day, reigning in a country on the borders of Persia, ignored the story of the wise men of the East, which was found in their own gospel, with all of its implications about the truth of the religion of Zoroaster? And why did Zoroaster's followers refuse to accept the news that their own magi brought back from Bethlehem about the fulfillment of their own prophecies? In short, why did the religious leaders of both sides turn away from the fruits of the spirit, which could have led to a rapprochement between their civilizations—a uniting of East and West? Alas, small-minded religious leaders have so often failed to lead. They have been so concerned with their own power and positions that they have failed to open themselves to the larger truths."

Ardeshir continued, "Even at the time of Yazdegerd, it was just a small squabble between a local bishop and the local Zoroastrian priests that soured relations between the king and the Christian community during the final year of his life. The rulers that followed brought warfare between the empires. Roman Christianity was prohibited in Persia, although Nestorian Christianity, being independent of the Byzantium West, was allowed to grow. It became the main branch of Christianity in Persia."

"Yes," added James, "I've read of it. Sometimes known as 'the Church of the East,' it spread north and eastward across vast territories in India, China, and as far as Mongolia, becoming at one point the geographically largest church of all Christendom. Marco Polo himself wrote about some of these Christian communities he met during his travels there. And yet this church never had enough followers, nor the royal patronage needed, to become the main religion of any of these lands."

Ardeshir resumed, "Persia, of course, remained predominantly Zoroastrian until the early seventh century of the Christian era, when Islam appeared. By that time, the toll of the centuries of constant fighting between the Zoroastrian Persian empire and the Christian Byzantine empire had greatly weakened them both. The Sasanian rulers did not see it coming nor did the Byzantines."

"Indeed," noted James, "we have heard that story from our Muslim guide in the Galilee. Christianity lost much during the spread of Islam," added James, "but Persia lost much more for the whole kingdom was overturned."

"Islam," Ardeshir sighed, "a religion that destroyed in a few years the Persian kingdom, which had taken centuries to build."

At this point, Hasan, who had been helping with translation without comment, spoke up with his perspective.

"Zoroastrians and Christians both like to explain the spread of Islam by portraying it as a religion spread by force while ignoring the failings of their own leaders. They often forget that their leaders had become more concerned with enlarging their armies, empires, and wealth rather than their people's welfare and spiritual development. These two supposedly religious empires did not hesitate to conscript the young men of their kingdoms into warfare and to increase the taxes on the rest to pay for their dreams of conquest. Their religious leaders had strayed far from the path of the spirit. Otherwise, they would have recognized the similarities between the teachings of their own Messenger and those of the Prophet Muhammad. While He was in Medina, Muhammad wrote to both leaders, urging them to recognize the new Message that He brought. But no—these leaders had been corrupted by a love of power, prestige, and wealth, while their conscripts and the masses of the people suffered under their rule.

"Islam came to Persia and defeated its rulers in a few years, but they did not force Zoroastrians to convert. I offer as evidence two clear items: First, the force of the young religion of Islam, less than twenty years after the Prophet had departed from this earthly life, was nowhere near sufficient to overtake a land as vast as Persia if the Persian people had been enthusiastic believers in Zoroaster at that time. But the masses had grown tired of the unceasing wars waged in the name of religion, with its excessive taxation and the loss of their sons, brothers, and fathers. When the Islamic army arrived to fight against the ruling class, most of the common people were so dissatisfied with the old ways that they did not make any serious effort to support the old order. As the new Islamic order expanded into the Zoroastrian lands, there would no longer be constant fighting at the western boundary of Persia. And after it spread farther eastward, there would be no threat of fighting there either. It is true that Islam required a tax to assist the poor, but overall, it was a good deal less than the taxes that the Zoroastrian leaders levied to support their wars and their lifestyle. Moreover, the additional tax revenue from non-Muslims became a financial incentive to *avoid* any forced conversions. So, indeed, many of the poorer Persian people welcomed the change in leadership."

James interjected, "Well, yes, that seems entirely possible. It has often happened this way in history. The upper class seems to forget that their own well-being rests upon the support of the lower classes and depends upon their belief, shared by all classes, that their system of government is the best one possible—worth sacrificing one's wealth and even one's life for. The lower classes are not blind. When they see that the upper class is mainly concerned about its own well-being, the shared vision is betrayed. The lower classes may not be able to rebel, but their support for the status quo weakens or dissolves. And then, when even a small crisis arrives and the upper class calls upon the people to sacrifice in order to save their wonderful society, it falls on deaf ears. There remain too few who are willing to sacrifice themselves to preserve an existing order that is unjust.

"I think of any human civilization," James continued, "as being like a house that rests on an unseen foundation, which, in turn, rests upon the soil. The foundation is the working class, while the soil below them is the underlying belief in the goodness and justice of their system of governance. Ultimately, all societies rest on some kind of spiritual vision, and society remains firm and strong as long as that belief remains firm and strong. That is why Jesus said, 'But seek ye first the kingdom of God, and His righteousness; and all these things'—that is, all the things you need—'shall be added unto you.'[18] He brought a host of spiritual ideals and laid a vast spiritual foundation upon which the Christian civilization was built.

"This 'mandate of heaven'—a sense of common vision and purpose that binds society together—can be withdrawn. But I don't believe that it is withdrawn by God. Rather, it is lost by short-sighted leaders who fail to understand it, who have no spiritual vision. It doesn't take too many such leaders, whose prime concern is their own fame and fortune or the fortune and power of their family or their class, before the erosion and weakening of the foundational beliefs begins. Unless it is quickly reversed, the foundation itself begins to crack, and before much longer, the cracks appear in the walls above, and the whole structure is weakened to such an extent that it will collapse even in a small storm."

They all paused for a moment to consider the implications of these ideas. Then Hasan added, "And who can truly inspire a new spiritual vision other than a Prophet of God? Who else could ever provide the new mandate from heaven? Indeed, isn't this *exactly* the reason that God sends a new Messenger?"

Zach reflected on how amazing it was that whole civilizations, with all their material development, ultimately rested upon inspiring ideals and upon the devotion that the masses of people were willing to give to those ideals. How dangerous, how utterly foolhardy, it was for the leading group in any society to betray those ideals.

While Ardeshir was mulling this over, Hasan continued: "My second piece of evidence that Islam did not force the Persian people to convert is nothing less than you yourself and the entire Zoroastrian community in our land. If Islam had conquered people by the sword, there would be no members of your community left. But instead, most Persians remained Zoroastrians for several generations after Islam defeated the Zoroastrian ruling class. Gradually, over a few centuries, these people became acquainted with Muhammad's revelation and saw that it contained many of the same truths and concepts that they knew from Zoroaster's teachings. Gradually over the centuries, most of them, but not all, accepted the new teachings.

"The only thing that the followers of Muhammad overthrew was the self-serving upper class, who loved their wealth and positions and whose priests were fully a part of that class. The priests had lost any true spirit of faith and service and had become more devoted to protecting their own positions than to sacrificing themselves in order to provide true spiritual guidance for their leaders and for their people. As our friend here has suggested," he said, nodding at James, "they had lost the love, the devotion, and the strong support of most of the people over whom they ruled."

Ardeshir thought this over for a moment. Then he murmured, as if talking to himself, "Is it any different among the ruling class and the mullahs of Islam today?" But immediately after saying this, he was seized with fear, realizing that he could be easily taken into the street and flogged to death for such a comment.

There was a long pause, which made Ardeshir very uneasy. Hasan's first impulse was to respond in an accusatory manner, but then he began to think of all of the problems that the orthodox branches of the Shiah hierarchy had caused for Shaykh Ahmad and Siyyid Kazim. The leaders of that hierarchy were just as jealous of their positions of authority as the leaders of the Zoroastrian religion had been at the time of the Islamic conquest. Yes, they clothed their words in Quranic verses, but Hasan and many others could see through them, and they saw that their true intent was self-serving.

Finally, Hasan simply said, much to Ardeshir's amazement and relief, "Alas, you are right.... We have come full circle. The devotion to a truly spiritual perspective, to justice, and to the service of society has, over the centuries, eroded away from Islam too. Instead of striving to understand the spiritual realities, our leaders are often striving to find ways to increase their material wealth. In place of the self-control created by prayer and fasting, they have developed a desire to control others. And instead of ideal leadership by force of example, they have descended into leadership by force, punishment, and fear.

"Many of our religious leaders have become as hungry wolves, who wear the garb of religious teachings but who, inside, wish only to strengthen their power and increase their wealth while forcing their views on others."

"Wolves in sheep's clothing!" interjected Zach, recalling Jesus' description from the book of Matthew.

"Indeed," added James, "we can even see some of that in our countries back home. It seems as if the winter season of religion is come upon us all. And we are *all* awaiting the springtime of renewed guidance from God."

He paused and then added, *"But this is exactly why we are searching for the Promised One now!* It is not simply that our understanding of the prophecies has guided us here. It is also that in the great cycle of human civilizations, we can perceive the gradual but inexorable decline that is eating into the foundations of society—yours and also ours. People are declining into a material pattern of thinking. They think only of the physical things, and it leads them to crave wealth and power. Even among the religiously inclined, the material perspective surrounds them and leads them to understand their prophecies in literal, physical, or material terms. It is *precisely* at times such as these that God's Messengers have appeared in the past."

Their discussion of the details of the history of the Zoroastrian faith, as well as the Christian and Islamic faiths, continued until late afternoon, when Ardeshir stood up and said, "We have so much to learn from each other. Would you be willing to stay with us for dinner?"

James, Zach, and Hasan all felt that although they had learned a lot and had broken through many barriers, there was still much more to learn, so they accepted Ardeshir's kind offer. Their discussions and learning between the four members of three religions continued through dinner and well into the evening. At length, James, noting the time, suggested that they should return to their caravanserai.

"But there is so much more to tell," insisted Ardeshir. "Now that you know the historical background, we must discuss more about our understanding of the future."

Zach and James said they would be happy to do that and pledged to return within a couple of days to continue the discussion.

*    *    *

HAVING LEARNED MUCH FROM each other's perspectives and having had a day to reflect over them, their next meeting was easier and more cordial, and they enjoyed some tea as they continued their discussion.

Ardeshir reiterated some of the concepts that Zoroaster had taught. The idea of a single God, or Lord of Wisdom, was easily understood. So also was the idea that there were heavenly spirits that could assist man in his efforts and the idea that there were wicked forces that could inspire men to do evil. Zoroastrians believed that a time would come in the future when all would be called to account for their deeds and that those who were good would go to heaven, while those who were evil would suffer in a fiery hell with a river of molten metal. James and Zach recognized this as being not so different from what they had read in the latter part of the Book of Revelation. And just as in that book, there was mention of the Promised One returning after a thousand years, at the end of time.

This raised a question for Zach. "You mentioned yesterday that many in your religion believe that God would send Messengers in intervals of about a thousand years. It is now about 3,000 years since Zoroaster appeared. Are His followers expecting the Saoshyant to appear anytime soon?"

Ardeshir reflected a bit before responding. "There are some amongst us who believe that He may return sometime soon—within this century at least."[19]

"Did you see the brilliant comet in the skies last spring? Does that indicate anything to your followers today, as it did to the Magi in the time of Jesus?"

"Of course we saw it—how could anyone have missed it? And yes, it was a cause for much discussion here. And even more, we heard news of sailors returning from the southern seas that spoke of a brilliant new star that was clearly visible in all parts of the south. It appeared in the same month as the comet.§ But alas, in the surviving text of our religion, there was no indication of the *exact* time or place for us to search."

Zach replied, "You are no doubt aware that there is a great expectation among the Muslims, especially the Shiites, that their promised Qaim will arise this very year. In my own country and in James' country, there are many who expect that Jesus will return this year also."

"So I have heard," said Ardeshir. "And if one or the other comes to pass, one religion will be proven correct and the others will be shown to be wrong."

---

§ The binary star Eta Carinae, a rare Type V supernova, erupted to peak brilliance in mid-March 1843, becoming the second-most luminous star in the skies for a brief period that year but visible only south of 30 degrees N latitude.

"This is exactly what I once thought," said Zach, "but there is another possibility. What if all three come to pass?"

"If the Saoshyant, the Qaim, and Jesus all appeared at the same time?" asked Ardeshir with great surprise. "Then there would no doubt be a tremendous battle!"

"No, no, no," replied Zach. "I mean, what if a single Messenger appears who fulfills the prophecies of Zoroaster, Jesus, and Muhammad?"

Ardeshir looked puzzled while he considered the idea. Then he replied, "Clearly impossible! That would suggest that all three religions were correct, and we all know that it cannot be so. If Christianity were a true religion, why did they fight against us for 300 years, nearly destroying our Sasanian-Zoroastrian kingdom and preparing it for its final destruction by the Muslims?"

"I asked a similar question when I first considered Islam," returned Zach. "Christian civilization has been fighting with Islam—theologically and often militarily—for more than twelve centuries. To suggest that Islam was a true revelation would be to suggest that a vast amount of conflict between the religions should never have occurred. It also suggests that overly ambitious kings and their religious leaders have failed to understand the true spirit of the teachings of the revelation that created their religion. Sometimes they may have misunderstood, but sometimes they have not even tried. Sometimes the kings may have been misled by religious leaders that were more devoted to increasing the number of their followers or protecting their positions than they were to a deep understanding of truth. And all too often these religious leaders have tried to bend the teachings of their religion toward their own political ends, leaving the people with a distorted religion that is far from the true intentions of its Founder."

Ardeshir was mulling this idea over. Then he said, "But Muhammad did not come 2,000 years after Zoroaster. He came only about 1,700 or 1,800 years afterward, so he could not have been one of the Saoshyants."

Hasan interjected at this point. "It is true that Islam is dated from 622 years after the birth of Jesus. However, His revelation continued to divinely guide us not only through the end of His life but also through His son-in-law, Ali, and through Ali's sons and then onward through to the last of the 12 Imams, who disappeared in 260 AH. So this expression of God's guidance lasted until almost exactly 2,000 years after Zoroaster's time. Therefore, it is very possible that the second Saoshyant was indeed Muhammad."

"Well," Ardeshir finally said, trying to be polite, "that is a *very* strange thought. I'm not sure that it is even possible...but I suppose we can just wait to see what the new Saoshyant has to say about it when He appears."

"Yes," replied Zach slowly, "and I think we may find Him soon."

"I have another question," said James. "The Jewish people believe that there will be two Messengers—Elijah first and then the Messiah. Some of us Christians are also expecting two—the return of Elijah, which is John the Baptist, and then the return of Jesus. The Shiite Muslims also expect two—the Qaim followed by the return of Husayn. And the Sunni Muslims expect two—the Mahdi followed by the return of Jesus. So I would like to know whether the Zoroastrian community expects the return of two Messengers also."

Ardeshir thought for a moment and then said, "Yes. Many of us expect that the Ushidar-Mah will appear first, followed by the Shah Bahram."[20]

James and Zach were interested to hear this answer. James asked the next question: "Where do you expect that He will appear?"

"It is hard to say," replied Ardeshir. "Some say from China, some say from Hindustan, some say He will arise from the holy Lake Kasaoya in Sistan province in the southeast, and some say He will come from Fars. But no one knows for certain."

"Where is Fars?" asked Zach.

"It is to the south, in the southwestern part of Persia—a province whose capital is Shiraz, near the ancient Persian city of Persepolis."

"Is there any distinctive feature we should look for?" asked James.

"He will have innate knowledge, as Zoroaster did. From earliest childhood, He will be able to answer questions with knowledge that hasn't been taught to him."

"Yes, we have heard the same from Christian and Muslim expectations. Is there anything else?"

"Yes, He will be a mighty warrior, who will gather a large army from the east and will come forth to destroy all those who persecute us."

Zach thought of how the Jewish people held similar hopes during the time of their oppression under the Romans and how God's fulfillment with the coming of Jesus had not met their expectations. He could tell from the expression on James' face that he was thinking the same thing, but neither of them was inclined to disabuse Ardeshir of his hopes.

James simply commented, "Sometimes smaller religious groups have hoped that God would relieve them of their sufferings directly rather than listening for new spiritual insights that would enable them to resolve their own spiritual problems that lay at the root of their outward sufferings."

Ardeshir paused to consider these thoughts. As he was thinking over all they had discussed, Ardeshir remembered something from their previous meeting: "You had told me earlier that you wished to visit the Tomb of the Wise Men. Let us meet early tomorrow afternoon at the *Jameh Mosque* on the south side of the city. If you can help us enter," he said, nodding toward Hasan, "I will be pleased to show you what I know about it."

Zach was eager to pursue this possibility, so they parted for the day.

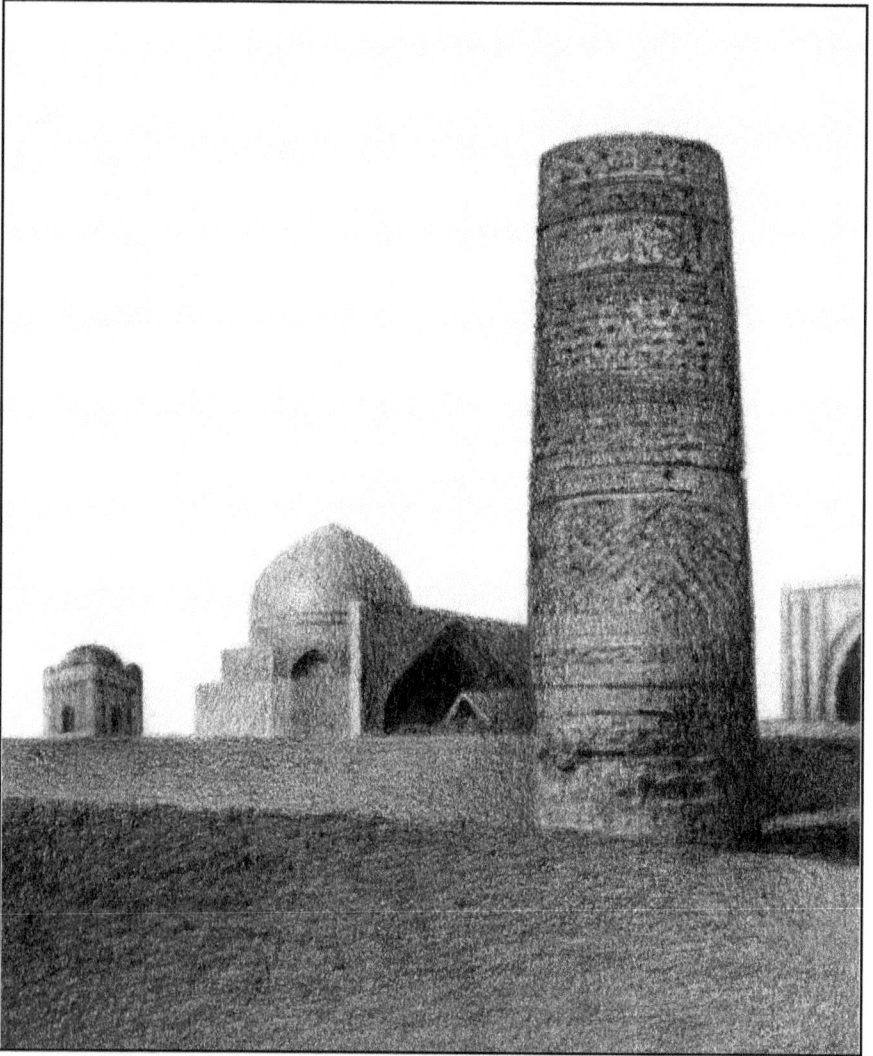

The Jameh Mosque in Saveh,
with minaret on right and
tomb of the Wise Men on left

# Chapter 6

# LAYERS OF FAITH

THE FOLLOWING MORNING, ZACH brought his diary up to date with all that he had learned from Ardeshir. It was, by now, the fourth day of Jamadiyu'l-Avval in the Muslim calendar—May 22 in the West. He thought of how beautiful the spring must be back in his hometown, with flowers and trees all in bloom. He had by now become adapted to the arid climate of the Middle East, but he missed the rich greenery of his native land.

The three men met Ardeshir at the place he had described—at the base of a large minaret adjacent to the Jameh Mosque. The minaret was ornately decorated in protruding brick in geometric patterns, some of which appeared to form Arabic inscriptions. Hasan, being a Muslim Persian, had no problem leading the group into the mosque compound. One of the mullahs seemed to be eyeing this diverse group suspiciously, but Hasan simply said, "I'm told that this is a holy place of Muslims and of Christians and even of Zoroastrians," and the mullah let them pass.

The dome of the mosque itself was covered in beautifully patterned gold and blue tiles, as was the inside of the main mosque. It faced Mecca, as most mosques do, which meant it faced southwest over a barren plain beyond the outskirts of the city.

"I have heard it was built about 700 years ago, but it was built on foundations that are older than that," said Ardeshir.

"Then this mosque was the one that Marco Polo and his uncles saw when they passed through Saveh in about 1271," said Zach. "It must have been even more beautiful back then."

"Possibly," replied Ardeshir, "but they came here shortly after the Mongolian invasion, when so much of northern Persia was damaged or destroyed.

"The mosque had been built on the remains of a church from pre-Islamic times—a church that may well have been built another 700 years before the mosque by the Nestorian Christians, who were, at that time, reasonably well tolerated by the Sasanians because they had dissociated themselves from Roman Christianity."

"So that was around 400 AD," James added.

Ardeshir nodded and continued. "They might have built their church here because they had heard that this might be the resting place of the Magi who are mentioned in your scriptures. Perhaps the earliest Christian communities had heard of them from the Zoroastrians themselves. Some Christian communities were quite well established here within 200 years of Christ's birth, and the earliest Christian individuals probably arrived by the end of the first Christian century—not soon enough to find your 'Wise Men' still alive but probably soon enough to hear the stories of their travels from their children or their grandchildren. Whether those Magi built a fire temple here or simply worshiped at one that already existed here, we cannot know, but below the foundations of the Christian church, there is clear evidence that this was originally the site of one of our fire temples."

Zach drew a deep breath. "Goodness me! When you explain it like that, it seems so near at hand that I can almost touch it!"

Ardeshir smiled. "If you would like to touch it," he beckoned and nodded his head to the right, "follow me."[21]

He turned to Hasan to confirm that he would protect them if any of the mullahs found them and raised objections to their being in some of the non-public places.

"Certainly," replied Hasan.

So Ardeshir led them quietly into one of the side rooms and, from there, through a doorway. He pulled a small oil lamp out from beneath his cloak and ignited it to give them light as they proceeded toward the end of a narrow passage that was bricked over, except for a small hole. They took turns squeezing through it and then found themselves at the top of a narrow flight of spiraled steps.

A couple dozen steps down, they came upon a large room and then another stairway leading yet farther downward. At the bottom of this, they entered a room with walls of polished limestone blocks. On these were carved repeatedly a symbol that was a composite of the Greek letters chi and rho.

"The ancient Christian symbol!" exclaimed James in wonderment. "These are the first letters in the Greek word for Christ. They are the symbol that Constantine saw in his vision, which led him to become a Christian!" He ran his fingers across the letters to make sure this was not a dream.

Then, gazing further around, he said, "Look here! Inscriptions of the Greek letters alpha and omega. This is clearly a reference to Christ's statement in the Book of Revelation about being the Alpha and the Omega—the first and the last!"

"Yes!" added Zach with excitement. "There is no doubt that this was once a Christian church—and a very ancient one at that." They both stared in wonder.

"But what of this?" Ardeshir asked as he pointed his lamp toward a large slab of granite, perhaps ten-foot square, near the center of the lowest section of the room. The slab had a large saucer-shaped indentation in its upper surface, which was covered in soot.

"I have no idea...." replied James.

"This," said Ardeshir proudly, "is a fire altar of the type that my ancestors have used over the last three millennia." He smiled. "Yes, below the Muslim layer and below the Christian layer, this site was first of all a Zoroastrian place of worship."

Zach, James, and Hasan stood in silence for a long moment as they tried to imagine the immense span of time that separated them from the day that simple slab of granite was hewn and the devoted efforts of the men that originally carved it and placed it there.

Finally, Zach asked, "Do you think the Magi are buried here?"

Ardeshir explained that it was likely that many people were buried here. The bones of some Zoroastrians, especially venerated ones, were buried near their temples. And many Christians and Muslims would have been buried in the area or sometimes even in hidden vaults behind walls and in areas that are now sealed off and forgotten. "If you dug in any direction, you would likely find some burial sites before long. But if you were looking for the burial vaults of the Wise Men of your Bible, how would you recognize them?" He shrugged.

On the way back up, Ardeshir took them through the room at the middle level to a place where they could see three large stone sarcophagi. These seemed to be very ancient but had no markings or ornamentation to indicate their exact age. They were empty. Grave robbers had apparently been here many years—or perhaps many centuries—ago. He shrugged again and said, "How would you know?"

While returning to the public areas, James inquired, "How did you ever find this place?"

"As a young boy, I had a good friend among my Muslim neighbors. He was an adventurous fellow, and after finding it himself, he led me here to show me what he had found. Adventurous young boys often know more about the small, hidden places in their vicinity than their parents do." He smiled.

Ardeshir then took them outside of the mosque compound and around to the area to the south. There, a short distance from the compound's outer wall, was a smaller square structure with a small dome above it.

"A Zoroastrian tomb," offered Ardeshir.

"How do you know?" asked James.

"It is a typical Zoroastrian style," he answered. "And see how it is oriented..."

They could all see that it was at an angle with respect to the mosque, so it was certainly not facing Mecca.

"One side faces exactly north," continued Ardeshir, "one side south, one side east, and one west. We studied the stars. We set the beginning of our year according to the spring equinox. We set our temples according to the natural order of the directions. We had a sense of the orderliness of God's creation," he said wistfully.

A quote came to Zach's mind, which he remembered from Marco Polo's book and now recited:

> *In Persia is the city called Saveh, from which the three Magi set out when they came to worship Jesus Christ. Here, too, they lie buried in three sepulchers of great size and beauty. Above each sepulcher is a square building with a domed roof of very fine workmanship. The one is just beside the other.*[22]

"Well, it is certainly square with a domed roof. The "great size" part may have been a bit of an exaggeration, unless the sepulchers down below are larger than the buildings above. But then, I've heard Marco was sometimes given to exaggeration. Where do you suppose the other two buildings are?"

"Possibly destroyed during one of the many invasions that have cursed this land," offered Ardeshir. "Or possibly they once stood where the other buildings of the mosque compound now stand."

"So do you suppose one of the Magi is buried in this one?" James asked Ardeshir.

"This is called the 'Tomb of the Master and the Disciple.' But which master? And which disciple?" Ardeshir shrugged.

As they walked back toward the minaret, James and Zach expressed their gratitude to Ardeshir for the tour of the mosque/church/fire temple of the Wise Men and for all his time and hospitality. They bid him farewell and continued to the caravanserai with thoughts of the great amalgamation of history that had occurred on that site.

"It is an amazing and yet very sad story," James mused. "Can you imagine how different history would have been if the people of Persia had listened when the Wise Men returned?"

"Yes, the thought had crossed my mind," replied Zach.

"If those men had had even a small following, and if they had sent someone back 30 years later to learn from Jesus during the years of His ministry and then taken His teachings back to Persia, they would surely have established a church, which would have grown. Persia might well have become the first Christian country instead of neighboring Armenia.

"Imagine if Constantine and all the Christian emperors who followed him for the next three centuries found that they had a peaceful Christian neighbor to their east instead of the traditionally feared Zoroastrians."

"Or even," suggested Zach, "if the Christian kingdoms of Armenia and Byzantium had treated the Zoroastrian empire as one that was inspired by a true revelation, as evidenced by the accurate prophecy of Zoroaster."

"Either way, the better part of three centuries of intermittent warfare between East and West would have been avoided.

"And if the Zoroastrian religion had accepted the Christian one, the idol-worshipping tribes of western Arabia would have been surrounded on all sides by the combined Christian–Zoroastrian–Judaic civilization since the Zoroastrian faith dominated eastern and southern Arabia, while the Coptic Christian religion dominated from Egypt to Ethiopia and across the southern end of the Red Sea into Yemen. It seems likely that they would have learned of monotheism before Muhammad ever arrived."

"The nature of Islam would have been entirely different," replied Zach. "In addition to eliminating the fighting that occurred between the Christian and Zoroastrian empires, it is entirely possible that the fighting between Islam and the Christians and Zoroastrians might never have occurred. Can you imagine how different history might have been?

"I'd bet that those who refused to listen when the Wise Men brought home the news of their success in finding the infant Jesus had *no idea* of the enormous consequences of their refusal! If they can now view the long chain of tragic events that have happened in this world through the centuries from their vantage point in the spiritual world, those people must have spent ages bewailing their failure."

"True indeed," said James. "Not unlike the consequences for the Jewish religion after their rejection of Jesus. Their desire for a political leader instead of a spiritual one brought on their destruction by Rome, and thus they have been without a homeland for over seventeen centuries."

"But then," Hasan added, "what of the consequences for Christianity for having ignored the teachings of Islam? It could have healed the many theological divisions that plagued and weakened Christian civilization at the time, and the combined benefits of both Jesus' teachings and Muhammad's would have accrued to the West about seven centuries earlier than they did."

They all sighed. "Oh, the utter folly of men!" declared James. "How carelessly we have tossed away the revelations that God has offered us! How arrogantly we have asserted our own opinions over the teachings of God's Messenger! And how utterly blind we have been to the vast consequences of these rejections!"

"Let us hope," Zach added wistfully, "that the pattern will not be repeated when the Promised One appears again in our new age."

*       *       *

THEY HAD BEEN AT Saveh for almost a week now, learning all that they could from Ardeshir and inquiring about Zoroastrian prophecies of the coming of Jesus and whether they had any prophecies of the time or place of His return. They had found a dramatic reference to the coming of the Promised One of the Zoroastrian faith: Two figures would appear—first the Ushidar Mah and then the Shah Bahram—very much like the two figures expected in the Jewish, Christian, and Islamic prophecies. They had found that there was also an expectation among many Zoroastrians that this would occur during the current century, which, according to Zoroaster's prophecy, marked the end of the third millennium from the time of His original appearance. All of this was reassuring and served to reinforce their understanding of Zoroastrianism as a true revelation, with prophecies that were parallel to what they knew from both the Old and the New Testaments as well as what they had learned from Islam, Hinduism, and Buddhism. But frustratingly, they had not found anything more specific about the exact time and place for the appearance of the Promised One than what they already knew from the biblical and Islamic references. They found it interesting that the Shah Bahram—the second of the two Messengers—was to be a descendant of the former kings of Persia. They had not heard that from the disciples of Siyyid Kazim. They also knew it would soon be time to move onward from Saveh.

They were more cognizant than ever of the awful toll that centuries of fighting can take on any civilization and how its most treasured gems of knowledge and history could disappear in a cloud of smoke whenever ignorant invaders succeeded in breaking through defenses and coming in to kill, burn, and pillage. It had now been about thirty centuries since the appearance of Zoroaster. He had laid the foundation for one of the most enduring religions on earth. Yet its length also meant that it had been subjected to attack and loss for an immense span of time. It seemed as if the physical fate that the ancient Zoroastrian temple had suffered was similar to the fate of the religion itself—covered over by layer upon layer of more recent history until it was difficult to get a clear picture of what the original had looked like.

As they returned to the caravanserai, both Zach and James were feeling downhearted at the results of their efforts. The Wise Men of Jesus' time had reached Jerusalem and had received guidance from the king and his advisers on where to look. It seemed so simple! But here they were, in the much larger land of Persia. They had been on the road and searching for two months, and yet they were still without a clue regarding exactly where to find Him.

# Chapter 7

# TOWARD THE SUNRISE IN THE SOUTHERN SKY

THE EVENING WAS CLEAR and warm, with a waxing crescent moon setting in the west. Zach asked James' leave that he might retire to the grounds of the mosque of the Magi to pray for guidance. There, as he sat with his back to the southwest wall of the mosque looking out at that small, ancient fire temple of the Magi and, beyond that, across the large, open plain toward the mountains in the distance and toward Mecca and Jerusalem beyond the horizon, he thought long and hard about everything that had led them to this point and all of the discussions that they had had with the people of so many different religions and backgrounds. Had he been wrong to start on this quest? He thought about how much he had learned, but he also thought about how many places they had seen and how many people they had asked; yet in spite of all of their efforts, they still had not found the One whom they sought.

Tears started to flow down his cheeks as he began his prayers, acknowledging his powerlessness and asking for God's guidance, sincerely beseeching Him to lead them aright. As he thought of the successful search of the Wise Men of Jesus' time, as well as the successful searches of Bahira, Waraqah, Nestor, Ibn al-Hayyaban, and Salman during Muhammad's time, he prayed that they might look down upon him and guide him as they themselves had been guided. He felt blessed at having discovered the meaning of the year 1260 and the Islamic dimension of the search as well as all of the signs pointing toward Persia as the right country in which to look. But the country was so huge! They would surely need much guidance. As he prayed,

95

he began to think of his father, who had sent him on this journey and who had said just before he passed away that he would do whatever he could do to help him on his quest.

His prayers were longer and more earnest than he had ever prayed before. In this state of intense longing, he seemed to gradually lose touch with his physical surroundings. The light from three stars appeared behind him, and he felt himself being rapidly lifted up by them as they rose, soaring upward and southward across the sky. As they reached an apex, they let him go, and he floated gently downward in a far-off place. As he looked around, he found himself standing on the roof of a fortress with turrets at each corner. He watched the three stars continue southward across the sky, beyond a narrow valley that now lay in front of him and, beyond it, a mountain rising on the other side, with another more distant mountain slightly to the right. The moon had set, and he was gazing up at the clear, star-lit sky.

Gathering of the Heavenly Host

96

As he looked, he saw a new, much more brilliant light gradually descending from the southern sky in the distance—a light much brighter than the Great Comet he had seen the previous year. It illuminated all of the surrounding earth until it settled slightly below the southern horizon, but it continued to light up that horizon like the early dawn. As he looked, an archangel appeared above that horizon, who cried out with a thunderous voice, "O Children of God! The great Day hath arrived! Arise from your graves and come forth from your distant lands! Witness and behold, for indeed the promised Day hath come!"

Then there was a blast of a multitude of trumpets so forceful that it knocked Zach down. The sound seemed to reverberate around the entire globe. He was trembling as he slowly rose to his knees. He was amazed to see, as if awakened by this mighty trumpet blast, a vast number of specks of light arising from every direction and heading toward the point where the light had settled. When a few passed nearby, he realized that each was a radiant angel. All were heading, with awe and great excitement, to witness the most marvelous event. They were thrilled and enraptured with the news, greeting each other with great joy and gladness and shouting to each other, "The great Day hath come at last!" He sensed that many of them had been waiting for centuries to witness this very moment.

So huge was this multitude that they seemed to be brilliant clouds all circling around now. As Zach watched, he saw one angel in the distance who paused and then started drawing closer toward him. The angel called out to him, saying, "Fear not: for, behold, I bring you good tidings of great joy, which shall be to all people." Zach immediately recognized these words as the ones the angel had spoken to the shepherds at the birth of Jesus. As he drew closer, he could see the angel's face, and he recognized that it was none other than that of his own father, who was beaming with the most wondrous smile.

Zach called out, "Father! I am here! We need your help in our search!"

His father drew near to him, still smiling. "My son," he said lovingly, "you have my help. You have had it all along. Did you not realize this?" He paused long enough for Zach to consider it, then continued. "Who do you suppose inspired Jeremy to ask you about whether you would be willing to make some changes in your own perspectives shortly after you first set out? And did you perhaps think that it was just by chance that Mr. Miller remembered the letter from Elijah Goodman and gave it to you? Did your persuasive argument that convinced James Lawrence to join you come to your mind by chance? After you had prayed for guidance in Rome, did you suppose that the riverboat captain overslept by chance on the morning of your departure, thus causing you to visit Akka first? Did you think that the Turkmen on the ship mentioned the year 1259 by chance? Or that Shaykh Hakim overheard the captain's mention of you by chance? Or that any of a dozen other critical connections that led you to this place could have occurred by chance?" He threw back his head and laughed with a long, deep booming laughter, as if the very notion of this was the funniest idea he had ever heard. Zach smiled and started to laugh too.

"Yea," he continued, "most of what men consider luck—both good and bad—is almost always guidance from us, as unseen helpers of the heavenly realm. If only men would listen! Sometimes a blessing, sometimes a test but guidance in either case. Surely, my son, I have been with you, and I will not stop helping you now."

Zach was thrilled to hear this. "Of course!" he said. "Of course we have been guided! And if we have been guided this far, you will surely continue to guide us."

Josiah glanced over his shoulder as if he was getting ready to go.

"But, Father, I want to go with you this night!" Zach shouted.

His father smiled and said, "The dead in Christ shall rise first *and then* the living."

Zach immediately recognized this as the passage from St. Paul's description of the return of Christ in I Thessalonians, chapter 4.

As Zach looked up at the angels streaming in from all lands, a thought crossed his mind: *If these are the Christians who have died before Christ's return, why are they coming from all lands? Shouldn't they be coming mostly from the West?*

But his father looked at him again with a patient smile—the same way that, when Zach was a boy, he would look upon him when he was learning something new and he would wait quietly while Zach thought things through.

Then it dawned on Zach: The Christ was much more than Jesus! The Christ is the Messiah, the Anointed One—that special One who is above and beyond the comprehension of any ordinary man. He who had also spoken to us in the person of Abraham and again in the person of Moses. He had spoken to us when He appeared as Zoroaster, as Muhammad, as Buddha and Krishna, and, no doubt, as others before we had the means to record Them. The Christ-spirit is eternal. That was why He was truly able to say, "Before Abraham was, I am." This eternal title, "the Christ, the Messiah, the Anointed One," all meaning the same thing, though taken from three languages, was never intended to refer solely to Jesus!

Zach realized, therefore, that the "dead in Christ" were all of the believers in any of God's Messengers who had died before the fulfillment of the great promise. And today they were drawn from all over creation. The elect were being gathered from the four winds just as Jesus had foretold and were being granted what had been promised to them for so long: the opportunity to witness, from on high, what would one day come to be regarded as one of the three greatest events in the entire history of the human race— each associated with one of the numbers given by Daniel in the last half of the last chapter of his prophetic book.

A broad smile broke over his father's face. He seemed to be able to read Zach's mind. "Now you understand," he said kindly.

"Father, you are truly one of the wise men of this age for recognizing the manner of His coming and our need to search."

Josiah smiled slightly and said, "Mr. Miller was certainly one of the wise men for reading the prophecies correctly concerning the time. And you and James will also be regarded as wise men of the age for discovering the location once you've brought your search to a successful conclusion."

"But the path is so long." Zach sighed. "Why did you not tell me at the beginning exactly where I should go to find the Promised One?"

His father paused for a moment, looked at him intently, and said, "The purpose in life is not simply its destination. It is also the journey. Through traveling this path, you learn, and your spirit grows. The path to knowledge is often long and difficult, but it is a path you must tread if you are to learn and if you are to bestow the blessings of this knowledge upon others."

Zach thought about all that he had learned through his travels and through his discussions with so many different people—how utterly ignorant he had been of the world of Islam as well as the history and teachings of Zoroaster, how much he still had to learn about Hinduism and Buddhism and other religions, and how small and restricted his life had been when he remained in America. He had to agree that the journey had been as important as the destination.

He looked at his father and said, "How much longer must I wait?"

"Fear not—your time of discovery is coming soon," said his father, who then looked toward the heavens and said with a smile, "It shall be...about four hours."

"But how shall I find Him?" Zach pleaded.

"*Seek,*" replied his father, as if to emphasize the importance of making an effort, "and ye *shall* find. *Knock,* and the door *shall* be opened." His father's face beamed again with that knowing smile, and his words were reassuring. Then he added, "And remember, when you find Him, you must do exactly as He asks of you."

"I will certainly remember," Zach replied.

"Then give praise unto God for this night. For you have been given to see what no mortal eye hath seen and to hear what no mortal ear hath heard."

Then, glancing toward the southern sky, Josiah simply said, "And now I must go." With that, he was soaring upward and southward, toward the light on that horizon that was soon to dawn.

Then Zach heard the most wondrous chorus of voices that he had ever heard—the voices of millions, all singing their praises to God. Indeed, he was certain that it was the most wondrous chorus that he could ever hear, so perfect were the harmonies, so strong and clear the melodies. He thought, *Surely, this must be what the shepherds heard on that night of Jesus' birth!*

He thought about the three extraordinarily brilliant stars that had brought him here from the north. He realized that these were the three Magi, who had succeeded in finding Jesus through the prophecies of Zoroaster.

And then, looking toward the southwestern sky—toward the direction of Mecca—he saw five more brilliant stars heading toward the light. He understood these as being Bahira, Nestor, Waraqah, Ibn al-Hayyaban, and Salman—the Christians, the Jew, and the Zoroastrian who had each successfully found Muhammad through careful study of their prophecies. And now, as Zach looked down on the scene, he saw eighteen similarly brilliant lights on the ground, each heading toward the Dawning Point. The first of these had reached the Point, and its brilliance seemed to be streaming profusely from that meeting. Zach felt certain that this connection had initiated the whole series of miraculous things he was witnessing. He wondered whether the remaining seventeen were other followers of Siyyd Kazim, who were even now finding their way to the Promised One.

Then he heard the words of the archangel again booming forth: *"Lo, the Lord thy God is come, and with Him is the company of His angels arrayed before Him!"* [23]

Zach recalled the verse from the first chapter of the Book of Acts, which explained that He would return in the same manner that He ascended—that is, accompanied by a host of angels and passing through the clouds of men's ignorance.

The light below the southern horizon grew stronger and stronger until, at last, the upper tip of a dazzling sun rose above the horizon. Its brilliance penetrated Zach's eyes, and he awoke to find the actual morning sun coming up over the eastern horizon and shining on his face.

He jumped up, surprised to find that he had spent the entire night in the yard in front of the mosque of the Magi. He ran back to the caravanserai to awaken James and Hasan and excitedly shared with them all that he had seen in his dream. They both marveled at his telling of it.

James asked, "Was this a dream of the future or the present?"

"I cannot tell," answered Zach. "My father said that the time was coming soon when we would find the object of our search. He looked heavenward and said, 'about four hours.' If by this he meant heavenly hours, then this is one sixth of a day. And following the day-for-a-year pattern, it would suggest that we will find Him in about a sixth of a year, that is, within two months. But based on what I saw in my dream—which seemed so real!—I wonder whether someone may have already found the Promised One last night. In any case, I feel we should move forward with all haste to find Him for ourselves."

James recalled his dream on Mt. Tabor and how at the end of it, he had seen a new light getting ready to dawn in the east. Now they were here in the east, but Zach's dream seemed to suggest a light that was dawning toward the south. "That is good," said James. "We have already discussed how the next place we would like to investigate is Shushan, where Daniel was at during the time of his prophecies, and that is southwest of here. Perhaps your dream is guiding us there."

Hasan said, "The route to Shushan is south for two easy days to Salafchegan and then southwest through the Zagros Mountains, with many climbs and descents. Finally, the last quarter of the trip follows a valley that leads southeast out of the mountains and down to Shushan."

"How long will it take?"

Hasan thought for a moment and then said, "Altogether, about four weeks or perhaps five."

"Let's start right away!" urged Zach.

They checked at the caravanserai and found a caravan that would be leaving for Salafchegan on the following day. They visited Ardeshir one more time to advise him of their plans and to thank him for all of the knowledge and the hospitality he had provided. Then they made ready for their departure.

*   *   *

THE TRAVEL HAD BEEN much as Hasan had predicted. The initial march south was across level terrain to Salafchegan. Turning westward there, the mountains were in sight, while the trail remained on the plain. The town of Arak seemed to be the gateway to the mountains, and for the next two weeks, there was an endless series of mountains and valleys. They were grateful for the valleys and for the mountain passes discovered long ago by earlier travelers. But the terrain dictated a path that zigzagged, thereby increasing its length considerably. The summer heat was growing, relieved only slightly by the greater altitude.

After Arak, they were bound for Khorramabad, the capital of the province of Lorestan. It had been an arduous day's march over some hills and through a long valley. Although the trail did not require serious climbs on this particular day, the mid-June weather had been very hot, and some of the animals had to stop more frequently for water from the stream along the trail that the caravan followed. These stops slowed everyone down.

They had converged with another caravan coming northward from Dorud, also bound for Khorramabad, so now they were a single large caravan. The slow pace through the heat and the larger size of the caravan delayed their progress, so the sun had already set behind the hills by the time they arrived in Khorramabad. They were looking forward to some well-earned rest in this provincial capital.

The city lay at a point where three travel routes converged. On this particular day, other caravans had already arrived from the north and from the west, and every room in every caravanserai within the city was filled before James, Zach, Hasan, and many members of their caravan were able to find a place to rest.

When they inquired of the attendants at the caravanserai what they should do, they were told, "Go to the *Falak-ol-Aflak*." Some of their fellow travelers knew where this was since they had stayed there previously when the normal accommodations were full.

As they crossed the river in the city, ahead of them they saw an enormous castle built on a massive rock outcropping and surmounted by twelve towers. It looked ominous, especially as it was now surrounded by the darkening skies of the evening. James commented that it looked like some of the medieval castles of England with its round turrets on each corner and the entire perimeter of the rooftop fortified with battlements for protecting the castle's defenders. Indeed, they discovered that it had been built some 1,600 years before and still served as a military fortification for the provincial governor. The steep approach to the castle, coming up the rocky hill from every side, was clearly planned to make any attack even more difficult.

"Something about this place seems familiar," said Zach, but he couldn't put his finger on it. He had certainly never seen any fortification like this in America.

"Well," said James, "it looks like a lot of castles I've seen back home. I don't suppose it is very comfortable, but it is better than staying with the animals in the stables."

Zach chuckled at the reference to the original Christmas story as they approached the massive entrance gate.

"Welcome, gentlemen," said the jovial head guard who met them at the gate. Raising his arms skyward, he added, "We welcome you to the Heaven of Heavens!" Indeed, the castle's name meant "Heaven of Heavens." The head guard was always pleased to have the occasional influx of travelers as it would provide him with some supplemental income. Although the barracks normally housed soldiers, the current complement of soldiers did not fill all the rooms, so there was adequate, if still uncomfortable, space. They unpacked their belongings, thankful to have a secure place to rest. After a hearty meal, they were soon fast asleep.

James awoke as the eastern sky was beginning to show some light. He glanced over to where Zach had been sleeping and noticed that he was not there. Concerned, he arose to look for him. When he could not find him in the immediate area, he inquired of one of the guards, who pointed him to a stairway. Following it upward for several flights, he arrived on the roof of the castle. There he found Zach, staring southward, in tears.

"Oh, James!" cried Zach as soon as he noticed his approach. "This is the place!"

"What place?" replied James.

"This spot is the exact place I saw in my dream when I spent the night in front of the Mosque of the Magi back in Saveh!" Zach was trembling with excitement.

"I had a strange feeling when we arrived that it seemed familiar. I didn't recognize it because I had only seen it from the rooftop in my dream. When I awoke early, I couldn't get back to sleep, so I came up here for some meditation and prayer. And after praying awhile, as morning twilight began, I turned and realized exactly where I was.

"And look there!" Zach pointed to the large mountain across the valley and a smaller one farther to the right. "That's *exactly* where the light on the southern horizon was shining from!"

James was so surprised that he didn't know what to say at first. "Uh...so you think the Promised One will arise from somewhere in that direction?"

"Positively sure of it!" exclaimed Zach. "I'm ready to head out this morning, alone if necessary, to reach the spot!"

"Well," said James, sounding a note of caution, "let's see what lies in that direction first."

As soon as the head guard had arrived at his post, they explained that they needed to find a map of Khorramabad and the surrounding territory. With a modest contribution to the guard's coffers, he located a map of the local area. Then they plotted a line from the castle to the point on the horizon Zach had seen and extended it. But they found nothing but mountains in that direction. They then asked for a map of the entire province and surrounding areas and extended the line, but again they saw only a vast string of mountains. Finally, they asked for a map of all of southwestern Persia, and they again replotted the line. This time, it led straight to the city of Shiraz, the capital of the province of Fars.

"That is it!" cried Zach. "I'm sure that's where we must go!" Zach's heart was still pounding with excitement. "Wasn't that one of the regions that Ardeshir mentioned as a place where the Promised One of the Zoroastrians might arise? We must head out now, straight for Shiraz!"

The head guard laughed. "You cannot go *straight* from here to Shiraz!" He laughed again and shook his head. "There are at least 300 miles of the most mountainous land in all of Persia on a straight path between here and Shiraz. We hardly even have any trails through there and certainly no regular villages or caravanserais where you could stay. No one would ever travel such a route!"

James, taking a more practical approach, simply asked, "Tell us, then, what is the best route to Shiraz from here?"

The head guard leaned back and thought for a moment. "Well, there are two. From here you could go back to Dorud and then southeast overland via Aligudarz and Isfahan to Shiraz. Or you could go down out of the mountains to Shushan in the southwest and, from there, to one of the towns on the Persian Gulf, from whence you would take a ship to Bushehr. From there, it is perhaps a week's journey up to Shiraz."

"Which way is faster?"

The guard shrugged. "They are both about the same from here. If you fear travel on ships, then take the land route."

They certainly had no fear of traveling on ships.

"If we wish to take the route through Shushan, which road should we take?" inquired James.

The guard pointed to the river that surrounded the base of the fortress on two sides. "Follow the Khorramabad River. It will lead you to Shushan."

James and Zach thanked him for his helpfulness and retired to their room to discuss their next move. Once Zach had calmed down enough to think straight, he understood that a direct route through the mountains would be both slower and more hazardous than either of the routes that the guard had suggested. The western route through Shushan, as originally planned, seemed to be the obvious choice. They could see if there was anything to be learned there from the spot where Daniel had seen his visions some 23 centuries earlier. Then they could go on to Shiraz from there.

*       *       *

THE CARAVAN JOURNEY TO Shushan seemed to drag on. The caravan followed the river, which ensured that there was no lack of water for man nor beast in spite of crossing through much arid land. This was critical as the June weather was getting hotter and the dry season had begun.

However, the river was guided by the mountains, which often meant that it took an indirect route. While the general direction of their travel was southwest, it was blocked by the many rows of the Zagros Mountains, which ran from northwest to southeast—almost exactly perpendicular to the direction they wanted to travel. Yet, time after time, they would find that the river had found a place to slice a notch through the mountains, and they could move forward.

At one point, they saw a notch cut in one set of mountains with a steep wall of additional mountains directly behind it. *There is simply no way that we can scale a mountain range like that!* Zach thought. But the river and the caravan moved forward. As they passed through the first notch, they could look to their right and see that a tightly constricted valley existed between these two sets of mountains, through which the river passed. After a couple of miles, there was a break in the second row of mountains, and they were able to follow the river through.

"It's a good thing that we're in a caravan," said James. "Otherwise I would never have guessed that we could pass there."

"I agree," mused Zach, "and it reminds me of how often in life, when we are looking for a way through, we see an obstacle that seems insurmountable. If we would pray for guidance and push forward instead, we might discover that a previously unimagined passageway exists that would enable us to reach our goal."

"A good lesson to keep in mind," agreed James.

At length, as the mountains funneled them into another small pass, they came out upon the city of Pol-e Dokhtar, with its spacious and well-watered farms. There the caravan rested for a couple of days and restocked from the marketplace in preparation for the next leg of their travels.

Soon it was time to set out again, but by now the late June days were sweltering. So this time they left in the late afternoon, with a setting sun in the west and a waxing moon high in the sky.

The heat of the day was declining, and they were soon moving through the desert in twilight and then guided only by moonlight. They were traveling in what seemed to James and Zach like a magical landscape. The night air was at first cool and pleasant, eventually becoming chilly but invigorating. The cloudless sky and the treeless landscape created a vast panorama free of shadows and brilliantly illuminated by the moon's cool light.

Around midnight, they entered a barren valley that stretched southeast and northwest, as far as the eye could see. The trail swung to the southeast to follow the valley. "Shushan ahead," the caravan guide noted, pointing in that direction. "Hills, yes, but no more mountains."

As the moon was setting, they reached the next village and rested there through the heat of the day. Then they started the process again. Each afternoon, the moon rose a little later, fuller, and brighter. They greatly appreciated the nighttime travel. The sky offered a spectacular display of stars, with the milky band spread across its zenith. Zach felt certain that the Wise Men of the East must have witnessed many similar scenes on their way to find the infant Jesus more than 18 centuries earlier. He thought of the star that led them to Bethlehem and imagined what the great comet, which he had seen last year, would have looked like from here. He thought too about how both the Wise Men and Joseph had been guided by dreams, which preserved the life of the infant Jesus, and how both he and James had also been guided in their current quest by dreams. In this nocturnal deserted valley, he felt somehow comforted and guided, with a growing sense that they were indeed on the right path.

James commented on how significant a role the lunar cycle played when caravans crossed deserts, and he wondered whether this may have been one main reason that the Muslim calendar was based on lunar months and was thus about eleven days shorter than the solar year used in the West. The cool air also meant that the animals did not need to stop to drink water often. This enabled them to shorten the trip as they could follow a more direct route and did not need to closely follow the meandering river.

Finally, with one last turn to the southwest, they descended onto the fertile plains surrounding Shushan.

# CHAPTER 8

# IN SHUSHAN AT DANIEL'S TOMB

THEY RETURNED TO DAYTIME travel for their entry into Shushan, or "Shush" as it was sometimes called. As they came down out of the hills, they drew near to the Karkheh River, into which the river from Khorramabad had emptied.

"Once known as the Ulai River," noted James, "it's the site the prophet Daniel saw in his vision." They paused briefly as they contemplated this river, which had fed the ancient civilization of Elam and its descendants for six millennia.

Passing a road that diverged to the right, Hasan pointed and said proudly, "The famed '*Royal Road*' of the ancient Persian Empire. From here, swift riders carrying royal messages would set out to reach Sardis, near the Aegean Sea. The messages would pass without stopping from rider to rider, thus moving ten times faster than the normal traveler. Swift communications were vital to the success of the Persian Empire and were the envy of the Greeks."

"Yes," acknowledged James, "I remember reading of this. *Herodotus*, in the fifth century BC, admitted that it was the fastest traveling service in the world and said that 'neither snow nor rain nor heat nor gloom of night stays these couriers from the swift completion of their appointed rounds'—a standard to which many postal services have aspired ever since."

"A system like this would be very valuable in our country," Zach mused, "especially if we continue to grow into the vast Oregon territories on the Pacific Coast."¶

Hasan repeated his earlier explanation of how Shushan was one of the five capitals of the ancient Persian empire—the westernmost of the three in the south.

"And where did you say Persepolis and Pasargadae are located?" Zach inquired.

"Just a couple of days' journey northeast of Shiraz."

Thinking ahead to their anticipated trip to Shiraz, Zach noted how fascinating it was that the ancient prophecy of Daniel, revealed in this city of Shushan, might be fulfilled in the relatively nearby city of Shiraz.

As they drew closer, Hasan had them break away from the caravan and directed them up a side path to a vast platform area east of the river. "Gentlemen," he said grandly, "I give you the temple of Darius, built by him and used by his son, Xerxes, and grandson, Artaxerxes."

It was an immense empty square. Zach and James looked around and tried to imagine the huge palace that must have stood on so vast a space.

"That means," said James, "that it was here that the decree of Artaxerxes was issued on the first day of spring 2,300 years ago, as explained in Ezra 7:9, which directed his Jewish subjects to return to Jerusalem and rebuild their city."

Despite the heat, Zach felt a chill of wonderment. "The starting point was right here! The event that marked the start date of Gabriel's prophecies, which Daniel recorded in chapters 8 and 9, was right here!" He gazed around and tried to imagine the event.

Hasan walked to the southwest corner and pointed toward the river, "And that, if I'm not mistaken, is Daniel's tomb." It was just a short distance away. "But let us first find a caravanserai and rest a bit."

*    *    *

---

¶ A very similar system, known as the "Pony Express" would be instituted in America in 1859, but it would be superseded just a couple of years later by the completion of the first transcontinental telegraph line—yet another example of the close of the old age and the opening of a new one.

AFTER RESTING THAT NIGHT at the caravanserai and refreshing themselves in the morning, they went straightaway to visit the tomb of Daniel.

The fact that it was still preserved here, after all of these ages, seemed to Zach a minor miracle in itself. "Perhaps his remains were preserved by the Jewish community that stayed here after most of the others had returned to Jerusalem," he said.

Tomb of Daniel, on the east bank of Ulai River

Hasan added, "I've heard that it has also been preserved by the Muslims since they took over this area 12 centuries ago. We regard the Jews as 'people of the Book,' and Daniel was certainly part of the book, even though he was not specifically mentioned in the Quran. It was the Muslim authorities who decided, long ago, to build the current tomb."

The tomb was on the east bank of the river and built up against its embankment. It was a solid-looking structure with a stone-arch entranceway. The roof was surmounted by a tall, narrow "dome," if one might call it that, very unusual in its architecture and looking almost like a narrow, inverted pinecone.

The shrine was open during the daytime, but a guard eyed them warily. *Did the guard notice that James and I are foreigners?* Zach wondered.

The thick stone walls helped keep the atmosphere inside cool, providing a welcome relief from the midday heat. The interior was ornately decorated in polished stone and finely crafted metal sheets embossed with Quranic quotations. An ornate metal cage surrounded the sarcophagus itself.

This time it was James who was inclined to remain longer in prayer and meditation after Zach and Hasan had left to return to the caravanserai. He was sitting in an alcove, deep in his meditations and apparently unseen by the attendant, for when he finally arose from his prayers, he found, much to his dismay, that the sun had set and he had been locked inside. He considered making a loud noise to rouse someone to his aid, but the silence and the sanctity of the place weighed against this. So he decided to simply remain inside and extend his prayer vigil through the night.

While in that state that is somewhere between prayer and sleep, an angel appeared and addressed him, saying, "O son of man!" James recognized this immediately as the same salutation that the angel Gabriel had used when speaking to Daniel in this very city in his vision concerning the 2,300 days. "Hath the sanctuary been cleansed?"

James recognized the phrase from chapter 8 of Daniel's prophecy, but he was unsure of which sanctuary the angel was speaking.

The angel seemed to sense James' uncertainty and so provided an answer: "The sanctuary of thine heart."

James thought briefly of all of the things he had let go of in order to join Zach in the quest—not simply his home and his work but also the opinions of friends and colleagues who had expressed doubts about his understanding of the prophecies and about his plans to search. And during his travels, he had let go of his negative attitudes toward foreign religions, recognizing that truth could be found in each of them. The angel seemed able to read James' thoughts and then smiled broadly, saying, "A thousand praises be unto thee that thou hast detached thyself from thy home and thy friends and from all their imaginings, and from all human limitations in order to seek thy Lord in these lands!"

James was heartened to hear this as the angel continued, "And praise be unto God, for that thou hast both heard and understood the words of thy Lord and the prophets!" This reminded him that it was both Jesus and Daniel who spoke of the prophecy of the 2,300 days and how Matthew, when referring to the prophecy, had added parenthetically, "let the reader understand."

James felt himself trembling by now, and his tears started to flow as he thought of the long months and wearying efforts of the travel that had brought them there. And in spite of the guidance they had received in their dreams, they were still searching. He responded, "I am but a humble seeker who has been on a long quest. Now I have arrived, yet still I know not how to find the Promised One nor where exactly I should seek."

"Fear not, O patient seeker! For thou shalt soon discover the object of thy quest. Follow the banks of this ancient river," the angel replied, nodding toward the Ulai River outside, "until thou cometh upon the Stream of the Arabs." He paused and looked James straight in the eye. "There shalt thou hear the mighty trumpet blast! There shalt thou be uplifted in rapture!"

His words seemed to pierce James' soul and so startled him that he jerked, bumping his head against the stone floor, which awakened him from his vision.

In the morning, the guard was upset to find that James had stayed in the shrine during the night. Zach arrived and was relieved to find that James was unharmed.

"Wait here!" demanded the guard. Zach sat down with James and listened intently as James recounted the vision that he had received. Here they stood, in the same city where Daniel had received his vision some 23 centuries before. It was the city from which the ancient Persian king, Artaxerxes, ruled and from which his decree had gone out in 457 BC to the recently released Jewish people, commanding them to rebuild Jerusalem. One of Daniel's visions had specifically said that "cleansing of the sanctuary" in the latter days would begin 2,300 years after this decree was issued. The start date and the method of understanding the prophecy had already been established by the accuracy of Daniel's prediction of the appearance and crucifixion of Jesus, in chapter 9 of his book. And Jesus Himself had specifically pointed to this prophecy when, in Matthew 24, His disciples inquired about the time of His return.

So here they stood—at the appointed time and place. They had sought guidance through their intense prayers and meditations, and here it arrived in what seemed to be clear instructions of where to find the "trumpet blast" of the new revelation.

But what exactly did it mean? Where was the "Stream of the Arabs"? It did not take them long to figure this out. When they translated it into Arabic to inquire, they soon discovered that the "Stream of the Arabs" was simply the Shatt-al-Arab, the name of the river formed by the confluence of the Tigris and the Euphrates, which flowed southward into the Persian Gulf. It was the border between the Persian Empire and the Ottoman Empire and a place of frequent skirmishes between them in recent years. It was also the end point of the Karkheh river—the ancient Ulai River in Daniel's time that had flowed down from Shushan. At the end of the river was the city of Mohammerah,** and so Mohammerah immediately became their next destination.

But the dream caused Zach some consternation. He was certain from his earlier dream that the answer to their search would be found in Shiraz. Yet James' dream seemed to indicate that they should search in Mohammerah. How could both be right?

As they were pondering this, the guard returned with a local mullah close behind. "Throw them into the prison!" the mullah declared.

"What?!" cried Zach. But it was too late. The guard had brought an assistant, and they seized James and Zach, bound their hands and feet, and placed them on a cart, which carried them to the local prison.

---

** Present day Khorramshahr

*　　　*　　　*

ZACH AND JAMES HAD always known of the possibility of local problems but had managed to sidestep them all until now. They languished in prison for two days and two nights with little water and very little edible food. Their cell was mostly dark, and a worn prayer mat was the only thing that separated them from the cold floor at night.

Finally, at the beginning of the third day, Hasan appeared.

"Thanks be to God! I have found you at last!" he nearly shouted. "I've been going mad these past two days wondering where you had gone and what had happened. I've been asking all over town, but no one seemed to know. Finally, the beggar who sits near the shrine told me that he had seen the guards carry you off."

"I accidently missed the closing of the gates at the shrine," said James. "I would not have thought that peacefully remaining inside would be a cause for imprisonment."

Hasan said he would inquire about the charges. When he returned, he had a grim look on his face. "It is not just about your unauthorized presence in the shrine," he said. "It seems that someone overheard our discussions at dinner on the night we arrived—someone who is adamantly opposed to the teachings of Shaykh Ahmad and Siyyid Kazim and who believes very strongly in the literal arising of the 12th Imam from the well in Samarra. He reported it to his mullah, who was similarly incensed by the very mention of the names of our teachers."

"Surely you can explain to him that we mean no offense," Zach pleaded.

"That's where the problem is," replied Hasan. "The officers here tell me that the mullah left town yesterday on a journey and will be away for no less than three weeks. And they don't seem to know exactly where he's gone."

"Three weeks!" Zach gasped. "How will we ever make any progress if we are spending all of our days in prison?" James shook his head at the thought of the wasted time.

But there was nothing Hasan could do except bring their necessary belongings and a regular supply of food and water to the prison. Although the circumstances were grim, it did provide Zach with the opportunity to update his diary of their travels. He also thought back to his dream and to his father's assurance that they would be guided. But it was hard for him to imagine how being stuck in a prison could, in any way, be guidance. *How can you be guided when you aren't moving at all?* he wondered. James was also incensed, feeling that they were so close to their goal but were now stuck in prison for God only knew how long. The angel had told him to "Fear not." Had the angel failed to see this danger?

*  *  *

"THESE ARE DANGEROUS PEOPLE!" The mullah banged his fist on the table when Hasan was finally able to obtain an audience with him after his return. "And you should be wary of associating with them! The teachings of Shaykh Ahmad and Siyyid Kazim are a heresy—some say punishable by death!"

Hasan was careful to avoid suggesting that he shared any of their beliefs, implying that he was simply their hired guide. He gently explained that they were foreigners who would soon leave the area and who posed no danger. "They are guests in our country. Are we not required to show all courtesy and hospitality to our guests?" he asked humbly, calling upon these ancient values of their culture.

"Are they not Muslims?" the mullah inquired.

"They are of Christian background," Hasan explained carefully.

"So they are idolaters! Why should such wretched people be traveling in our country?"

"Not all Christians worship statues," Hasan explained, hoping to mollify the mullah's outrage. "They are Protestants. Protestants have no statues to face during their prayers."

"Do they not worship empty crosses?" retorted the mullah.

"Perhaps," acknowledged Hasan, but a quote popped into his consciousness, and so he responded, "Even if they are idolaters, they have requested our protection. Do you not recall the verse in the Holy Quran, in which the Prophet, peace be upon Him, says, *'If any of the idolaters shall demand protection of thee, grant him protection, that he may hear the word of God: and afterwards let him reach the place of safety.'*"

"I don't recall reading that," groused the mullah.

"Perhaps you might find it in chapter 9, verse 6," replied Hasan gently. He had been reviewing the Quran for much of the past three weeks in anticipation of this meeting.

The mullah strode over to the stand that held his copy of the Holy Book, found the appropriate page, and reviewed it. He then returned and, without further comment, simply asked, "And they will be gone by tomorrow?"

"They have urgent business to attend to elsewhere," Hasan assured him.

The mullah paused and then said, "Inasmuch as the holy month of Rajab†† has recently started, I will grant them clemency." Then he added with a sinister grin, "There is only the matter of the fee for the cost of the lodging we have provided while they were under our care."

Hasan was appalled that his friends should have to pay for such unwanted "care." He did his best to negotiate downward what seemed to him like an exorbitant fee. When he brought the news to Zach and James, they were just happy to be freed at last and paid the final charge without complaint.

*    *    *

THEY WERE GLAD TO be heading south at last, toward the Persian Gulf, following the banks of the ancient river just as James had heard in his dream. Zach's dream, back in Saveh, of seeing the sun rising in the south, had convinced him that the new revelation was dawning in Shiraz, and he felt that they should move in that direction. Heading south along the ancient Ulai River from Shushan was also the best route to Shiraz, if they preferred sea travel. The traders told them that they could board a ship in Mohammerah sailing to the Persian Gulf port of Bushehr. From there, they could follow the road to Shiraz and reach the city in perhaps a fortnight.

The region around Shushan was a rich agricultural district with wide, flat lands and plentiful fresh water descending from the mountains to the east and north. Clearly the inhabitants here could produce more than they could use. As Zach knew from his life in New Jersey and New York, this meant there would be goods to

†† One of the four holy months in the Muslim year

117

export—materials that would go down to the nearest port. As at home, the rivers led down to the port—Mohammerah in this case, which was one of the last towns on the Shatt-al-Arab before it emptied into the Persian Gulf. However, the Ulai River was not navigable at Shushan, so goods for export were carried overland to Ahvaz, below the last set of rapids. Here riverboats could be found.

It was not difficult for them to find a caravan that was leaving for Ahvaz the following day. They were told that it would take at least a week to reach the port of Mohammerah. The sun at this time of year was blazing hot. The caravan would start off at earliest light, travel for about five hours, stop to set up shade tents for the heat of the day, then complete the day's travel in the late afternoon and, at this time of the month, under the light of the evening's moon before it set in the west.

They finally reached the small town of Ahvaz, about halfway to Mohammerah. At the end of the long, hot day, they found the caravan-serai there, secured a room, and went to find a meal at a nearby coffee shop. The waiter was a friendly fellow and, recognizing them as foreigners, started to ask about their journey and what had brought them to this place. James shot a glance of caution toward Zach. He had no desire for a repeat of their difficulties in Shushan. But Zach had a good feeling about the waiter's sincerity, so he explained quietly that they were searching for any news of anyone who seemed to possess innate knowledge from the time he was a very small child.

"Oooohhhh," replied the waiter, squinting a bit while pulling on his beard. "Are you Shaykhis?" he said quietly.

A wave of panic shot through James, Zach, and Hasan for they now knew just how dangerous this topic could be.

"We have some friends," said James cautiously, "who know something about the Shaykhis.... They have asked us to inquire wherever we go. What do you know of the Shaykhis?"

"I know of many of them. They are good people," replied the waiter, much to the relief of the travelers. "I know especially one from the time when I worked at the caravanserai in Mohammerah a few years ago. The owner there is a Shaykhi and a good friend. Other Shaykhis passing through would always stay there while traveling between Karbila and all points along the Gulf.

"And as to your question," he leaned down and lowered his voice, "I remember meeting one of the Shaykhi travelers in particular, many years ago. He was a schoolteacher named *Shaykh Abid*.[24] I told him that I felt I could never be a schoolteacher—I felt it would be too troublesome dealing with those small children every day. He told me with amazement that it is not always that way. He explained that he once had a student who was amazingly gifted—a mere child who seemed to know all the answers to questions that fully educated religious men would have difficulty puzzling out.

"What was more remarkable," the waiter continued, "was that this child came from a family of merchants. If the child had come from a family of mullahs, I might have thought that perhaps he had picked up some ideas from them. But such was not the case. Although the family wore the green turbans that signify that Muhammad was one of their direct ancestors, the family was entirely of the merchant class."

All three of the travelers sat up abruptly with interest at the mention of a child who met two of the main criteria they were seeking. They introduced themselves to the waiter, whose name was Mustafa.

"How old was this child, and how long ago did you meet his teacher?" Zach asked.

"He didn't say how old the child was nor how long ago he had taught him, but it must have been at least ten years ago that I met him."

"Where was this schoolteacher traveling to, and where was he coming from?" asked James.

"Being a Shaykhi, I suppose he was most likely heading toward Karbila, to learn from Siyyid Kazim," Mustafa replied, "and as I recall, he'd said that he had been teaching in the city of Shiraz."

Zach shot an excited glance toward James. Then he asked Mustafa, "Did you say that the owner of the caravanserai in Mohammerah was a friend of this Shaykh Abid? What is his name and the name of his caravanserai?" Zach's tone betrayed the sense of urgency that had suddenly built up in him.

119

"You may ask for Hajji Yacob‡‡," replied the Mustafa quietly. "He is the owner of the town's main caravanserai. But remember that Shaykh Abid was probably just an occasional customer of the caravanserai, so Yacob might not know much more about him than I do."

But that was enough for Zach and James. Here was the closest clue that they had found in all of their travels. The answer lay either in Mohammerah or, if they could find nothing there, they would certainly inquire for Shaykh Abid in Shiraz. They would surely find something soon, they felt. They thanked Mustafa profusely and retired for the evening.

---

‡‡ Hajji is a title given to those who have completed the pilgrimage to Mecca. Yacob is Arabic for Jacob.

# Chapter 9

## THE MIGHTY TRUMPET BLAST

THE FOLLOWING DAY, THEY found the small port on the river and soon negotiated fare on a boat that was being loaded with people, goods, and animals for the trip downstream to Mohammerah. They were grateful for the opportunity to rest in the shade of the boat's canopy, out of the blazing July sun, as they sailed slowly down the meandering river.

It was a few days later, in the late afternoon, when they reached Mohammerah. They went straight to the caravanserai and asked for Hajji Yacob.

"He is at prayer," replied his assistant.

"We will wait," replied James calmly.

After waiting twenty minutes, they decided to ask for a room and arranged for care for their animals. When they returned, Hajji Yacob was not yet back. They went for some food for themselves before returning once again.

But again, the assistant said, "He is still at prayer."

"How long is he usually there?"

"This is very unusual. He has been at prayer all day."

"We do not wish to trouble him," replied James, "but could you give him a note?"

James wrote a simple note from the Arabic he had learned in Egypt: "Friends of Mustafa of Ahvaz, friends of Siyyid Kazim, wish to have the pleasure of your audience."

The assistant returned quickly and said that Hajji Yacob would like to see them immediately. He led them down the walkway and ushered them into the large, well-furnished apartment at the head corner of the caravan-serai then withdrew.

After a moment, an older Persian gentleman appeared. His eyes seemed aglow with a special fire and he greeted the three of them warmly, although Zach noticed what appeared to be the streaks of tears on his cheeks. Then, looking more closely at Zach and James, he quietly asked Hasan, "These are...Shaykhis?"

Hasan explained how these Westerners had come a great distance seeking the promised Qaim alongside the other Shaykhis and how they had met Mustafa a few days ago in Ahvaz, who had directed them to him.

Zach added, "We have been traveling and searching for a year now. It has been more than four months since we left Karbila, searching the entire route to Saveh, from thence to Khorramabad and then to Shushan, and now to Mohammerah for any clue that might lead us to the Promised One. Although we have not yet found Him, our prayers for guidance have been answered in the dreams we've received. The last of these has guided us to this very city. If you know anything of the child with innate knowledge whose schoolteacher was, perhaps, a man by the name of Shaykh Abid, we beseech you to share what you know."

A broad smile broke out over Yacob's face. "Indeed," he said, "I know of Shaykh Abid and a good deal more." He then took them quietly to an inner room, closed the doors and drew the curtains, bade them to be seated, brought them some tea from the samovar, and then sat down with them.

"Have you ever met one of Siyyid Kazim's disciples by the name of Mulla Aliy-i-Bastami?" Yacob inquired.

"Why, yes, of course," said Hasan. "I traveled with him and others last year as we accompanied Siyyid Kazim on his final trip to Kazimayn. James and Zach met him also when we were all in Karbila. He set out on the search from there several months ago, a few weeks before we did."

Yacob paused and looked at them intently before speaking in a hushed voice. "He was here just last night. He is now on his way back to Karbila."

"Really?" Zach was incredulous. "Why would he be returning to Karbila? He seemed to be so focused on his search."

"There could be only one simple reason," replied Yacob. An expression of wonderment filled his face, and with his eyes gleaming, he said in a ringing voice, "All praise be unto God! *He has found the promised Qaim, Who has arisen in the city of Shiraz!*"

This news hit Zach, James, and Hasan like a thunderbolt as they tried to fathom the implications. Could it be, after all their travels, searching, and praying, that the Great Promise had indeed been fulfilled?

After a moment of silence in which they tried to fathom the significance of what they had just heard, Zach, in dazed wonderment, said, "Then the dawn in Shiraz is exactly as I had seen in my dream."

"And," added James quietly, "this news is indeed as a stunning trumpet blast. It has been sounded here in Mohammerah, exactly as foretold in my dream."

Up until this moment, it had all been prophecy, all open to speculation and various interpretations. But *now*, as of this very moment, they knew something had actually come to pass.

They sat silently for another moment, contemplating what all of this meant. Finally, Yacob added, "Mulla Ali arrived last night, badly scarred and bruised. He had been beaten severely by a man he encountered while leaving Shiraz, who regarded the very idea as a heresy. You must understand how heretical and dangerous this news is for many. I have been pondering and praying about its implications all day."

"Yes, we know very well how dangerous it can be. We have spent most of the last several weeks in prison for it," James replied, adding a brief explanation of their experience.

Yacob continued, "Yet Mulla Ali had no concern at all for his condition. He was aglow with the fire of the knowledge that the promise has been fulfilled! And he had been commissioned by the Qaim to carry the news, along with some of His first revealed writings, back to Karbila and to spread the news there. He left here this very morning, determined to reach Karbila as quickly as possible."

With his heart still pounding, Zach implored, "Tell us His name. How many seekers found Him and when? And how did they know that He was the Promised One?"

"As to His name," Yacob replied, "he told me that all of the disciples are sworn to secrecy for now. Such momentous news should be revealed gradually and only to those whose hearts are ready. He will tell us when it can be revealed. But He has taken the title of "the Gate." For although He bears a revelation from God, He said that the prime purpose of His revelation is to prepare the way for a yet greater Messenger who will appear within the coming years. He is, thus, the doorway or gate to that even more glorious revelation of the One whom He simply called "Him Whom God shall make manifest.'"

Zach gasped. "The two Messengers! It is exactly as Shaykh Hakim had foreseen when we were in Akka, like John the Baptist and Jesus!"

"Yes," added James, recalling their discussion with the Shaykh regarding chapter 4 of Zechariah, "the two anointed ones! And since 'anointed one' means 'messiah,' there must be two Messiahs at this time. Zechariah described them as the two olive trees, providing golden oil for the two candlesticks."

Zach said, "And the title He has taken—the Gate or the Door—fits exactly with what John said in chapter 10 of his gospel. Christ will return by coming through this door. John wrote, 'But he that entereth in *by the door* is the shepherd of the sheep.' And the good Shepherd will, in this age, gather all of the folds of sheep together!"

Yacob continued, "Mulla Ali said that He met every criterion that Siyyid Kazim had described, and much more importantly, the verses of revelation that come from His blessed lips are of unrivaled beauty and wisdom. The greatest poets would take months or years to compose something equal—if they could accomplish the task at all! And yet these verses come from Him so rapidly that the disciples can scarcely write them down before more are uttered."

Zach and James marveled. James inquired, "Is He a gifted scholar and a poet?"

"No!" said Yacob. "Mulla Ali told me that one of the most amazing things was that He has no training in religious matters or poetry. He, like others in His family, has previously worked as a simple merchant. He was raised by His uncle after His father died. Many of us who follow Siyyid Kazim had assumed that He would be a man with at least some religious training and background. But no! Recall that Muhammad was a driver of caravans. Jesus Himself was a carpenter. It seems that the clear channel whom God chooses for delivering His message is not the person whose mind is preoccupied with human understandings of religion. The fact that none of Them were from the religious class seems to me to be yet one more proof that revelation does not come *from* Them but instead comes *through* Them, from God Himself."

"Then He is certainly the One of whom we heard from your friend, Mustafa, in the coffeehouse in Ahvaz."

"Yes indeed—the One whose childhood teacher, Shaykh Abid, found how impossible it was to teach Him since He already seemed to have an answer for any question he asked—insights that showed understandings far surpassing those of the teacher himself."

Yacob explained all that he had heard from Mulla Ali. The Gate (*the Bab*)§§ had been living under the care of His uncle. Mulla Ali was not the first to find the Bab. That honor had gone to another seeker, Mulla Husayn, who described how the Bab had met him at the city's gate and invited him to His home. There, Mulla Husayn explained about his search and asked Him some questions. The Bab revealed verses that answered each of Mulla Husayn's questions with stunning clarity. This continued all night long. Mulla Husayn was so overwhelmed by the Bab's announcements and explanations that he could barely speak the following day.

"Mulla Husayn himself described that blessed night," continued Yacob. "He summarized his overwhelming joy and empowerment, saying,

'I seemed to be the Voice of Gabriel personified, calling unto all mankind:

> *"Awake, for lo! the morning Light has broken.*
> *Arise, for His Cause is made manifest.*
> *The portal of His grace is open wide;*
> *enter therein, O peoples of the world!*
> *For He who is your promised One is come!"'*[25]

---

§§ The "Gate" in Arabic is the "Bab"—the name by which He is known to history.

They sat in silence for another long moment, trying to imagine what all of this meant to them. Finally, Yacob said, "Yes, I have been at prayer all day, attempting to fathom its implications."

After further silence, Zach inquired, "How long ago did it happen?"

"Over two months ago. It was in the evening, after the fourth day of Jamadiyu'l-Avval."

Zach reached quickly into his bag to retrieve his diary. "Yes!" he shouted. "That was the very night that I had my dream about the Dawn of the new Sun in the southern sky, just before we left Saveh!" He explained to Yacob all that he had seen in his dream and how it had pointed them toward Shiraz.

Yacob read more of the details he had scribbled as he had heard them from Mulla Ali: "The Bab had insisted that Mulla Husayn could not reveal his discovery to anyone at the beginning—not even to his two traveling companions. He said that eighteen people must find the Bab *on their own* before He would allow any of us to leave and to start to carry the glad tidings outward to others. One by one, through various visions, dreams, and inspirations, all seventeen of us found Him. He called us the *Letters of the Living*."

Zach and James found this entirely understandable in view of the dreams and guidance that they had received. But Zach's curiosity was piqued by one thing. "Did he say earlier that there were eighteen?" he inquired. "I thought I had seen eighteen lights in my dream. Or did he say seventeen?"

"Well, yes, Mulla Ali told me about the poetess in Karbila, by the name of Qurratu'l-Ayn. Did you meet her?"

"Yes indeed. She was unforgettable," replied James, recalling her clear teachings and her vibrant presence, though she stood behind the curtain.

"She, of course, cannot travel as easily as men can in our realm, but she was certain that her sister's husband, Muhammad Ali of Qazvini, a devoted follower of Siyyid Kazim, would find the Promised One. She had already seen Him in the world of the spirit, and she wrote Him a letter, which she gave to her brother-in-law to deliver. He was, indeed, among the seventeen who found the Bab, and so he delivered her letter to Him. Upon reading it, the Bab declared that she, too, was one of the Letters of the Living for, in the realm of the spirit, she had found Him. Thus there are eighteen, although only seventeen were physically present in Shiraz." [26]

"Then it is exactly as I had seen in my dream. Those eighteen lights had found Him."

"Mulla Ali told me that he and several of the others had been led to Him through similar dreams and visions," said Yacob to Zach.

James wanted to stay and hear every last detail from Hajji Yacob, but Zach was too overcome with this overpowering news. He excused himself and went out to wander the now quiet streets of the nighttime city while trying to digest the staggering significance of this discovery.

Here he was, in the land of the prophet Daniel, who had received this incredible vision 2,300 years ago—a vision so extraordinary that Jesus Himself had singled it out from among all of the prophecies of the Jewish Bible as the answer to His disciples' question concerning the time of His return. And here, *exactly on time,* 2,300 years after the start date given in Daniel's prophecy, the revelation had appeared! And as if that was not enough, St. John's prophecy from chapter 9 of his Book of Revelation had suggested even more specifically, as James had explained while they were on the ship to Rome, that it would occur between late April and early June of that year. And now, it had appeared, on May 22–23, just as predicted.

And if any more certainty was needed, the predictions coincided exactly with the year 1260 in the Islamic calendar, another date that both Daniel and St. John had referred to and which turned out to be the same year as 1844. More amazing still, the Muslims were expecting their own Promised One to appear that year. Beyond this, the Jews, Zoroastrians, Hindus, and Buddhists were also expecting their Promised One. Each of these religions described conditions similar to the present day, even if in their cases, their prophecies that pointed to the exact year of their fulfillment were less clear.

This was so big that Zach felt that his head would break if he tried to imagine all of its implications. He found himself in a state of rapture, heedless of where he was wandering. He came to the riverbank and looked up at the silent stars as he tried to think about the vastness of the implications of what they had found. He had already lamented the needless centuries of persecution and war that had occurred between the Christian, Muslim, Jewish, and Zoroastrian religions. He thought also about the strife and bloodshed that he had heard of that existed between Hindus and Muslims, between Buddhists and Hindus, and even in some places between Buddhists and Muslims.

If the people could understand that the one God of the universe had sent the Founders of all these religions to mankind as a part of a single educational process, then all of the hatred and misunderstanding could be washed away forever. "The sanctuary," which Daniel had written of, could indeed "be cleansed." The Founders had delivered exactly what was needed for the age in which They lived. There was no legitimate reason for any of the religions to be fighting each other. They were simply sheep of the different folds, as Jesus had explained in John 10. And now—at last!—the time had come for the gathering of these folds into one flock following the one good Shepherd, Whose coming all of the religions had foretold, and Who would enter by "the gate." The idea was so vast, so all encompassing, he was overwhelmed by its significance.

How sad to think of the many times that people had misunderstood the Messengers and how religious leaders had allowed their pride, lust for power, greed, or a sense of tribalism to cause their followers to fight against the followers of other religions while imagining they were doing God's will!

But now, if they could see that the prophecies of all of the religions were being fulfilled together, all by a single new Messenger—or pair of new Messengers, as he had now confirmed—they would see that all of the religions had come from one divine Source. The future implications of this realization were beyond his wildest imagination.

It was as if humankind had turned the mightiest corner in its history. And here they were to witness it! Although the thought of the opposition he would receive from every religious congregation back in America had weighed on him, now it seemed a trifling matter. He no longer cared what they thought. The great news that the promise had been fulfilled was so glorious that they could crucify him and he would still praise God for having been enabled to be among the first to witness this wondrous fulfillment. These teachings were the new glad tidings—literally the new "gospel." It was indeed like the blast of a trumpet, calling all the dead to arise, so clear and stunning was all that he had learned. He thought of chapter 15 of Paul's first letter to the Corinthians: *"In a moment, in the twinkling of an eye, at the last trump; for the trumpet shall sound, and the dead shall be raised incorruptible, and we shall be changed."* He felt as if he had been dead indeed prior to hearing this stunning news, and now, in the twinkling of an eye, he had been raised up and born again into an entirely new life, exactly as Paul had described.

He thought of James' vision. Here, in ancient Elam, this stunning trumpet blast had been sounded in the very same land where Daniel's prophetic visions had occurred.

He started spinning around and around while gazing up at the stars, in complete abandonment of all earthly concerns. He felt as if he had indeed been lifted up into the air, for nothing on earth mattered to him. And he started to chant:

> *Tonight I am raised up!*
> *Tonight I soar, enraptured in God's love and wisdom*
> *Knowing His ancient promises have been fulfilled*
> *Exactly at the time foretold!*
> *Yea, indeed, His great promise is certain and true!*
> *The archangel Gabriel has shouted out the truth!*
> *The stunning trumpet blast has been sounded!*
> *Yea, indeed, all things have been fulfilled!*

As he whirled, he thought of his dream from that night in Saveh. He thought of all the misunderstandings that people had about the prophecies, which had clouded their vision, and how he had now been enabled to see through these clouds. The words from I Thessalonians chapter 4 came to his mind: *"For the Lord Himself shall descend from heaven with a shout, with the voice of the archangel, and with the trump of God: and the dead in Christ shall rise first. Then we which are alive and remain shall be caught up together with them in the clouds, to meet the Lord in the air: and so shall we ever be with the Lord."* And here, in his state of rapture, it was happening to him!

Around and around he spun in passionate exaltation, repeating the phrases over and over again, with his gaze to the stars above, oblivious of time and without care of what anyone within earshot might think. At length, his travel-weary body collapsed on the sand beneath his exhausted feet as his overloaded mind fell into unconsciousness.

*      *      *

HE DID NOT KNOW how long he remained there, but as the eastern sky grew lighter, he came to his senses. This magical night had slipped away, and dawn was almost upon him. He turned his steps to the caravanserai, knowing that James was probably wondering what had happened to his friend.

At the caravanserai, neither James nor Hasan had been able to sleep all night. They had been in a similar state of elation and were pondering, talking, and praying about all of the implications of this news.

However, as they walked to the courtyard with Zach, James started to explain "We have a problem."

"What problem could we possibly have?" asked Zach, still overwhelmed with joy. "The promise is fulfilled! Our quest has succeeded and is nearly over!"

"Yes indeed...but where shall we go next?" inquired James.

"Why, of course, we are going to Shiraz to meet the Bab Himself. We must go to the port this very morning to find the next available ship to Bushehr, and from there, we will travel inland to Shiraz!" He started to whirl around in excitement once again.

"Yacob says that he said the same thing to Mulla Ali," replied James, "but Mulla Ali repeated what the Bab had said: Now is *not* the time for more people to visit Him. Now is the time to carry the news outward to all of the waiting communities. Yacob said that if we wish to know more about the Bab, we should follow Mulla Ali and join him as he travels to Najaf and Karbila and make a copy of the Bab's writings, which he is carrying."

Zach sat down to contemplate this question. "Surely we can visit the Bab first and then go to Karbila."

Hasan said, "Yacob told us that this would be both dangerous and difficult. Difficult because we don't know whom to ask for in Shiraz—remember that the title of 'the Bab' is simply a new title that the people of Shiraz don't know. The eighteen Letters of the Living have been sworn not to reveal His given name. And in any case, they have all departed by now, at the Bab's behest. If He does not wish to make Himself known, we will never find Him.

"Also, it would be dangerous because there are many fanatical people along the way who are totally against the idea that the Promised One might appear without huge outward miracles. Surely you have not forgotten so soon our experience with the mullah and the prison in Shushan, have you? Can you imagine what he would have done if you had told him not only that the Promised One *might* appear without all of the expected outward miracles, but instead had told him that the Promised One *had already appeared?* His outrage would have known no bounds!

"Or consider Mulla Ali, who was badly beaten on his way here from Shiraz after telling just one person. And he is a mullah! If they have such little regard for a leader of their own religion, how much less regard will they have for two foreigners!"

"I don't care if they kill me!" said Zach boldly, still feeling the rapture of the previous night.

"I admire your courage," replied James, "and I share it. But if we are killed, we will be unable to carry this glorious news back to the West."

Zach acknowledged that James had an important point there, but still he felt as if he was being torn in half—one half heading east while the other felt compelled to go west.

"Furthermore, Mulla Ali told Yacob that the Bab is preparing to leave Shiraz to make the pilgrimage to Mecca, traveling by sea to make His announcement there. By the time we reach Shiraz, He might already be gone."

Zach thought hard and then said, "James, we have traveled for *so long and so far*—how can we stop now, when the object of our quest is within our reach?"

James, who had been pondering this question for a few hours already, replied, "The object of our quest is the discovery that He has appeared! And after that, which is more important—meeting Him in person or learning His teachings?"

Zach acknowledged that the new Revelation itself was the most important thing.

Hasan added, "Mulla Ali has a copy of most of what the Bab has revealed so far, so I feel that we should go find him."

Finally, in a somber tone, James said, "And, as I recall, you told me earlier that your father's last wish was not only that you should sail east to search for the Promised One but also that if you should find Him, you should do whatever He requested of you."

Zach reluctantly acknowledged that this was true.

"And according to Mulla Ali, He has requested us to get the initial message out to receptive communities. After we have safely gotten it out, then perhaps we can return for more details. But if we are to be true to your father's wishes, should we not now do whatsoever the Bab asks of us?"

This point was overwhelming. Zach knew his father had been watching over them, and he knew that he had promised to follow the instructions of the Promised One, as recently as during his dream while in Saveh. But still, this departure from their plans felt like a stab to his heart.

"Therefore," James concluded resolutely, "we *must* start our journey toward Najaf and Karbila immediately. Mulla Ali is a day's journey ahead of us, but I think that with a bit of luck, we might be able to catch up. Yacob has given me the names of several of the caravanserais along the route and the name of a Shaykhi who works at each. He said we can safely make contact, and these people will either show us to Mulla Ali, if he is there, or tell us exactly where he was heading, if he has already left."

Reluctantly, Zach went to gather his belongings, and they all prepared for a quick departure. This time, they would not wait for a caravan nor for sleep. They would head out directly on their own. They gave Yacob their profound thanks for delivering the joyful news to them. He cautioned them to be very careful in sharing it because he, too, was well aware of how dreadful the response could be from those who had no wish to be stirred from their deep spiritual slumber.

# Chapter 10

# RETURN TO KARBILA

HEADING UP THE SHATT-AL-ARAB toward Basra, James felt obliged to offer a bit of an apology. "In retrospect," he said, "I'm very glad that you were willing to speak with Mustafa back in Ahvaz. I must admit I was worried about it at the time. But without his help, we would never have found Yacob nor heard the astounding message from Mulla Ali. We might have gone on to Shiraz and missed the Bab there as well."

"Certainly true," replied Zach.

"I'm even glad that we spent those days in the prison back in Shushan," James continued. "Frustrating as it was at the time, I can see now that if we had not been detained, we would have arrived in Mohammerah too soon and would probably not have found Mulla Ali. He would have been traveling west while we were traveling east. And again, we might have missed finding the Bab."

"Yes indeed," Zach replied. "We see and know so little, while God and His angels see and know so much. Sometimes we just have to trust in Him. That is why I was not so upset for most of the time while we were in the prison. When something seemingly bad happens, after I have prayed for His guidance, I try to think about the ways in which this might be the very guidance we prayed for. And if I can't figure it out, I try to set it aside and trust that at some point in the future, I will see the wisdom of why things happened as they did."

James was pleased to be traveling with someone who blended an attitude of perseverance with an attitude of resignation to God's will in such an effective manner.

Traveling without a caravan enabled them to move more quickly than they normally did. However, the heat of late July was stifling, and their animals were not inclined to move swiftly in such heat. Taking a sailboat upstream would have been no better on this windless, sweltering day. Therefore, they were quite exhausted by the time they reached the caravanserai at Basra that evening. Hasan had noticed the nearly full moon rising as they arrived and suggested that they shift to night travel, as they had done when approaching Shushan last month, to avoid the heat and to hasten their progress. James and Zach happily assented to the proposal.

At the caravanserai, they asked for Jibril (Gabriel), whom Yacob had mentioned. He was not the owner of this caravanserai but its bookkeeper. When they found him, they explained that they had been sent by Yacob. His eyes suddenly lit up, and he said, "You have, perhaps, heard some important news from Yacob?"

"Yes, we have heard some wonderful news from Mulla Ali," replied Zach with quiet excitement.

Jibril gasped and then gave Zach a big hug. "It is the most glorious news!"

"It is the most wonderful news that anyone has heard in over a thousand years!" Zach affirmed. "We are hoping to find Mulla Ali to learn more from him. Is he, perchance, staying here?"

"He was indeed here last night, but he's now on his way to Najaf and Karbila. He left here a few hours ago that he might travel by night. He was determined to reach those cities as soon as possible."

They were pleased to hear that they were close to finding him. In spite of their exhaustion, Zach wanted to leave immediately to catch up with Mulla Ali. But Hasan pointed out that however eager they were to reach him, the animals were exhausted, and forcing the beasts forward to the point of collapse would not enable them to reach their goal. They decided to start tomorrow's journey at the earliest light in order to arrive at the next village, rest there at midday, and then start again in the evening in order to begin their night travel.

That evening they had dinner with Jibril and explained all about their search and how they were now hoping to learn of the Bab's teachings and read any of His writings that Mulla Ali carried.

"Yes," said Jibril, "His writings are exquisite! Mulla Ali recited some of the verses, and I asked him if I could copy some down. They come from His *Commentary on the Chapter of Joseph.*"[27]

"Please share them with us!" urged Zach.

So, Jibril drew forth from the pocket of his robe a small scroll and began to read slowly:

> *Verily I am the 'Gate of God' and I give you to drink, by the leave of God, the sovereign Truth, of the crystal-pure waters of His Revelation which are gushing out from the incorruptible Fountain situate upon the Holy Mount. And those who earnestly strive after the One True God, let them then strive to attain this Gate.*[28]

This reminded Zach of the water of eternal life that Jesus had offered to the woman in John 4. James and Zach had no doubts about who the Bab claimed to be as Jibril read further:

> *I am the Lamp which the Finger of God hath lit within its niche and caused to shine with deathless splendor. I am the Flame of that supernal Light that glowed upon Sinai in the gladsome Spot, and lay concealed in the midst of the Burning Bush.*[29]

With this, it was clear to all of them that the Bab was not simply claiming to be a reformer of Islam. Rather, He was claiming that the divine revelation that had appeared to the Founders of the great religions of the past had indeed been rekindled once again, in Him. And in the poetry of these Writings, they could hear the echo of the poetry of the Quran, which Musa had noted as they were sailing down the Euphrates.

\*　　\*　　\*

THEY AROSE AT THE earliest light of dawn to start the day's travels quickly in the hope of closing the gap that lay between them and Mulla Ali. Arriving at the next village by midday, they rested briefly but arose again in the early evening to start their journeys by night. However, they were now crossing the marshlands that lay between the Tigris and the Euphrates Rivers, and night travel here was not beneficial to those who were unfamiliar with this area. Here the tall reeds cast dark shadows in the moonlight, and thus crossing the many small streams of the marsh was arduous. Here also, Hasan warned them, they needed to move quietly lest they make their presence known to local thieves, who could hide easily amid the reeds. By the time they reached the caravanserai at Suq Al-Shuyukh on the western side, they discovered that Mulla Ali was actually now a day farther ahead of them.

The Ziggurat of the City of Ur, from which Abraham had fled

They pushed onward but were gradually becoming resigned to the thought that they would only be able to find Mulla Ali after he stopped to give the glad tidings to the Shaykhis in Najaf. By now, they were already halfway there.

On the following night, they were finally up on the dry plain west of the Euphrates when they saw a strange structure ahead. It looked like the lower part of a pyramid. As they approach, they realized that it was the remains of a large, ancient ziggurat. "What do you suppose that is?" asked James.

"*That*," Hasan said as he gazed upon the scene in the moonlight, "is where the story all began...several thousand years ago."

"What do you mean?"

"The first teachings of the oneness of God came through Abraham when He lived right here, in Ur."

"This is 'Ur of the Chaldees' from the Book of Genesis?" asked an astonished Zach.

"Yes, we have reached a spot from which you can see all that remains of the ancient city of Ur, where Abraham lived as a child. And this," he said, nodding toward the ruin, "is possibly one of the main temples of those ancient days—temples that were filled with many idols."

"Little is mentioned in Genesis about the nature of Abraham's life in Ur or why God told Him to leave," noted James.

"It is one example," replied Hasan, "of where the Quran has given us more of the story of the ancient Prophets than is found in either the Christian or the Jewish Holy Scriptures. Muhammad revealed the story of how Abraham, as a youth, objected to the idols in the temple. One night, when everyone had retired, He destroyed all but the largest one of them. When the people returned the next day, they were greatly upset and asked, 'Who has done this?' They suspected young Abraham and summoned Him, but He pointed to the largest idol and said, 'He did it.' He then suggested that the people should ask the idols for an account, if they could speak. The people wanted to say, 'You know very well that these idols cannot speak!' but they realized that this would only testify to the powerlessness of their idols. So they were vexed with young Abraham and wanted to burn Him, but God preserved Him and delivered Him safely from this land, sending Him to the Holy Land in the West."[30]

"Yes, I do recall reading that story in the Quran during the days we spent traveling on the Euphrates," said James, "and it is wonderful to see the actual site now."

"And the leader of Ur, who sought to burn Abraham, was that *Nimrod*?" inquired Zach.

"The name is not stated specifically in the Quran," replied Hasan, "but many think it may be so."

They headed onward as the late-night moon was now high in the sky. Zach was pondering all that had happened since those ancient days of Abraham. His thoughts of Abraham's "great crossing" from here to the Holy Land reminded him of the explanations that Shaykh Hakim had offered when they were first in Akka.

"Hasan," he inquired, "the Shaykhis we met in Akka told us that Muhammad reportedly said that the greater Prophet, Whose coming the Bab is announcing, will eventually go to Akka. They said He is destined to follow a path similar to Abraham and the Magi. Is that something that the Shaykhis here also believe, or are the Shaykhis of Akka just thinking wishfully?"

Hasan replied, "I have heard of the tradition of which they speak. This one is, as I recall, one of the more authentic ones. But I must confess, I have no idea why He would choose to go there."

"It seems to agree," Zach suggested, "with the prophecy of Jesus from Matthew 24: *For as the lightning cometh out of the east, and shineth even unto the west; so shall also the coming of the Son of man be.*' And then Jesus added, *For wheresoever the carcass is, there will the vultures be gathered together.*' What do you suppose He meant by that?"

Hasan paused a moment before offering, "I think the carcass is the dead body of religion, and the vultures are those who use their political or religious positions to feed off the mass of people who are spiritually lost."

"So," Zach inquired, "perhaps that part of the world will be particularly dead to the spirit?"

"God's messengers are often sent to the spiritually darkest parts of the world," Hasan replied.

They rode on in the silence of the night, each pondering the miraculous nature of the ways of God.

At length, Zach said, "You know, it is really an amazing thing to think of how mighty and wealthy the king of Ur must have been to be leading a nation that was building such great monuments and palaces. And yet, after more than three millennia, his whole civilization is nothing more than a crumbling pile of stones, abandoned by all and nearly forgotten on this dusty plain in Iraq."

Hasan added, "Yes, even the Euphrates River, which formerly ran through Ur, seems to have abandoned it, as it later changed its course, depriving the town of fresh water and access for sailing, hastening its decline."

Zach continued, "Abraham, on the other hand, was an outcast from this place and was seen by most of his family and neighbors as a trouble-maker. He was probably sent away with few worldly goods to sustain Him. Yet after all this time, His name is the one that is known across the world as the great patriarch of not just one but three religions—Jewish, Christian, and Muslim. Why, the only reason that anyone remembers Ur is because of Abraham's story."

"Human civilization," added James, "is subject to decline and decay. But divine civilization is built on spiritual principles. These true principles are enduring and are not subject to such decay. When human leaders build their civilizations on them, they last. But too often, success breeds hubris after a few generations, and then they fail to remain true to those enduring principles but instead stray onto the path of those seeking fame, power, and wealth."

"Moreover," offered Hasan, "those principles have been reinforced by the succession of God's messengers—Abraham, Zoroaster, Moses, Jesus, Muhammad, and now, the Bab. Were it not for the periodic appearance of new Messengers, I have no doubt that we, too, would wander astray, as so many human civilizations have done before us."

As they rode onward, Zach was reminded of a question from their meeting with Jibril in Basra.

"He mentioned a book that the Bab had recently revealed called the *Commentary on the Chapter of Joseph*. I've been reviewing the story of Joseph from Genesis in my mind—how his envious brothers sold him into slavery in Egypt and how, with God's help, he was able to rise to become the chief advisor to the Pharaoh. But I am not sure how that story relates to the coming of the Promised One."

"Ah, it is because you know only a part of the story," replied Hasan. "To you it may seem like it is merely the history of how Jacob and his family moved to Egypt. But in the Quran, it is explained how Jacob, in spite of the many long years of his son's disappearance, never really believed what his other sons had told him—that Joseph had been killed by a wild animal. Perhaps he surmised that Joseph might have been sold into slavery. In any case, he remained faithful to his belief that Joseph was alive and that one day he would find him. He cried so much in his yearning to see his long-lost son that he became blind, yet still he believed. At last, on the return from their third trip to Egypt, Jacob's other sons were bringing with them the news of Joseph's life and success in Egypt. They carried with them one of Joseph's inner garments as proof that he was, indeed, alive. Jacob was able to inhale its fragrance, even at a great distance, and was overjoyed. And thus understanding that his son was indeed alive, he also regained his sight.

"To Muslim poets over the centuries, the story of Jacob and Joseph has been a metaphor for a person's undying love and faithfulness to overcome every difficulty in order to find the object of one's quest, even over vast distances."

"And thus," James surmised from some of his earlier readings of Islamic poets and mystics, "the undying love of the sincere and dedicated believers can also find God's Messenger when He returns, even after centuries have passed."

"Exactly," replied Hasan. "Even though blinded by the sorrow of their long separation from Him, yet perchance they can use one of their other senses to perceive His presence. *We* are that Jacob, who have been so long separated from the true Joseph, and now, by God's grace, we have found Him!"

This explanation brought tears to Zach's eyes. He added thoughtfully, "My father was among the people in my country who inhaled a trace of this fragrance. He taught me to seek with a spiritual understanding. God willing, others may now be able to recognize the fragrance of the new teachings and thus overcome their blindness."

"Muhammad called the story of Joseph 'the most beautiful of stories,'" remarked Hasan, "and I can see why."

The faint glow on the eastern horizon announced the coming dawn. They would soon reach the next village's caravanserai to rest during the day as they continued their approach to Najaf.

*　　*　　*

HARUN (AARON) WAS ONE of Hasan's best friends, a Shaykhi who lived in Najaf. Upon their arrival, they went straight to his home to see if he had heard the good news.

"Indeed," he replied strongly, "and we were thrilled to the core when Mulla Ali arrived and summoned us, just two days ago, to tell us all about how the Promised One had been found! We begged him to stay and to start to proclaim the message right here. He promised that he would return soon but insisted that he first had to carry the message to the friends waiting in Karbila. We had to acknowledge that his reasoning was sound for the community of receptive Shaykhis here is smaller, and the voices of potential opposition are stronger than in Karbila. But before he left, he blessed us by sharing a few of the quotes he had copied from the Bab's teachings in Shiraz."

Again, they asked him to share them. Harun recited in beautiful Arabic:

> *O PEOPLES of the East and the West! Be ye fearful of God concerning the Cause of the true Joseph and barter Him not for a paltry price established by yourselves, or for a trifle of your earthly possessions, that ye may, in very truth, be praised by Him as those who are reckoned among the pious who stand nigh unto this Gate.*[31]

"Yes!" thought Zach. "How could anyone even compare this great news to the things of a normal life?"

Some of the verses felt like they were directed particularly to Zach and James and their countrymen:

> *ISSUE forth from your cities, O peoples of the West and aid God ere the Day when the Lord of mercy shall come down unto you in the shadow of the clouds with the angels circling around Him... Become as true brethren in the one and indivisible religion of God,*

141

*free from distinction, for verily God desireth that your hearts should become mirrors unto your brethren in the Faith, so that ye find yourselves reflected in them, and they in you.[32]*

"Yes!" he thought again. "How shall I remain still or settled in any city after this? Now we have the opportunity to do so much! And all who share this understanding do indeed become my true brethren, regardless of their religious background, because we all now recognize that all of the religions come from a single Source."

Harun explained that like Muhammad before Him, the Gate addressed the kings:

*O concourse of kings! Deliver with truth and in all haste the verses sent down by Us to the peoples of Turkey and of India, and beyond them, with power and with truth, to lands in both the East and the West.[33]*

It was clear to Zach and James that this message was not simply addressed to the Islamic world. Rather, it was addressed to the *entire* world, and they needed to deliver it to the lands of the West *in all haste.*

Although their hopes for meeting Mulla Ali in Najaf were dashed, James and Zach were consoled by the knowledge that Karbila was only two days' ride away. And so, requesting forgiveness from their host for their early departure, they set off for that city on the following morning.

\*      \*      \*

THEY ARRIVED AT THE home of Siyyid Kazim late in the day and were overjoyed to find at last that Mulla Ali was there. Though hungry, tired, and dusty from the long day's journey, they would not allow anything to prevent them from hearing the talk that Mulla Ali was giving that very evening. It had been less than seven months since they first attended the talk given by Mulla Husayn in that same house, but so much had happened in that brief time that it seemed like a different age.

Mulla Ali described how, after much prayer and fasting, he and his group of twelve others had been drawn to Shiraz. They had traveled overland around the north end of the Persian Gulf. He was surprised to find Mulla Husayn there in Shiraz, seemingly composed and no longer anxiously searching. After meditating on how this could be, it occurred to him that the only reason that a person who had been on such an intense search might cease his searching was that he must have found the object of his quest and yet was unable to speak of his success. So he spoke to him.

"'I adjure you,' I told him, 'to bestow upon me a portion of that holy draught which the Hand of mercy has given you to drink,' but he refused, suggesting that I should seek God's guidance."[34]

Mulla Ali explained that he conveyed this to his companions and that they started a vigil of prayer and fasting. On the third night of their vigil, he saw a light that moved, and he followed it. It led him to the Bab. Each of his twelve companions, as well as the companions of Mulla Husayn, independently found the Bab through dreams or while in prayer or meditations or visions.

Then he explained how *Quddus* had arrived after a long journey from the northern part of Persia. He was another student of Siyyid Kazim, who had departed from Karbila earlier in the previous year. He recognized the Bab almost instantly, simply by the way He walked and by the power and majesty that seemed to radiate from Him. The Bab confirmed that He had already met Quddus in the spirit world.

Finally, Mulla Ali also explained how the Bab had received the letter from Qurrat'l-Ayn and how pleased he was to bring back to her the news that the Bab had recognized her as one of the eighteen Letters of the Living—His initial disciples.

The news of the fulfilled promise had spread quickly among the local Shaykhi disciples who had been unable to join in the search. It was even more stunning to them than it had been to James and Zach, for while the Shaykhis were overjoyed with the news, they also knew that embracing it could easily lead to their own deaths. They knew that the religious leaders could, and probably would, falsely claim that accepting a new Messenger of God was equivalent to rejecting Muhammad as God's Messenger. It would be easy for these "scribes and Pharisees" of the Islamic world to remind their followers that the punishment for ceasing to believe in Muhammad was death. Thus, to accept the new Revelation was to put one's life at grave risk. And yet they were so thrilled by the awesome majesty of this greatest news that, like Zach and James, they felt themselves lifted up into another realm, abandoning any care or desire for their mortal life below.

Regular evening meetings were held, during which Mulla Ali read from the Bab's *Commentary on the Chapter of Joseph*. Whatever was read in the evening would be copied and recopied by the many followers during the next day as people longed to have a copy of their own and as a way to ensure that it would never be destroyed. It was a daunting task for the Bab had, over the course of 40 nights, revealed 42 verses of commentary on *each* of the 111 verses from the Quran's chapter of Joseph.

A few days later, Mirza Muhammad-Aliy-i-Qazvani and some of the other Letters of the Living arrived from Shiraz. They were part of the larger group who had been sent forth shortly after Mulla Ali had gone forth. He explained how the Bab had, in most cases, sent them off to their home provinces to start to spread the great news. He had been sent here initially to deliver the Bab's letter to his sister-in-law, Qurrat'l-Ayn, which confirmed that the Bab had indeed appointed her as one of His 18 initial disciples.

Her brother-in-law also carried with him the words that the Bab had addressed to the main body of the Letters prior to sending them forth. It was a powerful message galvanizing His disciples and followers to carry His message forth. He read it aloud:

> O My beloved friends! You are the bearers of the name of God in this Day. You have been chosen as the repositories of His mystery. It behooves each one of you to manifest the attributes of God, and to exemplify by your deeds and words the signs of His righteousness, His power and glory. The very members of your body must bear witness to the loftiness of your purpose, the integrity of your life, the reality of your faith, and the exalted character of your devotion. For verily I say, this is the Day spoken of by God in His Book: "On that day will We set a seal upon their mouths yet shall their hands speak

*unto Us, and their feet shall bear witness to that which they shall have done."* [35]

*Ponder the words of Jesus addressed to His disciples, as He sent them forth to propagate the Cause of God. In words such as these, He bade them arise and fulfil their mission: "Ye are even as the fire which in the darkness of the night has been kindled upon the mountain-top. Let your light shine before the eyes of men. Such must be the purity of your character and the degree of your renunciation, that the people of the earth may through you recognize and be drawn closer to the heavenly Father who is the Source of purity and grace. For none has seen the Father who is in heaven. You who are His spiritual children must by your deeds exemplify His virtues, and witness to His glory. You are the salt of the earth, but if the salt have lost its savor, wherewith shall it be salted? Such must be the degree of your detachment, that into whatever city you enter to proclaim and teach the Cause of God, you should in no wise expect either meat or reward from its people. Nay, when you depart out of that city, you should shake the dust from off your feet. As you have entered it pure and undefiled, so must you depart from that city. For verily I say, the heavenly Father is ever with you and keeps watch over you. If you be faithful to Him, He will assuredly deliver into your hands all the treasures of the earth, and will exalt you above all the rulers and kings of the world."* [36]

"Yes, He is very familiar with the words Jesus addressed to His followers in His Sermon on the Mount," said Zach.

"And He sends us forth in the same manner that Jesus sent His disciples forth in Matthew 10," added James.

The reading continued:

*O My Letters! Verily I say, immensely exalted is this Day above the days of the Apostles of old. Nay, immeasurable is the difference! You are the witnesses of the Dawn of the promised Day of God. You are the partakers of the mystic chalice of His Revelation. Gird up the loins of endeavor, and be mindful of the words of God as revealed in His Book: "Lo, the Lord thy God is come, and with Him is the company of His angels arrayed before Him!"*

*Purge your hearts of worldly desires, and let angelic virtues be your adorning. Strive that by your deeds you may bear witness to the truth of these words of God, and beware lest, by "turning back," He may "change you for another people," who "shall not be your like," and who shall take from you the Kingdom of God. The days when idle worship was deemed sufficient are ended. The time is come when naught but the purest motive, supported by deeds of stainless purity, can ascend to the throne of the Most High and be acceptable unto Him. "The good word riseth up unto Him, and the righteous deed will cause it to be exalted before Him."*

*You are the lowly, of whom God has thus spoken in His Book: "And We desire to show favor to those who were brought low in the land, and to make them spiritual leaders among men, and to make them Our heirs." You have been called to this station; you will attain to it, only if you arise to trample beneath your feet every earthly desire, and endeavor to become those "honored servants of His who speak not till He hath spoken, and who do His bidding."³⁷*

"He is calling us again for the self-same humility that the disciples of Jesus possessed," observed James.

*You are the first Letters that have been generated from the Primal Point,⁋⁋ the first Springs that have welled out from the Source of this Revelation. Beseech the Lord your God to grant that no earthly entanglements, no worldly affections, no ephemeral pursuits, may tarnish the purity, or embitter the sweetness, of that grace which flows through you. I am preparing you for the advent of a mighty Day. Exert your utmost endeavor that, in the world to come, I, who am now instructing you, may, before the mercy-seat of God, rejoice in your deeds and glory in your achievements. The secret of the Day*

---

⁋⁋ This was one of the titles of the Bab.

*that is to come is now concealed. It can neither be divulged nor esti-*
*mated. The newly born babe of that Day excels the wisest and most*
*venerable men of this time, and the lowliest and most unlearned*
*of that period shall surpass in understanding the most erudite and*
*accomplished divines of this age.*

"Of course!" Zach realized. "The advent of the mighty Day refers to the coming of the second Messenger, Who brings the mighty 'Day of the Lord,' which the Bible mentions in many places."

*Scatter throughout the length and breadth of this land, and,*
*with steadfast feet and sanctified hearts, prepare the way for His*
*coming. Heed not your weaknesses and frailty; fix your gaze upon*
*the invincible power of the Lord, your God, the Almighty. Has He*
*not, in past days, caused Abraham, in spite of His seeming help-*
*lessness, to triumph over the forces of Nimrod? Has He not enabled*
*Moses, whose staff was His only companion, to vanquish Pharaoh*
*and his hosts? Has He not established the ascendancy of Jesus, poor*
*and lowly as He was in the eyes of men, over the combined forces*
*of the Jewish people? Has He not subjected the barbarous and*
*militant tribes of Arabia to the holy and transforming discipline*
*of Muhammad, His Prophet? Arise in His name, put your trust*
*wholly in Him, and be assured of ultimate victory.*[38]

So resounding was this call for both Zach and James, and so stirring the poetry of the passage, that tears were streaming down their cheeks by the time they reached its end. Here was the clarion call, the Great Commission, a trumpet blast sending everyone forth to announce the joyful news of the coming of God's Messenger!

Zach was amazed to hear not only the Bab's references to the Quran but also the references to the story of Jesus. How could a young merchant, unschooled in religious studies and surrounded on all sides by the religion of Islam, be so aware of the verses that Jesus uttered unless He was hearing them from the divine realm? In hearing this message to the new disciples,

147

he could hear the voice of Jesus once again. In His call for deeds of stainless purity and detachment from all worldly affections, He was clearly calling forth good fruits from the lives of His followers—clear evidence, by Jesus' own standard, that this was a good tree, a true Prophet. Zach, feeling as if he had been transported back to those precious days when the earlier disciples were first learning the teachings of God at the feet of Jesus, couldn't help but cry out, "How greatly have I been blessed!"

They had spent weeks in rapt attention, listening to every word of those priceless lessons that Mulla Ali and Mirza Muhammad-Ali shared with the Shaykhis who were ready to accept the news that the Promised One had appeared. Zach and James had no desire to leave, but the Bab's call made it clear to them that this was what they must do.

They knew that this mighty news had to be shared carefully in the Islamic realms, knowing the dangers posed by religious leaders who were all too ready to bring the sword of denunciation down upon the necks of all those who were perceived to be heretics.

As September was starting, Hasan pulled James and Zach aside to provide some advice: "The holy month of the Ramadan fast is approaching. I have heard that during that month, Mulla Ali will start to proclaim this message publicly, first here and then in Najaf. I fear that this will ignite a firestorm of protest and denunciation and other hardships for all of the believers here. It will very likely result in his arrest and imprisonment. The same fate may fall upon his companions. If it is your intention to carry this message safely to your homelands, it may be wise for you to commence your journey soon—before this storm breaks."

# Chapter 11

# FAREWELL TO A FRIEND ON THE JOURNEY TO AKKA

JAMES AND ZACH WERE saddened at the thought that these days of bliss, basking in the glory of the newly revealed words of God, might be coming to an end. But after prayerful consideration, they took Hasan's advice and began their preparations for travel. The return route to Akka would necessarily be overland since, as they already knew, upstream travel by boat was not feasible. The first half of the journey would be easy, with food and water plentiful as they followed the Euphrates River up to the old fortress town of Deir ez Zor. From there, the route turned southwestward across the Syrian desert to reach Palmyra and from thence to Damascus. Although no one was available to accompany them this time, they felt they had learned enough of the Arabic language and customs that they could get by. They were no longer searching, so they could travel quietly with others in the caravan. And, as James noted, all of the desert portion of the journey would be during the holy month of Ramadan, when attack by marauding local tribesmen or others was less likely, making their travel safer.

After a few days of gathering provisions, they bid a very fond farewell to their good friend, Hasan, and to the other Shaykhis they had come to know in Karbila. They expressed the hope that they might be able to return after carrying the good news to the people of their homelands.

The September weather was still quite hot along the Euphrates, so they were thankful to have ready access to the river as the caravan followed it upstream. In Deir ez Zor, they purchased sufficient skins to hold the water they would need for the long stretches between the oases of the desert. Though they started their two-week crossing on the first day of autumn, it still felt like summer. The moon, however, was again in their favor, so the caravan was able to make the entire transit through careful timing of their daily departures, combining moonlit night travel with late afternoon or early morning travel. Thus, they avoided the worst of the heat.

They had been traveling for several days. During the long hours of travel over the parched and monotonous landscape, they had plenty of time to contemplate the events that had transpired over the past several months and the immense significance of their discovery.

Yet Zach was concerned. "I cannot think of anyone back home who will take this news well. Even my family will struggle to understand it, except perhaps for my young nephew Gabriel."

James replied, "We have learned so much. There is no going back now. As Jesus said at the end of Luke 9, 'No man, having put his hand to the plough, and looking back, is fit for the kingdom of God.' To move forward with the new Revelation is to let go of much of the past."

"True indeed," responded Zach wistfully. "One thought that has been nagging me since our departure from Saveh concerns the response of the people of that area to the news that the Magi brought. Apparently, no one came back to learn from Jesus thirty years later."

"Yes," agreed James, "the thought has crossed my mind too. Being 'Wise Men,' they were probably too old to return after thirty years. By the time Jesus started to teach, they may have been dead or at least too old to make the journey again."

"True enough," said Zach, "but don't you think they would have had some followers? I mean, perhaps not a whole mass movement but at least a few young followers—maybe only members of their family—who would have been young enough to travel thirty years after the Wise Men had returned to Persia? And if so, why didn't any of them return to the Holy Land to learn from Jesus and to carry His message straight back to Persia?"

"As I recall," replied James, "there were some Persians, 'Parthians and Medes and Elamites,' among the foreigners in Jerusalem at the time of the Pentecost, when people of all tongues could somehow understand what the apostles spoke, even though they were speaking in Aramaic. But there is no mention that they were connected to the Magi. If such a person was there, there is no record of it in history—as far as I've ever heard. When the early Christian disciples spread eastward, they surely would have recorded in their Church history the discovery of any Christian community established in Saveh by the children or followers of the Magi. But to the best of my knowledge, it never happened.

"And," he continued, "we've seen the site where they were supposedly buried. It was clear that a Christian community later occupied it as a church or shrine and added their symbols to the original Zoroastrian architecture. But if any Christian followers of the original Magi were ever found, they didn't leave any mark on history."

"I have read that *Thomas the Apostle* traveled to South India and established an early Christian community there," replied Zach. "If he traveled overland, he would likely have taken the same Silk Road route through Persia that we took and would have passed near Saveh. If there had been a community of followers of the Magi who expected to hear more about Jesus, he would surely have stopped there and would have sent word back to the other disciples."

"Perhaps he traveled to India by sea," offered James, "or perhaps he took the southern route. But tell me, why has all of this been bothering you?"

"Well," said Zach, "my concern is that in spite of the wondrous success of the Magi in using the prophecies of their religion to find the promised Messiah eighteen hundred years ago, it would seem as if, when they got home, they found that their countrymen were unwilling to believe it."

"And by extension," James finished the thought, "you are wondering whether the same fate awaits us."

"*Precisely*," replied Zach. "Perhaps the people who have not traveled to faraway places, and who have not experienced other ways of living, are incapable of understanding any perspective other than that of their fathers and the people around them. Perhaps their manner of thinking has not been stretched sufficiently. Perhaps it will be impossible for them to break away from their long-held beliefs and make the transition to the new ways of thinking about the fulfillment of the prophecies and, indeed, to accept any new teachings of the Promised One."

"Yes," acknowledged James, "perhaps the 'new wine' will not set well in the 'old skins,' as Jesus had taught."

Zach continued, "Convincing people that the great miraculous scenes, all of which they were hoping to witness, are spiritual or allegorical in nature—that would be difficult enough. But added to this now, they will need to learn that God has been working with all peoples, everywhere, sending Prophets and Messengers throughout history, and has worked through each of the resulting religions as well, however true they may have stayed to the teachings of the Prophet or Messenger who founded them. Our listeners will need to be humble enough to acknowledge that although their own prophecies were correct, they were not *exclusively* correct. Those who have looked for the appearance of the Promised One as a vindication and proof that they were right and everyone else was wrong—these people are going to be sorely disappointed, and perhaps very upset, with our good news. It will surely threaten the comfortable positions that some of our religious leaders have."

"Not unlike the Pharisees of Jesus' time," replied James. "It almost seems like we have come full circle, doesn't it? It seems as if the same story is being told, just with new actors."

"Yes, that is very true," Zach said thoughtfully. "But if we are indeed living in the time of the 're-turn,' it means that we have literally turned again—we've gone through a whole cycle and are now returned to the place we started. It is not only that Christ returns but also the opponents of God's Messenger return. The questioning returns, the upheaval returns, and the awakening of people returns. It is like the return of spring each year: It is not just that the sun returns to its spring position—no, there are thousands of other conditions on Earth that are also awakened by that change and return to their spring condition."

"But what I would like to know," asked Zach, "is what was the real benefit of the Wise Men? Why did God inspire them to travel to find Jesus if it would not lead to the rapid development of an early Christian community in the Zoroastrian East?"

After pondering a while, James replied, "I can think of two reasons: Firstly, it was an announcement to the Jewish people that the appearance of the Messiah was bigger than what they had imagined. It was bigger than just the fulfillment of Old Testament prophecy. This was not simply the appearance of the next Old Testament prophet with instructions to the Jewish people on how they must mend their ways. This was the birth of a whole new revelation, similar in importance to the revelation of Moses and with teachings that were universal enough to reach beyond the theological limitations of the Jewish people. This was something that would break the Jewish religion out of its mold.

"And in the event that the story of the appearance of the Magi did not help most of the Jewish people understand the scope of the new revelation, it had a second benefit: It would help the new Gentile Christian communities to understand the wide scope of Jesus' revelation. Here was something for the whole world. This was not just a new version of the Jewish religion, but a far larger truth. It went far beyond the narrow confines of Judaism to encompass the widespread religion of the vast Persian Empire. The fact that a foreign religion contained accurate prophecies of the appearance of the Christ Child was certainly a sign to the Greek and Roman world that something hugely important was happening here. For Who else, other than a universal God, could have implanted such accurate prophecies in the Persian religion, which was born a thousand years earlier and a thousand miles away?"

Zach said optimistically, "I hope we are more successful at teaching our people than the Magi apparently were." But whenever he thought of the vast majority of his fellow believers in America and how tenaciously they clung to their expectations that Jesus would descend from the physical sky, his hopes would wane. He thought also of Sa'id Hindi, the Bab's disciple from India, who was even now heading back, carrying the news to his home country. Would he have any success there? And what of the fearless Mulla Ali? He seemed to be headed into a maelstrom in the Islamic world.***

***Historical note: After proclaiming the news of the coming of the Bab, Mulla Ali was imprisoned in Baghdad for several months and then exiled to Constantinople in 1845. According to recently discovered records, he died in a labor camp while there. Thus he is regarded as the first Bab'i martyr. As to Sa'id Hindi, one person is known to have become a follower of the Bab as a result of Sa'id Hindi's efforts. That person went back to Persia while Sa'id Hindi continued on to India. No further record of him has been found to date. However small his direct impact may have been, his spiritual impact was, perhaps, far larger, for it is interesting to note that the new religion has, in recent times, spread faster in India than in Persia. India currently has the largest population of its followers of any country in the world.

On the next day, Zach was inclined to look further ahead. He had been thinking about this question for a while now. "Even if we find that no one will accept this—yes, even if there is none who will remember the story of our own success in finding the Promised One—still the accuracy of the prophecies of Daniel and the fact that Jesus pointed to them, as well as the prophecies in the Book of Revelation, which you explained to me when we were sailing here, will eventually be discovered. Some future generation of our Christian brethren will realize that the Promise was fulfilled *exactly on time,* even if the manner of its fulfillment was different from what most of our generation was expecting. That generation will be able to understand how prophecies from all of the world's great religions can be foretelling a single set of future events, even though they look at these from many different angles. But this comes into focus only if the followers of these religions realize that many of the aspects of the prophecies are intended to be understood spiritually rather than materially.

"At some point they will realize that not only is a universal fulfillment possible but also that it is one of the greatest testimonies to the universality, the oneness, the justice, and the majesty of God Himself.

They both paused as they contemplated the overwhelming significance of this point in history that they had recently witnessed.

Then Zach continued, "As for myself, I don't need the fame. It would be nice if people listen to what we've discovered, but if they don't, I know that their descendants will discover it. Who can stop the will of God? For myself, I will just be eternally grateful that He enabled me to be there, in Persia, at the right moment to witness this grand fulfillment after 2,300 years. Do you realize how incredibly blessed we are?"

James nodded in agreement. "That is true," he said slowly. "That is absolutely true. And as my thanks for this great blessing, I am happy to accept whatever God may have in store for us."

As he said this, a couplet came to his mind from the poetry of *Sana'i,* which he had heard years ago in Egypt and which spoke of the detachment of the saintly followers that arises from their deep love and firm knowledge of their Lord. He shared it with Zach:

*A lover is he who is chill in hell fire*
*A knower is he who is dry in the sea.*

And so they continued in their long trek across the sands toward the ancient city of Palmyra and, beyond that, to Damascus.

\*　　\*　　\*

REACHING THE CARAVANSERAI IN the Shiah section of Damascus on October 6, they noticed it was nearly empty that evening.

"They have all gone to the mosque," the innkeeper explained, "for the celebration of the Night of Power."

This was the holiest night in the Muslim year, commemorating the beginning of Muhammad's revelation and, as they both remembered, the time Hasan had said that the Bab's revelation would first be proclaimed in Karbila. They prayed that it would be accepted by as many as possible.

The following day, they continued their reflections on all that had happened as they made their way southwest from Damascus and, from there, past Mt. Hermon and into the northeastern corner of the Holy Land. The first rains of the season soaked them as they crossed the plains overlooking the east side of the Hula Valley. A chilling wind made them feel worse. As they gazed down into the valley, they hoped to find a warmer climate there.

The caravan moved down the path toward the northeast corner of the Sea of Galilee and stopped at a caravanserai of a small fishing village on its shore, a day's journey from Tiberias. Their rest here was troubled by the swarms of mosquitoes thriving in the swampy lands at the confluence of several streams and the river that entered the sea from this side.[†††]

Whether from the chilling rains or the lack of sleep or both, James was not feeling well as the journey resumed the following day, but he thought he would recover as they pushed on. Within a few hours, though, he developed a severe headache. They had not quite reached the village of Capernaum when he became very sick to his stomach and told Zach that they would have to stop there. Resting in a sheltered hollow in the shade of some trees

---

††† At the time, the mosquitoes were considered just another nuisance of travel. Their connection to infectious disease was not known in those days.

near a brook, Zach helped James dismount and noted how feverish he felt. Soon James started to vomit—several spells until his stomach was empty. He then suffered several bouts of diarrhea. When James returned to lay down, Zach started to swab his friend with a cloth with cool waters from the stream to bring down what now felt like a high fever. But James started to shiver from this, even while he was feverish.

"I think...I've got...malaria," he said weakly. "I've heard others describe it. It's common enough in these parts. I...n-need a blanket."

"Don't worry," said Zach. "I'll take care of you." But Zach himself was very much worried. He had no idea how to cure such an illness. If wrapping him in a blanket would help to stop the shivering, it would only make the fever worse. Bathing him in cool waters might reduce the fever, but it would make the chills unbearable. James was thoroughly exhausted by this point and wanted to sleep. Zach said he would go to the nearby village while James rested to see if there was anything or anyone who could help.

He returned soon with some powdered "fever tree bark," which was recommended and sold to him by a man in the village who vouched for its effectiveness. He heated some water on a fire and mixed some of the powder into it. James still had the fever as he awoke, and so Zach had him drink the tonic. In spite of his fever and the chills that still caused some shivering, James wanted to talk.

"I...I had the...most amazing dream!" he said in a joyful but quivering tone. "I met S-Siyyid Kazim! He...was overjoyed to know of our search! He pointed m-my gaze to Karbila, where Mullah Ali has lit the fire of the Bab's c-cause in the last few days with his public proclamations and how he w-was, even now, tr-traveling to Najaf to do the same there. He said it was already causing a gr-great commotion, as he knew it would.

"I was thrilled when he complimented us...on all of the efforts we'd made in our search. H-he said we had done well! He urged me not to worry about anything that might happen in this world, and he seemed to set every-thing into the context of the Greater Realm, which made all the normal cares of this world seem so...small. He made me feel completely at peace.

"And then he...said that the Bab would soon come to bring me home.

What do you suppose he m-meant by that? Do you think He will help us reach London?"

"I have no idea," replied Zach, although, with a sinking heart, he actually had an idea, but he didn't want to share it.

The sun was getting low, so Zach unpacked things they could use for staying out under the trees that night and gathered more materials for the fire. The sky indicated no threat of rain, so Zach felt it was best to remain here in the hollow.

The medicine seemed to be bringing the fever down somewhat, and James' shaking abated. He requested a pen and paper and set to work writing something while Zach started cooking some food for himself. Although James was in no condition to have food at this point, Zach prepared another cup of the fever tree bark tea, this time mixed with a bit of sugar he'd been saving.

"What are you writing?" inquired Zach.

"It is a notice," replied James.

"Who is it for?"

"Why, it's for you."

Zach thought that was a rather strange reply. "May I read it?"

"As soon as I'm done."

A little while later, James sat back and handed it to Zach.

"Oh no!" gasped Zach as he read its title. It was a simple last will and testament that James had prepared. "You don't need to write this! You must reach England and carry the news of our discoveries to your countrymen. You're not going to die!"

"Most assuredly, I *am* going to die," replied James with a note of finality. "Only the date may carry some degree of uncertainty. And just in case the time is soon, I wanted you to have that since I have no close family—at least none in this world."

Zach read the brief statement stating that all of James' possessions and property were bequeathed to Zach and listing some of the main items. He set it aside.

"Now drink that tea," Zach instructed confidently. "Tonight the fever will be broken, and by tomorrow we'll be able to move on to find Musa in

Tiberias, where we can take a few days for a proper recovery and perhaps benefit from the natural hot springs there."

"God willing," replied James with a gentle smile as he drank the tea.

But something in it did not agree with him, and before long, he was again retching the last of the liquid that had been in his stomach. Night had fallen, and feeling weak, he went off to sleep on the blanket spread on bunches of dried grass that Zach had gathered.

Zach said some prayers for his friend and tried to sleep after a while.

He was awoken in the middle of the night by James, who was sitting bolt upright and seemed to be looking up while having a conversation with someone, or at least a half-conversation in the dim light of what remained of their campfire.

"Why, look there, Zach," said James, pointing upward and ahead of him. "It's Elijah, come to visit us."

Zach looked but saw nothing. "Do you see the prophet Elijah?" he asked.

"No, no, no," replied James with a chuckle. "It's our old friend, Elijah Goodman, who's come from England to see how we are doing. Can't you see him?"

Zach still saw nothing.

Looking from side to side, James smiled broadly and said, "Zach, you were right about my ancestors. Do you remember what you told me in London? I can see them all smiling now—hundreds, nay, thousands of them! Why, look! Even my dear Caroline and little Joseph are here! And they are all beaming with joy, knowing what we have discovered. Ah yes, you were right indeed!"

Zach smiled and went to get some more kindling for the campfire while James returned to his conversation with the invisible Elijah Goodman, telling the story of all the places they had visited and all they had discovered. Zach realized that James' fever must have gotten worse and that perhaps this was making James delirious. He started making some more tea.

James continued the story, finally reaching the part where they first heard of the appearance of the Bab when they were in Mohammerah. He described their ecstatic joy at hearing the news. Then, pointing excitedly to the right, he said, "And look there! Here He comes now!"

And with that, a beautiful expression of joyous serenity came over James' face. His eyes closed, and he slumped back upon his blanket.

"Oh no!" shouted Zach as he jumped up to see what had happened to his friend. But it was too late. James Lawrence had breathed his last and slipped away, his body now lying limp on the blanket. But that most beautiful expression of serenity was still upon his face.

Zach wept.

*     *     *

AFTER MANY TEARS AND many prayers, the memory of James' comments almost a year earlier, while seated on the Mount of the Beatitudes above Capernaum, floated back into Zach's mind. He had spoken of the beauty of the scene and the serenity of the hills with the lake below. Had he not said that it would make a wonderful final resting place?

So at the earliest dawn, Zach assembled all their belongings onto the camels and secured James' body over the donkey. In Capernaum, amid his considerable grief, he explained his situation to a laborer, and together they traveled up the gentle slope of the Mount of the Beatitudes, to a beautiful spot slightly below where Jesus' first sermon had been given.

There, they dug a grave for James. The laborer was surprised at Zach's instructions that the grave should face not toward Jerusalem nor toward Mecca, as was the normal practice, but rather toward Shiraz. "Someday," he told the laborer, "you will understand."

Zach had found a plank in the village that he brought to use as a grave marker. Upon it, he now set to carving the following:

> *Here lies James Lawrence,*
> *who freed himself from all worldly concerns*
> *to seek the Promised One of God*
> *—and not in vain was his search.*

And then, echoing those beautiful words that Jesus had first uttered on that same hillside almost two millennia earlier, he added:

# FAREWELL TO A FRIEND ON THE JOURNEY TO AKKA

*"Blessed are the pure in heart: for they shall see God."*
—*Matthew 5:8*

*October 10, 1844*

James' final resting place, overlooking the Sea of Galilee

After more prayers, Zach spent the rest of the day on the road to Tiberias. He was sorely grieved by the loss of his dear friend and fellow traveler. He wondered whether, perhaps, he should never have encouraged James to make the journey. But when he pulled out the will that James had written, he noted that James had expressed therein his great gratitude to Zach for leading him to the most important discovery possible and for the wonderful meaning it had given his life. James seemed to have had no regard for the fire of malarial fever that had consumed him. The quote from Sana'i, which James had shared earlier, returned to Zach's thoughts: "A lover is he who is chill in hell fire." He remembered the expression of blissful contentment that remained on James' face.

In Tiberias, he made his way to the home of Musa, who was delighted to see him, although deeply saddened to hear the news of James' recent demise. After prayers for James, Musa arranged a fine meal for Zach, and together they spent much of the night discussing all of the wondrous things that had happened in the seven months since they had parted. Musa burst

160

into an ecstatic dance when he heard of the news of the appearance of the Bab, the Promised Qaim, jumping up and joyfully embracing Zach when he explained their success in finding Him. He spent the rest of the night memorizing passages from the Bab's writings, which Zach had read aloud.

*     *     *

TWO DAYS LATER, ZACH reached Akka and went straight to the house of Shaykh Hakim. He was disappointed to find that the shaykh had left, along with Youssef, to see Youssef's uncle, Suleiman, who had returned to his home in Mays al-Jabal. He was told that they would not be back for another month. To fulfill his promise of bringing the news of what they had found to the shaykh and Youssef, Zach spent the whole day at the caravanserai composing a letter describing all that had occurred on their journey of discovery.

On the following day, Zach went down to the waterside to inquire of the date of westbound ships. He was pleased to find a captain planning to leave for Malta in about four days' time, so he booked passage. He knew that Malta was a British protectorate and a major stopping point for British ships. From there, it would be easy to find passage onward to London.

On returning from the port, he was greeted by a familiar face.

"Salaam! Shalom!" shouted Moshe, greeting Zach with peace in both Arabic and Hebrew.

"Salaam! Shalom!" shouted Zach back, recognizing the man he had met at the Cave of Elijah. "What brings you here from Haifa?" he asked.

"Haifa is such a small village," he replied. "I come here regularly to purchase items that we cannot find there. But what of you? Have you been here in Akka all this time? And where is your traveling companion?"

Zach suggested that they go to the nearby coffee shop, where they could talk at length. He then recounted the story of his travels, all they had discovered, and the fate of James.

Moshe expressed his condolences regarding James and then added, "So you think the Moshiach has appeared in Persia? Surely He must come to the Holy Land."

"The Messiah will surely come to the Holy Land," Zach replied, thinking of what Shaykh Hakim had taught concerning the year 1290. "But the spirit of Elijah must appear first, as the prophet Malachi spoke of at the end of his book. And I tell you that the spirit of Elijah has indeed appeared in ancient Elam—that is, the land of Daniel's vision. He has taken the title of 'the Gate.'

"You taught me about the Zohar and its prediction that the *gates of wisdom on high* would be opened after 1840. Now, the first of these Gates has been opened, and He taught that an even greater One would follow Him soon. So these Gates of wisdom on high are being opened."

After a long pause, Moshe said, "I shall have to think about this. I have always thought that Elijah must appear here in the Holy Land and would return to Mt. Carmel."

Zach inquired as to whether anything of significance had happened in Haifa and Akka during his absence.

"Not so much here, but did you hear what happened in Constantinople in March? A most wonderful thing! The British, incensed at the Muslim practice of killing former Muslims who had converted to Christianity, prevailed upon the Ottomans to issue an *edict of toleration*, forbidding the practice. Henceforth, in all the Ottoman realm, they must show tolerance."

Zach replied, "Yes, I heard someone discussing this when we passed through Damascus. However, I didn't think it significant. So what possible significance could it have to the Jewish community?"

"Well," resumed Moshe, "you may recall me saying that the current sultan, who came to power in 1839, started reforms during our Holy Year of 5600—reforms called the Tanzimat. These reforms increasingly recognize that all subjects are equal before the law, *regardless of their religion*. We were not sure at that time whether his generous proclamation was just talk or whether it would find continued support. This most recent edict seems to weigh in favor of continued support. It may seem a small thing to you, being from America, but I see this as an important part of the beginning of the promised return to the Holy Land."

"I'm not sure if I see its significance," said Zach skeptically.

"Its significance is this," replied Moshe. "There are small Jewish communities all over the world. Some get along without too much persecution, but many are persecuted or mistreated. They have borne this burden for ages, thinking that they had no other choice. *But now they have a choice!*

Although our conditions may be difficult here, the Jews around the world now have the choice of bearing their own hardships as strangers in a strange land or bearing them here, in the land where they historically belong—the land that once belonged to our ancestor, Israel, that is, Jacob. More importantly, they have the option of fulfilling the promise of the return to the Holy Land, spoken of by Moses and many of the prophets of old and anticipated for almost two millennia now.

"Indeed, it shall be exactly as Yeshayahu (Isaiah) had prophesied in the 11th chapter of his book:

> *And it shall come to pass in that day, that the Lord will set His hand again the second time to recover the remnant of His people, that shall remain from Assyria, and from Egypt, and from Pathros, and from Cush, and from Elam, and from Shinar, and from Hamath, and from the islands of the sea. And He will set up an ensign for the nations, and will assemble the dispersed of Israel, and gather together the scattered of Judah from the four corners of the earth.*

"Many of those who live in peaceful communities may remain abroad, but those who are persecuted will increasingly make the choice to return here. Idealism and the inspiration of God for some and the persecutions of the world for others—these will gradually bring them here. As long as the sultan upholds his Tanzimat principles, we will be able to buy land and start to farm it. We can lay the foundations for many Jewish communities in the Holy Land, which will, one day, again be called the land of Israel. Mark my words—the gate that has for ages been closed against the return of the Jews has now been unlocked. The hand of Providence has done this."

Zach thought for a moment about the compelling logic of Moshe's argument. Then he said wistfully, "When your people have returned to the Holy Land in such large numbers that it becomes their country, then surely the whole world will know that we are indeed living in the latter days. It was clearly foretold by Moses and the prophets several millennia ago."

They parted as friends, both sharing a sense that they stood at the edge of an age of vast changes, which was just now beginning.

163

# Chapter 12

# TOWARD ENGLAND
# AND AMERICA

ON BOARD THE SHIP at last, Zach sat on the deck and recalled the momentous events of the past year. For it had been only slightly more than a year since he and James had been on a similar ship, plying the same waters while approaching Akka when that Turkish waiter had inadvertently mentioned the Islamic year in which they lived, opening their eyes to the equivalence of the year 1844 in the West with the year 1260 in the East. How much he had learned since that first encounter! His mind had been stretched by new discoveries in ways he had never imagined possible. He mused on how this discovery had led to so many others and how many unexpected doors had opened while much of what he had expected was nowhere to be found.

Not only had their minds been opened to the truth of Muhammad and the Quran but also to a fuller understanding of the truths of the Zoroastrian religion—the religion that had brought the Magi to witness the birth of Jesus. And then to learn, totally unexpectedly, that Buddhism and Hinduism had their own prophecies of the coming of their Promised One as well! The journey had yielded a much richer harvest than he could have possibly imagined. Indeed, he understood now that all the Founders of the great prophetic religions were endowed with this gift of being able to foresee certain essential details of the distant future. Each had spoken of the coming of future Messengers. Most spoke of a particularly great time when two Messengers would appear in close succession. And now he knew for certain that the first of those two—the Bab—had appeared during this, the promised year.

He was saddened when thinking of the loss of dear James—how valuable and perfect a travel companion he had been! Nevertheless, as he thought of all the seemingly fortuitous turns of events and the dreams that had guided them whenever they were unsure, he felt certain that God had answered James' most ardent prayer—to find the Promised One, the date of whose appearance the angel Gabriel had foretold 23 centuries earlier in the vision given to Daniel.

But how to convey all of this to his countrymen, so wrapped in their sole focus on Jesus and who, like most of the Muslim world, were thinking only of a material fulfillment of their Holy Book's prophecies? How could he open their eyes to the much larger world without causing such upset that they would close their eyes yet more tightly or even arise against him? How could he demonstrate that the claims to exclusivity, found in many of the religious scriptures, were not references to a particular historical Messenger but rather to the one universal Messenger, whose spirit has existed "before Abraham was"—a Spirit that had taken on several human forms and had each time taught according to the needs of the age in which He appeared? This was a puzzle that Zach would contemplate during the many weeks of his voyage.

*    *    *

THE GRAY SKIES AND late November air of London seemed especially cold to Zach as he disembarked. He took a cab directly to Elijah Goodman's home but found it dark and empty, with the yard somewhat overgrown. Inquiring from the neighbors, he was saddened to hear that Elijah had passed away recently, but this was mitigated by the thought that both he and James must by now know much more about the coming of the Bab than he himself did. When Zach inquired about the date, they told him that Elijah had passed on the evening of October 9.

Zach's mind immediately flashed back to that date. It was the same day that James had contracted malaria. "When he seemed to be speaking to Elijah in the middle of that night, I thought he was delirious," Zach chided himself, "but now I see that Elijah Goodman's spirit was indeed there. Perhaps I was the crazy one." He resolved to pay better attention to the reports of a dying man should the opportunity ever arise again. And he thought again of how they were all together, united with family and friends who had passed on earlier, all now clearly aware of the great "good news" that was just beginning to dawn on a sleeping world.

The neighbors explained where to find the church that Elijah and James had attended. Zach felt that he should at least notify the pastor of James' passing.

When Zach introduced himself, the pastor said, "Oh yes, you're the young man who took James Lawrence on your journey to the Holy Land."

Zach took some time to explain all that had happened and how James had died in the Holy Land when their journey had nearly ended.

The pastor winced. "I'm very sorry to hear it. He certainly was a fine young man and a devoted member of the church. We will have to organize a memorial service for him."

Then he added, "Your tale is quite an amazing story, but I'm not sure if you will find anyone who will want to hear it, either here or in America, given what has happened in the past few months with your William Miller. I used to be a follower of Mr. Miller's teachings myself, as Elijah may have mentioned."

Zach didn't like the sound of that, as if the pastor was distancing himself from Mr. Miller and his teachings.

"I'm just today coming from the ship and haven't heard any news from America nor much news of Britain in a long time," Zach confessed.

"Oh yes, that's right," the pastor replied, "Well, it has been quite a tumultuous year, especially in America. Firstly, you may perchance have heard of that young fellow from New York State with the golden plates."

"Why yes, you mean Joseph Smith and his group of Latter-day Saints."

"Yes—he's the one. Well, he was imprisoned in Illinois near the end of June when a mob, angered by his heretical ideas, assembled together. They broke into the prison and killed him."

Zach gasped. He knew that Mr. Smith's teachings had created controversy, but he would not have guessed that it was enough that people might be ready to kill him. His country prided itself on its religious freedom, didn't it? Zach was stunned. He couldn't recall a single case of a person being killed for his religious beliefs since the founding of the American republic.

After taking a moment to recover, he asked, "And what of Mr. Miller?"

"Well, nothing so violent there, thank goodness, and yet perhaps a fate worse than death. You may recall that he felt certain that Christ would return in 1843 or 1844, but he was reluctant to pick a particular date within these years."

"Yes," noted Zach, "I recall him saying so."

"Well, apparently one of his followers came to the conclusion that the exact day could be accurately predicted and that it was the Jewish Day of Atonement, which was October 22-not too many weeks ago. Although Mr. Miller was reluctant at first, he eventually came to agree with this idea and announced it publicly. So it seemed like the whole world was watching with bated breath to see whether the preacher's predictions would come true on that night."

"Oh, no," thought Zach, as he closed his eyes, bracing for a shock.

"And, yes, as we can all plainly see, Christ did not return on that date nor on any date since. We've just recently received news articles from America about what they are calling *The Great Disappointment* and how many of the faithful have abandoned Mr. Miller. Some of them had not bothered to plant their crops due to their expectations that the world was about to end, and they are now facing the prospect of ruin and even starvation this winter. And most put the blame squarely on your William Miller and his 'prophetic' preaching."

Zach gasped again. He had not thought about the implications of how people might behave if they were truly convinced that the end of the physical world was imminent. He thought back to his conversation with Father Timothy while on the ship to Rome, who had described the plight of Joachim of Fiore—the monk who mistakenly predicted the return of Christ as 1260 AD.

"He must feel utterly crushed," replied Zach sadly.

"Oh, you can be sure of that. And I'm afraid your newspapers aren't treating him very kindly."

"I must get back to him as quickly as possible. I will let him know all that James and I have discovered and that he need not despair. For he was correct in his understanding of the time of the return, even if he misunderstood the manner," said Zach firmly.

The pastor looked at Zach quizzically, but Zach sensed that he wouldn't be interested in the details of his story now. The pastor seemed to be so perturbed with the troubles that the teachings of Mr. Miller had caused that he understandably wanted to steer clear of the whole subject.

So rather than trying to explain, Zach wanted to get down to the docks to find the next ship sailing for America as quickly as possible. He thanked the pastor for sharing the news and then excused himself to hurry down to the Jerusalem Coffee House in the Cornhill section of London, where news of the sailing dates of all ships was commonly available.

Upon arriving, he was chagrinned to hear that a ship to New York had left earlier in the day and the next was not due to leave for another week. Ships sailed less frequently in the winter weather.

He found one was leaving within two days for Boston first and then New York, but he figured that this indirect route would take longer. Then he remembered the train line from Boston to Albany, the end of which he had seen on his journey through Albany almost two years earlier. "That's it!" he said to himself. "I'll take the early ship to Boston and the train straight to Albany, and then I'll travel up to Mr. Miller's farm from there." Although he wanted to see his family too, he felt it was crucial for him to reach the preacher as quickly as possible.

On the morrow, he visited the house that James had owned and bequeathed to Zach. It was a modest house, not far from University College, where James had taught. Zach spoke with the neighbor, a Mr. Harold Matthews, whom James had asked to serve as a caretaker-landlord in his absence. Zach explained all that had happened and indicated that he might return there one day. He wrote up an agreement extending Harold's role as landlord, allowing him to use part of the proceeds for upkeep and for his labor, as James had done. Zach hoped that he might return to meet the Bab, and so he might return to England and use the house as a base for a return visit to Persia. He registered James' will with the authorities and became a signatory to James' accounts. He also visited the college's central office to explain what had happened.

\*　　\*　　\*

DECEMBER WAS NOT NORMALLY the best month to sail across the North Atlantic, and this December proved to be no exception. They had sailed southwest toward the Azores before setting a more westerly course toward Boston. It was not the shortest route, but it was better to minimize the impact of the storms and cold weather and the risk of encountering icebergs. The southern track westward followed the prevailing winds more precisely so that the longer route caused only a slight delay.

The cold winds and colder ocean spray encouraged everyone to stay below deck and mostly in their cabins during much of the crossing. The quiet time provided Zach with the opportunity to review and augment the notes from his diary, while mealtimes provided some opportunity to learn about developments that had occurred during his sojourn.

The captain shared some interesting news about developments in the realm of shipping. He spoke of the SS *Great Britain*—that huge new steamship with an iron hull and a submerged rear propeller instead of sails or paddlewheels. It was so large that it had encountered some difficulties in moving from the shipyard into the open sea, but now it was undergoing its final outfitting and would be ready to make its first Atlantic crossing within a few more months.

They spoke excitedly about what this might mean for the world of shipping, trying to imagine a world in which crossing the ocean might become routinely safe, with a fully predictable schedule. How long, they wondered, would it be before the marvelous wind-powered ships that they had known so well would become a thing of the past?

At dinner one evening, one of the passengers mentioned the development of the telegraph.

"What's a telegraph?" asked Zach.

Everyone else seemed to have heard of the marvelous new invention that enabled messages to be sent from Washington to Baltimore in the blink of an eye. Zach was fascinated to hear that the date of this invention was May 24—the day after the Bab had first disclosed His mission to His first disciple. He was even more fascinated to hear the message that the inventor had chosen to send, from Numbers 23:23: *"What hath God wrought!"*

170

"What indeed," Zach mused, thinking of the revolutions in thought that lay ahead. That evening, as he sat on the deck in the brisk air, he looked at the stars and pondered, "What is the future in a world where ships will move on a reliable course, at a known pace according to constant steam power, instead of being at the whims of the wind? And what kind of a world will be created when news is flashing from city to city in the blink of an eye? Surely it will be a world in which people are traveling more. People of many types will be ever more frequently in contact with each other. But how can such a world work when their old religious views are in such conflict? If we try to put this new wine of a modern world into the old skins of old religious concepts, they will simply burst. The old ways cannot handle the new world.

"Jesus must certainly have known that once we were advanced enough to carry His message to all nations, we would also be meeting the peoples from those nations. And this would mark the end of the old age, as He stated in Matthew 24:14. He must have realized that we would need to understand new, wider truths at this time—truths that would have been too difficult for His followers to bear 1,800 years ago. And thus He told us, in John 16:13, that the 'Spirit of truth' would come forth to guide us to all truth—the truth about the wider nature of mankind, the wider nature of God's revelations, and a more universal understanding of God Himself. Thus, the new inventions must go hand in hand with the new understanding of God's revelations to all humanity. The new age cannot develop properly without both."

Later, additional dinner conversations continued the theme of new ideas and the possible effects they might have on the future. One of the passengers mentioned hearing a lecture by a young man named *Charles Darwin*, who told of his studies of geology and species in the distant countries of South America and the islands of the Pacific over the past decade and his conclusions that the earth is far, far older than previously supposed and that its creatures have evolved gradually over long periods through natural selection, in a manner slower but similar to the artificial selection that farmers often practice to improve their animals and plants.

Another passenger commented on how he had heard a lecture at the University of Cambridge a few years earlier by a *Professor Charles Babbage*, who claimed to be building an "analytical engine" that could be programmed to do mathematical calculations. He was amazed to think that such a thing might even be possible, but, he said, "apparently it is."‡‡‡

England at this time was becoming more and more industrialized. With that industrialization came the problems of long hours, low pay, child labor, dangerous working conditions, incessant smoke in the cities' air, and extreme income inequality between the factory workers and the factories' owners. One passenger spoke of a writer who had earlier in the year published *Outline of a Critique of Political Economy* based on research he had done of the working conditions in the industrialized town of Manchester.

"It seems to prove that this industrialized capitalist system cannot continue forever," he said.

"I doubt that much will ever come of that idea," offered one of the others at the table with a chuckle. Several others agreed. "Who was the author anyway?"

"It was written by a German fellow named *Friedrich Engels* and published by his friend *Karl Marx*."

The passengers were interested in hearing Zach's tales too—especially the Englishmen, who tended to take an interest in everything between England and their foremost colony, India, including most of the Middle East. They seemed eager to learn of the many perspectives that Zach had found during his travels, but most scoffed at the idea that any of the Eastern religions could somehow be compared to Christianity, much less be seen as a part of a universal religion. Those few who seemed to be willing to consider the idea were not particularly religious themselves. And linking his newfound beliefs with talk of the fulfillment of the prophecies as William Miller had outlined brought scowls of disapproval and laughter at the dramatic failure of his October 22 prediction, which seemed to be fresh in everyone's minds.§§§

---

‡‡‡ Often regarded as the birth of the computer era.
§§§ Historical comment: It is not known when the first news of the Bab's mission reached England orally. The first known written publication reportedly occurred on Nov. 1, 1845, in the Times of London. It was reprinted in America a few months later—in New York and Philadelphia in January 1846 in the Eclectic Magazine of Foreign Literature, Science and Art.

\*     \*     \*

IT WAS MORNING ON January 1 when Cape Cod first came into view. "The promised year is over," Zach reflected, "and my father was right—Jesus has not descended from the sky." However, he realized that what he and James had discovered was something even bigger than what his father or anyone else had imagined prior to the event—the fulfillment of the prophecies not simply of one religion but of all of them! The very idea was too big for some to even imagine. True enough, the prophecies were often fulfilled in unexpected ways. And clearly, disappointment was in store for anyone who had been hoping to use the fulfillment of their own religion's prophecy as evidence that theirs was the *only* true revelation. But a corner had been turned, and a milestone had been reached. Jesus had said that if we sincerely seek, we will find. Zach had done that. And *exactly* 2,300 years after the start date of Daniel's prophecy, the fulfillment had come to pass during the promised year. The promised year in the Islamic world, 1260 AH, would end in another nine days.

*Now the tough part begins*, he thought. *Trying to convince my own countrymen to see this larger picture.* He resolved to present his news as best he could and to know that the response to this news was ultimately a matter between God and his listeners.

After off-loading his belongings, he picked up a ticket at the train station for the first train to Albany, leaving next morning, as well as some supplies at the nearby general store.

\*     \*     \*

ON HIS WAY TO boarding the train, Zach passed the steam engine, all hissing and snorting and belching thick black smoke as well as white steam clouds from various points in the complex machinery. He was reminded again as to why he preferred sailing. Once aboard and underway, he had to admit that the ride was much smoother than taking a carriage would have been and, of course, much faster. Still, he found the occasional lurching, the creaking of the cars, and the clacking of the wheels disquieting, and the smell of the smoke and ash was very unpleasant on those occasions when the movement of the wind and the train combined to push the plume toward his car.

"Become accustomed to it," suggested a woman slightly younger than he. She was sitting across the aisle and had noticed his apprehension. "I'm told it is the way of the future."

"What do you mean?"

"Surely," she replied calmly, "you've heard all the talk in these past couple of years about the plans for building more railroads. Why, half of the wealthy class seems to be afflicted with 'railway fever.' I expect that within a couple of decades, all of the cities in America will be connected and all with the amazing new telegraphic communication lines strung alongside them."

"Actually, I'm just returning from a long journey to the East. I've been away for the last two years, and apparently I've missed a lot of news," he confessed.

She introduced herself as *Margaret Fuller*, the literary critic for the *New York Tribune*. Having recently moved to New York City to take the position there, she was returning now after a Christmas visit to her family in Boston. She took some time to fill Zach in on several of the many things that had transpired in America while he had been traveling, including the recently announced success of James Polk in the presidential election. Zach found it interesting to be back in a part of the world where he could speak openly to a woman in a public place—someone whose face and hair were not covered by the veils and wraps that all of the women in the East wore whenever they were in the presence of a man who was not a member of their own immediate family.

"You seem to be quite well informed," he said.

"I read quite a bit," she replied. "One must do so when one is working as a literary critic. But then, I have also traveled."

"Where?"

"I spent the summer before last traveling around the entire Great Lakes region and meeting with many of the Indian tribes there. Last spring, I completed and published a book about it."

"Fascinating. What exactly did you find?"

"I found, among other things, that the so-called savages of our land are not so savage at all when treated with basic respect and dignity. The Indian has a belief in, and a reliance on, God, or the 'Great Spirit,' that pre-dates all Christian contact with him. He has a belief in a life beyond our present life and a sense of right and wrong, which my own countrymen sometimes seem to lack. He prays and fasts on certain occasions, not unlike our Christian brethren. So I have come to have considerable respect for those whose presence here pre-dates our own."[39]

"That's very interesting," Zach replied. "I should very much like to read your book."

Then, recalling his discussion with Hasan, he added, "It reminds me of a teaching that I learned from the Quran, which says, 'Unto every nation hath an Apostle been sent.'[40] I am certain that God has not forgotten any of the peoples of the world. They may not have had the means to record the exact details of their Messenger, but nevertheless, He has taught them. Virtue and bravery—indeed all of the good qualities—do not arise from people themselves but come from Messengers whom God has sent to all peoples."

"And what of your travels?" she asked. "The various countries in Europe perhaps?" It was not uncommon for well-established young men to make the "grand tour" of Europe in those days.

But she was both surprised and fascinated to hear of Zach's travels to places far beyond what she had imagined. He provided her with a synopsis of his journeys and his new broader understanding of the religions of the East.

She said, "You would do well to correspond with some friends of mine. They call themselves the *Transcendentalists* because their thinking transcends the normal limitations that most people tend to impose. It seeks the broadest possible outreach. You would, in particular, enjoy speaking with one by the name of *Henry David Thoreau*.

"He has shared with me some parts of a book he is writing based on his reflections while spending a week on the Concord and Merrimack Rivers a few years back. You would like his observations on the religions of mankind." She reached into one of the compartments of her rather large bag and soon pulled out a sheaf of papers she had been reviewing. She read aloud:

*It would be worthy of the age to print together the collected Scripture or Sacred Writing of the several nations, the Chinese, the Hindoos, the Persians, the Hebrews, and others, as the Scripture of mankind. The New Testament is still, perhaps, too much on the lips and in the hearts of men to be called a Scripture in this sense. Such a juxtaposition and comparison might help to liberalize the faith of men. This is a work which Time will surely edit, reserved to crown the labors of the printing-press. This would be the Bible, or Book of Books, which let the missionaries carry to the uttermost parts of the earth.*¶¶¶[41]

"Yes indeed!" replied Zach. "That is *exactly* what I'm talking about. It sounds as if Mr. Thoreau reads the scriptures of various faiths and hears just a single voice. I would only add that if he studied the *prophecies* of all of the religions, he would find a most remarkable coherence in them as well."

They continued sharing observations for the rest of the journey, reflecting on the new age that humankind seemed to be entering. She gave him a copy of *The Dial*, the publication of the Transcendentalists, of which she had been the editor, as well as the name of her book, *Summer on the Lakes, in 1843*. They reached Albany before long and exchanged addresses before parting.

---

¶¶¶ This suggestion would be taken up in earnest during the latter half of the 19th century by Max Muller with his 50-volume project entitled *Sacred Books of the East*.

# Chapter 13

## RETURN TO WILLIAM MILLER

ZACH WAS ABLE TO travel from Albany to Ft. Edward by boat, even during the below-freezing days of early January, since the river itself was not yet frozen over. However, the journey from Ft. Edward to Whitehall was necessarily by horse-drawn carriage over a rutted and frozen road since the surface of the slow-moving canal had frozen during the previous month. He remembered with fondness the warm spring day almost two years earlier when he had traveled the same route to visit William Miller for the first time. It seemed so long ago! "Perhaps it's because I've traveled so far and learned so much during these past two years," he thought. His perspective had been enlarged dramatically.

While traveling, Zach realized that in his haste to reach the Millers' residence, he had not sent a message ahead to advise him of his planned arrival. So he rested on Sunday in Whitehall and penned a note, asking the preacher whether he might come by to visit. He paid a young man to carry it as special delivery to Mr. Miller that afternoon. A note came back the following morning, warmly inviting him to proceed up to the Miller farm. As the sleigh carried him over the snow-packed trail, he recalled the date. Today was once again the 12th day of Christmas, January 6, celebrated in much of the Christian world as the Feast of the Epiphany. He thought back to his young nephew, Gabriel, who had posed those questions about the Magi to Josiah two years earlier. How much he had to share with Gabriel when he returned to Perth Amboy! He was looking forward to that greatly.

He also wondered whether this day might be an epiphany for Mr. Miller.

When Zach arrived, he was surprised to see that the preacher seemed to have aged considerably during the past two years. Not only was he visibly older but he seemed less energetic and had a melancholy air about him. It wasn't difficult for Zach to understand why.

After exchanging greetings, Mr. Miller asked whether Zach had heard what had happened with the Adventists during the previous few months.

Zach affirmed that he had heard of it and expressed his great sorrow at the recent turn of events. The preacher explained how many of his former friends and followers had cut all ties with him or even turned against him. Some had not planted their crops in the summer or ignored other essentials, because they were so certain that the world was going to end—all based on his teachings and the teachings of some of the other leaders of the movement. He had just recently received the news that he, his family, and his followers in the Baptist Church of Low Hampton would no longer be considered members. It had been almost three months since the Great Disappointment had occurred—unquestionably the worst three months of his life. He wondered if perhaps Prof. George Bush had been right after all.*

Eventually he turned to Zach and inquired about whether he had made the journey to the Holy Land as planned, whether he had contacted Mr. Goodman, and whether they had discovered anything.

Zach took a deep breath and began, "I found Mr. Goodman in London—a wonderful gentleman, a bit older than yourself, and now, alas,- deceased, as I discovered sadly upon my return to London. But when I first met him, he directed me to one Mr. James Lawrence, closer to my age and experienced in both the Arabic language and in living among the Arabs. James agreed to join me in traveling to the Holy Land and beyond, and we discovered far, far more than we had ever hoped."

The preacher raised an eyebrow and then inquired as to whether they had found any indication of the Christ whom Zach had imagined.

Zach sighed and said, "Yes indeed, but this is a thing far, *far* larger than

---

*Prof. Bush (Chapter 5, Vol. I) had, in fact, written to Mr. Miller in March 1844, acknowledging the legitimacy of Miller's time calculations but stating, "You have entirely mistaken the nature of the events which are to occur" in that year. See *The Advent Herald*, March 6 & 13, 1844, pgs 37-38 & 41-43 respectively for details.

you or I or anyone could have imagined. Indeed, I hope it is not larger than you *can* imagine."

Mr. Miller looked startled and then inquired as to how anything could be larger than the return of Jesus.

"Suppose..." Zach began slowly, "suppose it turned out to be the return of the Promised One of *all* religions?" The preacher looked on quizzically as Zach continued. "We know that Christ's return fulfills not only the prophecies of the New Testament but also many of the prophecies of the Old Testament. Thus, He is also the Messiah the Jews expect. Both religions have prophecies regarding what will occur in the latter days.

"But Christianity and Judaism are *not* the only religions with prophecies," Zach continued. "We know from the story of the Wise Men who found Jesus at His birth that the religion of the Magi, which was revealed by Zoroaster about a thousand years before our Lord was born, was also capable of accurately predicting the time and, to some degree, the place of the appearance of God's Messenger. It turns out that their prophecies also predict another Messenger who is to appear sometime within this century!

"But it does not end there. The Muslim world expects to see their own Promised One coming soon. And a large part of that world—the Shiites—understands prophecies in the Quran that indicate that He will return in the year 1260 of the *Muslim* calendar. Did you know that the year 1260 on their calendar is the same as the year 1844 on ours? That same 1260 that Daniel spoke of, and which appears repeatedly in the Revelation of St. John, also appears, by an entirely different calculation, in Muslim prophecies.

"And as it turns out, even the Hindus and the Buddhists have prophecies about the coming of their Promised One—and that the conditions are ripe for the fulfillment of their prophecies."

Mr. Miller was surprised at the scope of what this traveler had learned, but he was still inclined to regard anything outside of the Christian fold as pagan.

"I can see that this is going to take a lot of explanation," replied Zach.

So Zach began to recount the story, starting with his meeting with James Lawrence and how he had turned out to be the best possible traveling companion with his familiarity with life in the Middle East.

He described his conversations with the Catholic monk and learning of Joachim's misunderstanding of the meaning of the year 1260 AD. He explained their astonishing discovery of the fact that the year 1844 AD was the same as the year 1260 AH and how they discovered, incredibly, that much of the Muslim world was expecting the advent of their own Promised One in the very same year. He recounted their trip to the Cave of Elijah on Mt. Carmel and their discussion with Moshe, the Jewish believer there, and their trip to Mt. Tabor and the amazing dream that James had there. He told of their failure to find any indications of the appearance of the return of Christ in the Holy Land itself and the several indicators that guided them to look farther to the East. He described what they had learned from the followers of Siyyid Kazim and their subsequent journey to Baghdad. He explained what they had learned from Arjan Singh while on the Silk Road about the religions of Sikhism, Hinduism, and Buddhism and then all that they had learned about the Zoroastrian religion while in the native city of the Wise Men. He recounted his amazing dream while near the fire temple/ church/mosque of the Wise Men and how the scene on top of the castle in Khorramabad pointed them toward Shiraz.

And finally, Zach told him of James' dream after they had been visiting the tomb of Daniel and how it led them down the river to Mohammerah, where they learned that Mulla Ali had found the Promised One, the first of the two Messengers. They learned that the Bab, like Jesus and Muhammad, was known to be endowed with innate knowledge and that He fit, in every respect, the description that Siyyid Kazim had given his followers. He described their haste to return home with the great news, his profound sadness when James passed away while returning through the Holy Land, and how the news of the "Great Disappointment" of October 22 had reached him while in London, which motivated him to hurry back to Low Hampton even sooner.

"I know that my discoveries present a picture of the Return that is far different from what you have expected. Indeed, the results are far different from what either James or I expected. But let us think about it seriously: Should the truth be conditioned by our own expectations? If we close our eyes to all except for those things we expect to see, are we not in danger of missing many things? Might we not end up putting ourselves among those who are blind? If we tell God that we refuse to believe unless He acts according to *our own* expectations, are we not actually exalting ourselves above God? Surely a little humility before God—a frank acknowledgement of our own limitations—is a virtue, is it not?

"I have no doubt there are many who cherish the hope that God will fulfill the promises of their own holy scriptures, and *only* their own holy scriptures, and will thus vindicate their claim to be the *only* ones who are right, thereby proving everyone else to be wrong.

"But now, as a result of my travels, I have lived in the land of the Magi and have deepened my understanding of the truth of their religion, as supported by the Bible. Now I have learned extensively about the teachings of Muhammad and have come to understand many of the undeniable connections between His teachings and those of Jesus. Now I find it impossible to believe that the coming of the Promised One will be strictly according to the interpretation of one denomination or one religion and not any of the others. I now see that *all* of the prophecies can be fulfilled, and indeed they *are being fulfilled*—but only if we see them with spiritual eyes and hear them with spiritual ears, as Jesus asked us to do.

"For instance, we as Christians believe that our Savior will return from the sky. Much of the Muslim world believes that their Savior will arise up from the ground. How can both of these expectations be fulfilled? It happens only when we realize that the true intent of the prophecy was that He would return from an unseen place—a place that we cannot see with our physical eyes. That is to say, He will come from the spiritual realm, just as the spirit of Jesus came to us from the spiritual realm 18 centuries ago, even though His body was born of Mary, as the Bible describes.

"If, as Jesus says in John 10:16, there are other folds of His sheep that He will gather into one fold, then surely this tells us that His spirit has appeared before in other places to establish God's teachings and to provide guidance for these people of the other folds. And surely it implies that each of the folds must now move a little—that is, they must each change a little—in order to come together as a single fold.

"Moreover, if God has promulgated all of the religions that expect the coming of a Promised One, and if each of these diverse religions insists that the Promised One should appear only according to their own expectations, then all will be disappointed. All will need to look again at their prophecies to understand them with open spiritual eyes. Is this not exactly what Jesus asked us to do—to stay spiritually awake?

"And although He comes to fulfill the promises of all religions, He must necessarily arise from a location where one of the religions is dominant and from a family that follows one of the religions. This may disappoint the followers of the other religions, but it is wise to note that He comes from the ancient land of Elam, the same land where Daniel's vision of the 2,300 days originally occurred."

Mr. Miller had been listening intently. Yet, clearly, there was so much here that was new, and it was difficult to take all of it in at once.

There was a long moment of silence before he finally inquired as to whether Zach had abandoned his belief in Jesus in order to believe in Muhammad and this "Bab" from Persia.

Zach paused for a moment then said slowly and earnestly, "I have not abandoned anything. I am a follower of Abraham, who taught the oneness of God though it caused Him perpetual banishment.

"I am a follower of Moses, who spoke of how His people would be scattered to all nations and how, in the latter days, they would be gathered back together once again in the Holy Land.

"I am a follower of Jesus, who affirmed Daniel's prophecy, who described the spiritual conditions of the time of His return, and who linked it to the time that we could reach all nations with His message, which we have now accomplished with the development of our sailing ships and the missionaries who have used them, bringing this prophecy to fulfillment.

"I am a follower of Zoroaster, who accurately prophesied of the time and place of Jesus' birth, enabling some of His followers to find the infant Jesus—a thousand years later and at least a thousand miles away.

"I am a follower of Krishna, who described so clearly how, in each age, whenever goodness grows weak and evil increases, His spirit makes a new body, and thus He steps forth into our world to destroy the sin of the sinner and to establish righteousness.

"I am a follower of the Buddha, who, some 24 centuries ago, foretold of a future Buddha of Boundless Glory and who told His followers that He would appear sometime during this current century as the moral conditions of mankind declined.

"I am a follower of Muhammad, who was the last of the Prophets to foretell of the coming of this mighty Day, the Day of the ingathering of all mankind—an ingathering that is even now starting as travel between countries becomes ever easier and the intermixing of people and their religions becomes ever more common.

"And finally, I am a follower of the Bab, who teaches that all of God's Messengers are a single Holy Spirit, which has appeared in many bodies and has always revealed God's Word according to the needs and capacities of the people of that age.

"There is no point in trying to distinguish one Messenger from the other, for in the voice of each of Them, I hear the voice of God calling us. Since it is *one same Voice*, I find it impossible now to accept just one expression of it while excluding the others. My only choice now is whether to believe in *all* of Them or *none*. And thus, in order to continue to believe in Jesus, I now find that I must also believe in Muhammad and in the Bab, and, indeed, in all of God's Messengers.

"And so I bring to you today this new Evangel, the new Gospel—*this great good news that God's promises were not in vain!* Nay, rather He has begun to fulfill them exactly in the year foretold by Daniel, by Jesus, and by all of His Prophets so many centuries ago. If it is not in the manner we expected, then perhaps it is time for us to reexamine our expectations and to humbly consider that perhaps our own pride or hubris has kept us from looking toward other possible explanations."

There was another long pause as Mr. Miller considered all of these thoughts. He and Zach looked very intently at each other.

Finally he said, "You ask a lot of me." He paused, and then he reminded Zach of how badly he had been disparaged since that day of the Great

Disappointment on October 22. His name, he noted, had been maligned and drawn through the mud publicly; many had fallen into disbelief and cursed him privately and some even publicly.

He was now pacing the floor. He asked Zach what people would think of him if he now started teaching that Christ had returned but that He was from a Muslim land and that Muhammad himself was a true prophet. He felt certain that people would say he had gone from being absolutely wrong to being utterly mad. How, he asked, could he explain such a thing to a world that already held him in such contempt?

The preacher said that he would much rather admit that his calculations might have been slightly in error, and it was true that some others had already suggested that the correct date should be 1847 or 1848, or another time in the near future, by slightly different calculations. He further explained that he had decided to refrain from advocating any specific date. He would instead simply wait patiently.

He also indicated that even if he were to accept Zach's fantastic idea that Christ might return first as a child, in a manner similar to the way He appeared 18 centuries earlier, He might appear anywhere. How could he be certain that other travelers with similarly fantastic stories might not appear from various places around the world and report their claims about other events that happened during the past year? Or perhaps that He was indeed born in 1844 but He would not be grown and ready to start His teaching work for another thirty years. Such were the concerns that the preacher expressed.

A voice in Zach's head was screaming, *Don't say "Let us wait"! That's what the Jewish leaders said when Christ came to them! That's what the Zoroastrian leaders said when the Wise Men returned with the news of Jesus' birth! That is what many of the Christians and the Jews said when Muhammad appeared! "We don't like what God may have sent—so let us wait and see if He will send someone more to our liking!" And who are you to judge —you who would not so much as open the new Book to read with an unbiased mind?*

But then another voice—the voice of his dear friend Youssef, who had guided them through much of the Holy Land—arose in his mind, saying, *Patience. There is no compulsion in religion.*

Zach was tempted to answer by repeating what he had already said concerning the various prophecies that had guided him and James to look further east than the Holy Land and, ultimately, to Persia and why they felt that the *revelation* of the new Messenger should have begun in 1844 rather than His *birth*. But then he sensed that some quiet time was needed now rather than argument—time to allow these ideas that were so wildly different from previous expectations to sink in. And in any case, time would tell. So he simply said, with some reluctance in his voice, "How long will you wait before you are willing to reconsider?"

Mr. Miller sighed, and then, with a slight smile, he suggested that he wanted to wait "a week."

Zach smiled back and said, "I would be happy to remain here with you for the next seven days, but I take your meaning to be "a week" in prophetic biblical terms, which is to say seven years."

Mr. Miller nodded and noted that the prophecy from Daniel 9 described the time of Jesus' crucifixion in terms of weeks. He suggested that perhaps he had misunderstood this by one week.

He also noted that he had heard of various swamis and gurus from the East who had made claims, gathered a following briefly, and then disappeared. He wanted to know what would happen to Zach's "promised one" and his followers after a few years.

"You are perhaps confusing Persia with India," Zach replied. "I, too, have heard of several such people from India. In that land, making a new claim and starting a new group is generally tolerated or even respected. But in the Islamic world, you will find no such tolerance. Indeed, many of the people I met during the course of our travels there spoke of persecution, imprisonment, and death as the near certain response in store for anyone proclaiming a new revelation from God. Even advancing the idea that the fulfillment would occur in an unexpected manner could be cause for severe persecution. Mulla Ali was beaten nearly to death just for answering a few questions about it after leaving Shiraz. James and I were imprisoned for three weeks simply for asking about it. No one in Persia who has any concern for his own life would ever advance such a claim," Zach insisted.

"And yet," he continued, "I don't expect this to go away easily. There are so many people in that land who are expecting His appearance. And from what I saw and heard while we were there, the Bab is certainly capable of fulfilling those expectations. Even more than here in America, the entire country of Persia is a tinderbox of millennial anticipation. And now," Zach concluded ominously, "the flame has been lit."

Zach was disappointed but, in the end, not surprised that Mr. Miller was not able to immediately accept the great news he had brought. He had known that it would not be easy, especially for someone who had not traveled to the East and experienced all that Zach and James had experienced. He thought of the words of his father from his dream in Saveh about the importance of the journey, not just the destination. Perhaps it was too much for any person to take in all at once. He and James had learned so much over the course of the past year and a half. How could he expect the preacher to understand it all in just a few hours? Perhaps it needed to be contemplated for a few years. And in any case, something amazing *had* happened during the expected year, 1844. Although it had not happened in the manner that the Christian world expected nor in the manner that most of the Muslim world had expected, nevertheless, something amazing had happened. Zach knew that the news would eventually spread. Time, he felt, was on his side.

Still, there was one thing that bothered him. His mind jumped back to James' discussion with Ardeshir, the Zoroastrian and his description of how the rest of the magi in Persia failed to accept the news of the appearance of Jesus as the fulfillment of Zoroaster's promise, how it probably began with a decision to "wait and see" and how such decisions to wait had led both the Zoroastrians and the Jews into a period of interminable waiting, which had continued now for almost two millennia.

But Zach also considered how seven years would provide him with an opportunity to return to Persia to meet the Bab at last and to ask Him questions and thus be able to provide a full explanation of the teachings of the new faith.

"So shall we set a date?" he proposed. "Seven years from now will be January 1852. You shall wait here in America to see if Christ returns in the manner you expect. Meanwhile, I shall return first to England, where

I shall study all I can find about the Persian language and their customs for a couple of years in order that I may become so proficient that I can move easily amongst the people of that land. From thence, I shall return to Persia, to Shiraz, to meet with the Bab Himself. I will send reports back to you on all that has happened and all that is happening while I am there. I will endeavor to obtain answers to all of your questions. And in the autumn of 1851, I shall commence my return trip to meet you here once again, on the Feast of the Epiphany in 1852, to review all that I have discovered."

Mr. Miller agreed to this meeting if, and only if, Christ had not returned from the sky by that time, as the preacher expected.

"If He returns from the sky," Zach replied calmly, "then I shall meet you there, for I assure you, I am still a believer." Then he added, "Before I leave, I would like you to write down the questions you would like me to ask when I reach the Bab. Are there any particular aspects of the prophecies and their fulfillment that you would want Him to explain?"

Mr. Miller said that he would spend the rest of the evening preparing a list.

And so Zach retired, contemplating plans for his next trip to the East. In the morning, the preacher provided Zach with the list as Zach was preparing to leave.

"Very well then," said Zach. "I am now ready to depart on my second journey of discovery and shall look forward to meeting you here again after seven years." He paused and then added, "As you know from the sad experience of James' death, there is always the possibility that I might not be able to return. While I was traveling over these past several months, my main hope has been to be able to complete my journey and to safely bring the news here to you in America. Now at least I can say that I have achieved this goal. But if it should happen that on this second trip I am unable to return, and if Christ does not return in the manner that you expect, please keep your eyes and ears open for news from Persia as I have described. If I do not return here, be sure to write to your followers in London and ask them to inquire from their Foreign Office concerning the status of the teachings of the Bab in Persia."

Mr. Miller assured Zach that should Zach fail to return by the spring of 1852, he would surely make the inquiry. And with that, Zach hoisted his sack onto his shoulder and bade Mr. Miller a heartfelt farewell once again.

\*  \*  \*

ALAS, THE HOPED-FOR RENDEZVOUS would not come to pass. William Miller would not survive to reach the planned meeting date. But that is not all. A few months after Mr. Miller's passing, the Bab Himself, after several years of teaching, persecution, and imprisonment, would be executed in July 1850 for claiming to be the Promised One. By late 1852, most of the 18 Letters of the Living, including Qurratu'l-Ayn, along with almost all of the other leading exponents of the Bab's faith and tens of thousands of followers, would be martyred as the existing religious authorities of Persia, fearful of losing their positions of power, combined their forces with those of the government in a ruthless effort to completely extirpate the new faith.

Among the leaders of the Bab's religion, there was just one who remained alive. He was a Persian nobleman, a descendant of the Sasanian kings of Persia as well as a descendant of the Jewish King David, the son of Jesse. He was arrested during the latter months of 1852 and languished in the Shah's subterranean dungeon known as the "Black Pit" in Teheran, bound in mighty chains. His fellow prisoners, who were also followers of the Bab, succumbed one by one to the horrific conditions of their captivity or to execution at the hands of the Shah's guards. But it was there, in the midst of that dark and vermin-infested dungeon, that the dazzling light of a new revelation, heralded by the Bab and promised in the scriptures of all religions, burst forth once again.

This time, the authorities decided not to make Him a martyr to avoid fanning the flames of a new faith, as had happened with the Bab. They decided instead that He should be banished to Baghdad. From there, the Ottoman sultan would later summon Him to his capital in Constantinople and then banish Him to Adrianople and ultimately to a remote walled city, plagued with putrid air and disease, in a far corner of the Ottoman Empire. They hoped He would either die there of its diseases or simply be forgotten due to its distance from Persia. And so He was exiled to that far-off prison city in the Holy Land—the city of Akka.

But *that* is another story.

# Chapter 14

## FAREWELLS

THE DAY WAS CRISP and clear, and Zach soon found a sleigh heading to Whitehall, which carried him swiftly over the brilliant snow-blanketed landscape. He was preoccupied, however, with making plans in his mind for his next journey to the East. He figured he could live in the house he had inherited from James and perhaps study Persian at University College there. Perhaps a professor could introduce him to some of the Persian residents in the area. Perhaps he might find work eventually at the Persian diplomatic mission in London.

After a bumpy carriage ride heading down to Ft. Edward, he was pleased to be once again in the peaceful cabin of a schooner, with time to review the questions that Mr. Miller would have wanted to pose to the Bab and to think of his own questions. Combining both in his mind, he drafted the following list of twelve questions:

1. What exactly is meant by the statement in Matt. 24:29, "Immediately after the tribulation of those days shall the sun be darkened, and the moon shall not give her light, and the stars shall fall from heaven, and the powers of the heavens shall be shaken"? Similar references were made by several of the Old Testament prophets, yet Peter said at the Pentecost in the second chapter of Acts that this was fulfilled even in Jesus' time. How shall the powers of the heavens be shaken?

2. What is "the sign of the Son of man" that is to appear in the heavens? (Matt. 24:30)

3. What exactly is intended by the statement in Matt. 24:30 that the Christ will be seen "coming in the clouds of heaven with power and great glory"? Is this to be understood physically or metaphorically?

4. What is meant by the sending forth of angels "with a great sound of a trumpet" and the gathering of the "elect from the four winds"? (Matt. 24:31)

5. And what is meant by "Heaven and earth shall pass away, but My words shall not pass away" (Matt. 24:35). In what sense will there be a "new heaven and a new earth" (Rev. 21:1)?

6. What of the dead arising from their graves or the "day of resurrection"? (or "resurrection of the dead"?) (Matt. 22:23–31) Or the resurrection at the last day? (John 11:24) Is it only in the spiritual world, as I saw in my dream?

7. Will He come as a king ruling over a material kingdom? (Rev. 17:14 and 19:16 and I Timothy 6:15)

8. What is the full meaning of "the return"? (whether it be of Elijah or of Jesus or both)

9. What exactly did Jesus mean when He said He was "the beginning and the end, the first and the last?" (Rev. 22:13)

10. Who exactly was intended by the term "I" when Jesus said, "Before Abraham was, I am"? (John 8:58). And who exactly was intended by the term "me" when He said, "no man cometh unto the Father, but by me"? (John 14:6)

11. What exactly is meant by the "bread from heaven"? (John 6:51)

12. What is the meaning of the "New Jerusalem" or the "city of my God" that comes down from heaven? (Rev. 3:12 and 21:2)

He felt certain that an accurate understanding on these points would open the hearts of many to the realizations that he had gained through his travels.

\*      \*      \*

As Zach reached Perth Amboy, his family members were amazed to find him disembarking from a riverboat rather that arriving directly from London on one of their packet ships.

"We have been anxiously awaiting your return," said Daniel, "checking each ship coming from London. We never expected you to return on a riverboat!"

"Sometimes a return can occur in unexpected ways," Zach replied with a knowing smile. "But come.... We have much to discuss."

The family joyfully welcomed him and urged him to tell the whole story of his travels and discoveries. Daniel and Clara invited Sarah and Isaiah and their children (who now included the nearly eighteen-month-old Matthew, born shortly after Zach's departure) to hear the entire tale. Zach also requested that his earlier traveling companion, Jeremy, should join them. During the course of several dinners and evenings in the parlor by the warmth of the fireplace, Zach explained the many episodes of his grand adventure and his growing awareness of the underlying commonalities behind the different religions as well as the linkages between their prophecies in spite of their surficial differences.

At the end, Zach explained how Mr. Miller seemed skeptical and wanted to wait to see what would transpire over the course of the next seven years. He also explained his plan to return first to England to study and then to go onward to Persia again. He noted how James Lawrence had willed his home and all that he owned to Zach, and thus he felt that he would likely need little additional financial support from the family's shipping business.

Neither Daniel nor Sarah were very pleased to hear this part of his news. Daniel had been looking forward to Zach's return and his assistance with the shipping business. Sarah had been hoping that Zach would be available to help occasionally with Gabriel and Timothy since she was busy now with little Matthew and was also expecting their fourth child.

But Zach explained, "I would love to stay here and help with the business and the family, But this thing that I've found is far too big to ignore. If God has sent us the Promised One, exactly as foretold, we cannot simply ignore it. We must get this news out! This is exactly what our father had hoped to see!"

Daniel shot a glance at Sarah, which Zach noticed. "Well, okay," he admitted, "maybe it is a little different from what Father and I had expected. But it is essentially the same, as he made clear when I saw him in my dream."

"And besides," continued Zach, reflecting on one of the meditations he had had on his return trip from London, "we must courageously look to the future."

"What do you mean by that?" inquired Daniel.

"Daniel, let us look carefully at the future. What do you see?"

"I don't know. Probably more shipping, more work, and more money, if all goes well. What do you see?"

"Yes, I see more shipping but not just more business. Plans are well underway in England, and even here, to build steamships with metal hulls and submerged rear propellers instead of paddle wheels. This will enable them to cross the oceans on predictable schedules, independent of the weather. Ships of larger size, faster than our fastest clippers, will soon be built. This is unavoidable since shippers like us will always be willing to pay for faster, larger, and more reliable ships."

"That sounds good to me. We are in the right business!"

"Yes, Dan, but the goods that the ships move are just a small part of the story. They also move people. Trade causes people to move. And political, religious, and economic upheavals also cause people to move and to resettle in distant lands. And as it becomes easier to move, more and more people will decide to do so. Moving will become the commonplace solution to all of these problems.****

"Indeed, in the last chapter of the Book of Daniel, we find him identifying the 'time of the end' as a time in which 'many shall run to and fro, and knowledge shall be increased.' Is that not exactly the time we are moving into right now?

"I see a future in which there will be great intermixing of peoples. But people always bring their ideas, their customs, and their religious teachings with them. And *not a single one of the religions today is prepared for this kind*

---

**** Historical note: As an example, the Irish potato blight was already gathering momentum at this point and would burst into full famine later that same year, leading to approximately one million deaths, with at least another million emigrating, mostly to the United States--the first wave of many modern mass migrations.

*of intermixing.* As long as they insist that they alone are right, there will be an endless amount of conflict arising from such mixing. Mark my words! An age of intermixing of ideas, with all the conflict it creates, is the future toward which we are inexorably heading.

"And how will we find a way out of this mess? No religious leader has the ability or the authority to convince or compel other religious leaders to accept his views. The only way out of these unavoidable conflicts is for God to send again the Christ-spirit—that Holy One who can receive the Word of God for our age and convey it to us in spite of the resistance such a new message has always engendered. He is the One who is willing to sacrifice Himself, if necessary, that the new Word of God might live among us. And I believe that this same Spirit has now arrived, at the promised time foretold by Jesus. He is now starting to promulgate the new Word of God—that New Jerusalem that is even now descending from above and which the world will desperately need soon enough. If we do not respond, terrible clashes will arise between contending peoples of the world, leading to greater suffering than the world has ever known.

"I believe this is why Jesus said that the end of the age would come when His message had reached all nations. No doubt He knew that the very same capability that allows us to reach all nations—our ocean-spanning ships—is the thing that will cause the intermixing of peoples and ideas and necessitate a new, much larger understanding of God's purpose for mankind and the development of a new world. Isn't this exactly what He meant when He said that He would return to gather the many folds of His sheep into one fold?"

Then, turning particularly toward Sarah and Isaiah, he said, "Perhaps not your children but your grandchildren, and certainly your grandchildren's grandchildren, will witness these horrific conflicts unless the new Word of God can start to spread out and to transform the hearts of people today."

They all sat in silence for a moment, contemplating the picture of the future that Zach had foreseen.

Eventually Daniel stood up and said, "Well, that future may come, but we all have more pressing problems of the present to deal with, don't we?" The conversation drifted off into the details of what they saw as the needs of the coming year. Although most of the members of his family did not explicitly agree with Zach's views, they seemed at least a bit more supportive after this.

*       *       *

SOMETIME AFTER THIS DINNER discussion, as Zach was sitting in the parlor, Gabriel and Jeremy, who had been listening intently to the discussions, came into the room to ask more about Zach's adventures. Gabriel had a faraway look in his eye, as if imagining every detail of what Zach had been describing. When Zach mentioned again his plans for returning, Gabriel stood up and said boldly, "I want to go with you!"

Gabriel was still a young lad, not quite 11 years old now. Zach smiled, knowing that he was far too young to be brought along on such a journey. "Not this time," answered Zach, "but I will be back after seven years. By that time you'll be almost 18. So when I start my third journey, you'll be a fine age for starting your sailing career with me!"

The offer of this promise seemed to dissolve any disappointment in being too young to sail immediately. Gabriel stood up tall and said, "It's a deal! I won't forget—I promise!" and he thrust out his hand to seal the deal with a handshake.

"Now, you remember," cautioned Zach with a wagging forefinger, "you must tend to your studies while I'm gone, *and* you must practice obedience to your parents. All good sailors know how to obey orders!" Gabriel promised that he would, and he skipped out of the room with glee. Zach asked Jeremy to keep an eye on him while he was away and to take him on occasional river trips as he got older.

Jeremy assured Zach that he would help in any way he could. Then he added, "I, for one, want to compliment you on achieving your goal. Not only have you traveled to the Holy Land but also all the way to the land of Daniel and the land of the Wise Men of the East. I have no doubt that in the future, they will refer to you and Mr. Lawrence as the 'Wise Men of the West.'"

Zach chuckled at the notion. "Well, maybe so, but it was only by God's grace, and with the aid of my father and Mr. Miller, that we were able to reach our goal."

*       *       *

THE FOLLOWING EVENING, AS Zach was contemplating the details of his next journey, the remembrance of James made him contemplate the possibility that he himself might not be able to return. This led him to think of how disappointed Gabriel would be, not only for the loss of his uncle but also for the loss of the chance to join him in his travels. With this in mind, he decided to write a letter to the future 18-year-old Gabriel. On the outside, he wrote in large letters: *To Gabriel: Not to be opened until your 18th birthday.* And below that, he added: OBEDIENCE! The following day, while visiting Sarah and Isaiah's house, he managed to slip quietly into the boy's room and tucked the letter into the back, bottommost part of one of the drawers that held some seldom used blankets, knowing that it would probably never be seen until such time as they emptied out the drawers to move the furniture—probably several years from now anyway. Zach had every intention of retrieving the letter himself upon his return, before Gabriel's 18th birthday. But he wanted to leave it there as a precaution against the chance that he might not return.

Although Zach was eager to sail soon, he was also cognizant of the difficulties of sailing in mid-winter in the North Atlantic. Unlike his previous journey, he was not under an immediate deadline this time. He thought of publishing the news of his discoveries. He felt he could use a part of his time in England to draft a manuscript. *Surely once it is published, I shall find several people who are open-minded enough to consider adopting the new discoveries,* he thought to himself. He wrote to Margaret Fuller to suggest this idea, and she wrote back encouraging him to pursue it.

He also spent some time preparing a copy of his diary so that he might carry one for reference and yet leave one safely behind in the event he might lose the one he carried, whether by thievery or some other unfortunate accident. He had recorded a lot during the previous two years, and the process of copying was slow, taking several weeks. He also removed the question mark from its title and, with some satisfaction, inscribed an additional word so that it now read:

*The Wise Men of the West—A ^Successful^ Search for the Promised One in the Latter Days.*

195

He placed it in a leather pouch, which he had sewn tightly closed as a protection, and placed this on a plank between the rafters in a back corner of the attic to ensure it would remain undisturbed until he returned.

By March 12, Zach's preparations were complete, and so he boarded the *Lucy*—one of the Thompson's line of packet ships—headed for London. It was loaded mostly with wheat for sale in London and had few passengers. The captain said there would be many Irishmen in the steerage section on the return trip; the potato blight in Ireland was already making life there untenable for many.

As the ship set out into Raritan Bay, Zach gazed back at the town of Perth Amboy and thought about how much he had changed as a result of his travels. Perth Amboy was home, and yet somehow, he no longer felt fully at home there. The world, in his mind, was so much more real to him now, and he had to live in that larger reality. The perspectives of his family and friends seemed too provincial, too limited, to fit comfortably with this larger one. He had grown so much as a result of his travels and had learned so much from all the people he had met along the way. Thus he knew that his life could never quite return to the life of a shipping manager in the little town of Perth Amboy.

*    *    *

THEY HAD BEEN SAILING eastward for almost three weeks, with cloudy skies during the past several days. Zach wondered whether they might be getting near the Irish coast. He knew that it was hard to tell exactly where they were since the winds and the current varied and accurate navigation depended on the captain's ability to take readings on the locations of the stars and the time of the setting of the sun. Lately, overcast skies had made such readings impossible.

As he slept that evening, he had a most profound dream.

He dreamed that he was walking on a path, heading toward the top of a very large hill—the tallest in all the region. Surrounding the hilltop were four massive walls, each with three arched gates. At the top of the hill, rising above the walls and occupying the area within, was the most beautiful garden he had ever seen—lush trees of many types and brilliant flowers of all varieties blooming in great abundance. A fragrant breeze was wafting from this city-garden. Coming out of it and splashing through a fountain on each wall were four streams—one leading to the east, one to the west, one to the north, and one to the south. The streams seemed to vibrate with life-giving powers to irrigate the dry and distant plains. The morning sun shone brightly, while the sky was a clear and radiant blue and the air cool and invigorating.

Guardians at the Gate of Paradise

Zach was carrying four bundles—one pair of which was connected by a strap slung over his right shoulder while the other pair was similarly connected and slung over his left shoulder.

197

As he approached on the path leading to one of the gates, he noticed that the entrance was guarded by two flaming swords, which seemed to be twisting and turning, blocking the way to the city gate and the garden within. Immediately, Zach thought of how very much like the Garden of Eden this was—a paradise that was nearly impossible for man to reenter. Yet he greatly longed to enter the Garden.

As he approached, he thought about his four bundles and how difficult it would be to pass by the flaming swords with these bundles. One of the bundles seemed to contain all the things he owned. The second bundle consisted of all the expectations that his family members, friends, and neighbors had for him. (Although it might seem odd to think that these expectations could weigh him down just as much as the material things he owned, in the dream world, this was perfectly clear to him.) The third bundle consisted of his pride in his accomplishments and what he had achieved in the eyes of men. The fourth and final bundle contained all of the teachings of religion that he had heard since his childhood—all of the interpretations, explanations, sermons, and opinions about what was found in the Bible. In some respects, this seemed like the biggest burden of all.

Slowing down a bit as he continued to climb the path toward the entrance, he wondered if the flaming swords would allow him to pass. He gingerly approached them, but as he got within a few feet, in the twinkling of an eye, one sword spun with its tip toward him, passing immediately in front of the right side of his chest and upward, slicing through the strap over his right shoulder. Before he knew it, the tip of the other sword had slipped behind his back, between his left shoulder blade and the strap on that shoulder, and moving swiftly upward, it severed that strap as well. All four bundles fell to the ground and started to roll down the hill, away from the entrance to the great garden-city.

His first impulse was to run after them in the hope of recovering them, but he paused for a moment and thought to himself, *Shall I try to keep these things, or shall I choose to enter into the Garden of Paradise?* Fortunately for Zach, the decision was not too difficult to make. In pursuing his search, he had given up most of the things he owned, except the few things he needed on his journey. He had already turned away from his larger family—his brother and sister and their families. He did not have a wife or children to care for. He had also turned away from the opinions of friends and acquaintances, many of whom thought he had lost his mind in deciding to journey to the Holy Land in the beginning and who now considered him even worse for wanting to return there again. As to his accomplishments, he was not sure that they amounted to anything so far in his life, and he was never inclined to be prideful. And in his exploration of the truths that he found in his travels, he had given up many of the interpretations of religious teachings he had learned from childhood and had come to accept the truths he found common to all of the religions.

So he simply stood in place, watching the bundles roll farther into the distance and toward the edge of a steep ravine, from the bottom of which he knew they would be washed away in the next rain. As he turned around to look toward the entrance to the city-garden again, he was surprised to see that the flaming swords had stopped twisting. They seemed to be standing at attention, as guards might stand in the presence of an officer of high rank, and a voice was now emanating in deep tones from them, saying, *"Your study of prophecy hath carried you far. Yet it is not enough to enter this most sanctified City."* Then they tipped slowly downward, as if bowing to each other and blocking the way. They continued, *"We are Detachment and Humility—the guardians and protectors of the entrance to Paradise. None may enter the City of God, save those who possess us."* And then, to Zach's great relief, they swung open like a gate, both now pointing toward the city's entrance. Zach stepped forward carefully between them. As he passed, he noticed that the word "Detachment" was emblazoned on the blade of one of the swords, while on the other, the word "Humility" was engraved.

As he approached the spectacular, jewel-studded entrance to the glorious city, he now understood the meaning of the flaming sword from the Garden of Eden story in a new way. It was never intended to indicate that we could not return to Paradise. Rather, it was intended to show that the path leading to Paradise required detachment and humility: detachment from material things; detachment from the opinions of friends, neighbors, and family; detachment from the often errant interpretations of men concerning the teachings of God; and a humility that comes from recognizing that the new Messiah brings teachings from a realm far, far beyond our ability to imagine—teachings that may well be somewhat different from whatever we might have imagined they would be or should be.

Jesus' disciples had this kind of detachment and humility, as did Muhammad's early disciples, and, indeed, the early followers of each of the Messengers. It had enabled them to enter the Paradise of the presence of the Anointed One for their age. These qualities were almost always lacking among the existing religious leaders when He appeared, and thus they were barred from His presence, as surely as if flaming swords were blocking their way. These leaders, when separated from their bundles, would surely have chased them as they rolled down the hill. In doing so, they would have turned their backs on the gateway to Paradise.

As Zach passed through the gate, stepped into the Garden, and looked about, he realized that this Paradise was also, in many ways, the same as the "holy city" that St. John had described in the last two chapters of his Book of Revelation. Here, indeed, was the "city of God"—the New Jerusalem, as radiant as a bride. From the high point at its center, a large fountain poured forth the most pure water, welling up from an unseen source. It fed all of the beautiful and fragrant plants of this garden as it moved outward to form the four streams leading out in all four directions. He remembered his discussion with James and Musa concerning the four rivers described in the second chapter of Genesis that flowed forth from the Garden of Eden. He recalled a portion of the psalm of David, which read, "There is a river, the streams of which make glad the city of God, the holy place of the tabernacles of the most High. God is in the midst of her." He remembered also Muhammad's words from the Quran frequently mentioning the rivers flowing in the Garden of Paradise.[42]

Here, he understood clearly that this river was the flow of God's Word, sent forth to teach mankind. It was the spiritual wisdom that is as essential to our spiritual life as surely as physical water is to our physical life. His explorations of the religions of mankind had shown him how the teachings of all religions had welled up from a single, invisible Divine Source. They had spread outward from that Source to provide spiritual life to the various peoples of the world. He knew that in places beyond the Garden, these peoples had, often with the best intentions, benefited from these pure waters but had also added their own colorings and impurities to it, making it look different downstream, in the different lands through which it flowed. He knew that further downstream near the coasts, where most people lived—and where the water was least pure—each of the different groups argued, saying that their water was different and somehow better than the water of the other streams.

But back here, at the Source, *it was all one*, and it was all perfectly pure.

Drawing close to one of the streams, he saw how, on each side, was planted the Tree of Life, exactly as St. John had seen. The roots of these trees went down to draw their water from the River of Life. As St. John had noted, those who had followed the commandments of God were now able to eat from the Tree of Life. The fruits of this tree, as well as the leaves, were the teachings of God for the healing of the nations.

Looking at others here in the Garden, he was thrilled to see the Magi, as well as Salman and Waraqah, Bahira, Ibn al-Hayyaban, and Nestor, and also Mulla Ali and the other Letters of the Living—those rarest and most blessed of souls who were humble enough to understand clearly the spiritual meaning of the prophecies of their religions and who were detached enough to leave behind all things in order to find the newest appearance of God's Messenger. Beyond them he saw, to his utmost joy, that James was there, as was Elijah Goodman and Zach's father. They were speaking with none other than Daniel and St. John, who were explaining to them further details of the meanings of all the prophecies from the visions that had been revealed to them, which they had set down in their books.

He then gazed upon the Tree of Life on the near side of the stream. From it emanated those beautiful verses of the Bab, which he had encountered after hearing of His appearance. As he stepped to the side, he noticed that there was, behind this Tree, another one from which the verses of the Quran reverberated. And behind that, a Tree from which the sweet sayings of Jesus were sounding, while further up, also along the stream's bank, other Trees emanated the teachings of the Buddha, Zoroaster, Moses, Krishna, Abraham, Noah, and others of every hue, stretching back into the distant past and including Messengers whom God had sent to peoples that had not kept written records. Yet when he looked again, he saw only one glorious Tree, which was at once all of them. A deep voice emanated from this Tree, which seemed to be speaking to Zach of its unity in spite of multiplicity— that all of these Trees are the first and the last, the beginning and the end, the Alpha and the Omega, the one yet many, the seal yet also the starting point. "*I am all the Prophets.*" These words resonated in his mind like a mighty chorus. Zach realized that he was in a realm in which the distinctions between the individual Messengers were insignificant. The limitations that were required during the ages in which They lived did not exist here. Even the concepts of multiplicity and singularity grew fuzzy here. He recalled his lesson from Musa about how the singular sun exists eternally, although when we are on Earth, we may speak of multiple sunrises and sunsets, the sun of yesterday, today, and tomorrow.

Turning now to look at the Tree of Life on the other side of the stream, he saw, emanating from it, "the Spirit of Glory" (Baha)—a Spirit whom the Bab had foretold was soon to appear[43], who had been prophesied in the scriptures of all religions. Known by numerous names and titles from the various religions, including the "Return of Christ" to both Christians and Sunni Muslims, this Spirit was shining so radiantly that Its brilliant light seemed to illuminate everything in the Garden. This Tree was understood by Zach to be the One who would be forced to leave His homeland and would be exiled to the plain of Akka, as Shaykh Hakim's study of the traditions of Islam had indicated. Glory seemed to emanate from it. It reminded Zach of the description of the garden of paradise in the last two chapters of the Book of Revelation— how there was no need of the sun nor the moon, "for the glory of God did lighten it."

As with the Tree on the first side, there was a whole row of other Trees standing behind this glorious Tree. They, also, seemed at once different and yet all one. As he gazed upon Them, he realized that these were the Messengers who would come in the future. He understood from chapter 20 of the Book of Revelation that after the first Return, there would be a period of a millennium, after which there would be another Return. And if that were to happen, why not additional Messengers even further into the future? It was clear to him that man would always need God's guidance if he was to continue to progress. These future Messengers, as with those from the past, appeared from one perspective to be a single Messenger, but from another perspective, They appeared to be many.

As he watched, he heard the reciting of sacred verses that boomed forth like thunder from the Tree. As the words reverberated to the far horizons, the peoples of the distant lands beyond the Garden could hear them, even as they slept, and all were stirred to their very depths:

> *O My Friends!* (His words rang out at a slow but deliberate pace.)
> *Have ye forgotten that true and radiant morn,*
> *when in those hallowed and blessed surroundings*
> *ye were all gathered in My presence*
> *beneath the shade of the tree of life,*
> *which is planted in the all-glorious paradise?*
>
> *Awe-struck ye listened*
> *as I gave utterance to these three most holy words:*
> *O friends! Prefer not your will to Mine,*
> *never desire that which I have not desired for you,*
> *and approach Me not with lifeless hearts,*
> *defiled with worldly desires and cravings.*

Zach was indeed awestruck by the beauty, the power, and the majesty of the revelation of these words and how they seemed to support the lessons he had just learned from the flaming swords about the need for detachment and humility. After a pause, the verses continued in a slower, more measured cadence:

> *Would ye but sanctify your souls,*
> *ye would at this present hour*
> *recall that place and those surroundings,*

203

*and the truth of My utterance*
*should be made evident unto all of you.*[44]

Zach hoped that he would someday find more people who would sanctify their souls and thus awaken to this new evangel—this great Good News. He was enthralled by everything he saw in this wondrous Garden—all of the spiritual truths that seemed to emanate in the deepest and most brilliant colors and to dance in a joyous vibration from every flower, bush, and blade of grass as they exuded the most exquisite fragrances. Every beautiful bird, perched upon the branches of the trees within the Garden, sang glorious melodies in praise of God. One of the leaves of the Tree drifted downward and landed in Zach's outstretched hand. He instinctively put it to his mouth, and as he swallowed it, his mind was flooded with the knowledge of a simple teaching—that peace between the peoples of the world would be facilitated if everyone learned one common language in addition to his mother tongue so that all could communicate clearly. He then gazed upward at the Tree, which was full of thousands of such leaves—each one being a glorious new teaching—and he was reminded of the description of the Tree of Life in the final chapter of the Bible: "...and the leaves of the Tree were for the healing of the nations." *Yes indeed* he thought, *this is the age in which the healing will begin.*

He bent down by the side of the river to scoop up a handful of the crystal waters to drink and instantly felt his entire being suffused with the knowledge of a thousand truths of spiritual realities that he had never previously considered. He felt that he wanted to stay here forever and live among all of the wondrous souls who had been admitted into this glorious Garden.

As he was gazing over the beautiful scene, he heard a deep voice boom forth, saying, "Come up hither!" He did not understand the meaning of this, but as he looked, the scene seemed to dissolve. He heard the sound of waves, and he found himself awakening in the cold of his cabin on the ship, with the light of a gray dawn beginning to enter. He sat up and pondered for a while, wanting to remember every detail of this strange and marvelous dream and dearly wishing that he could return to that beautiful garden in the new Jerusalem.

He dressed quickly and climbed up onto the deck. The cold morning air chased away all vestiges of sleep. Though the sky was overcast in the east, he noticed darker, ominous clouds coming in from the west. By breakfast, the waves were growing stronger, and it was clear that a storm was coming up. The captain had a worried look and gave orders to trim the sails.

Before long, the storm was full upon them—a fierce wind with sleet that would freeze upon impact. The captain had furled all of the sails save one by this point. But now, with the icy coating and part of the tackle jammed, it was nearly impossible to reach the lines needed to furl the last one.

Zach, with his knowledge of sailing, knew the dangerous predicament they were in. He knew from the length of their sailing that they must be somewhere near the Irish coast. And while a sturdy ship tightly closed could weather all the waves that the storm might toss against it, the dashing of the ship against the rocks of the coast was another matter.

The waves alone could push the ship toward the coast, and with a sail stuck in place, it would move eastward much faster. The crew members strove for over an hour to reach the problem sail and to at least cut the lower ties free so it would only flap in the wind. But the first sailor who tried to climb out toward the end of the main boom was barely able to cling to the slippery wooden pole. As the growing waves tossed the ship back and forth, he lost his grip and fell into the sea and was lost, much to the horror of the rest of the crew. Finally, a second sailor was able to reach the tie lines of the stuck sail and, with his hatchet, cut it free.

But how close to the shore had the storm blown them? By this time the dark clouds were all around them, limiting their view, so there was no way to tell. At one point Zach thought he saw a bumpy horizon in the distance between a break in the clouds. Was it the coast? He could not be sure.

Another half hour passed, with the wind howling and the waves growing even larger, like living hills that were tossing the boat fifty feet up and then down again with each sickening pass. The passengers and much of the crew had taken refuge below deck while the captain did his best to steer the ship into the oncoming waves.

Then the captain saw the one thing he feared most: From atop the crest of one wave, at the bottom of the wave trough, he saw a splash of water. It was the tip of a sea mount—normally so far below the surface that ships would sail over it untouched but now exposed briefly when the deep troughs passed. He hoped that the coming wave would lift the ship up and far enough forward to pass over it. But then, as the ship dropped from the crest of the wave down into the next trough, there was a horrifying jolt and the sound of splintering wood and screams from inside the cabins below deck.

The captain and Zach, as well as all the sailors who had any experience, instantly knew what this meant: The ship was finished. A large hole below the waterline in the middle of a gale meant there was no chance that the ship might be saved. The ship started listing toward its starboard side as the hold filled with cold seawater. As the force of the next wave flung the ship upward again, the timbers on its port side began to split apart, sealing its fate.

Howling for God's mercy, some threw themselves into the sea in hopes of staying clear of the now flailing ship and hoping, perhaps, that they might be washed toward an unseen but nearby shore. Some became entangled in the fallen rigging. Some tried to cling to a part of the ship while looking for anything that might float.

But among all who were on board, as the icy waters enveloped them, no one accepted his fate with such calm acquiescence as Zach Thompson. His thoughts were fixed on the vision of the great city and the marvelous garden he had found therein. The meaning of the words he had heard at the close of his dream, "Come up hither!" were now clear to him. Holding briefly to the railing on the high edge of the ship, the words James had recited on their journey across the desert came back to his mind: *"A knower is he who is dry in the sea."* And with that thought, he flung himself from the railing and the listing deck outward, toward the frigid waters of the North Atlantic.

Yet ere his body plunged into the waves, he had already left it behind. He found himself soaring upward, returning toward his true home in that glorious city upon the hill.

\*     \*     \*

THE WAVES ALSO SWALLOWED his travel diary and the list of the twelve questions he had hoped to ask the Bab. Yet all was not lost. For one day, less than two decades later, after the Bab had been martyred and after the Holy Spirit had begun to speak to the One whom the Bab had foretold, a seeker would be inspired to ask those same questions, and more, to the new Messenger—the One who would come to be known as "the Glory of God." In a discourse that lasted two days and two nights, He revealed the answers to each question and more, opening the seeker's eyes to a spiritual perspective on the prophecies of all religions, illuminating their fundamental coherence and demonstrating how they must necessarily emanate from a single divine Source. These were written down in a book that provided spiritual certainty to its grateful recipient—a book now known to history as *The Book of Certitude.*

# Epilogue

THE STORY OF ZACH and James, our fictional Wise Men of the West, has ended. But the true story of the Promised One—the Bab—and His valiant followers had only just begun. It would come to include the successful search for the second of the two Messengers—the return of Christ to both the Christian world and the Sunni portion of Islam, the return of the Imam Husayn to the Shiah part of Islam, the "Lord of Hosts" and "Everlasting Father" to the Jewish people, the "Shah-Bahram" to the followers of Zoroaster, the reincarnation of Krishna to the Hindus, the fifth Buddha to the Buddhists, and "Him Whom God shall make manifest" to the followers of the Bab. [45]

Stepping outside of the fictional genre now, this epilogue is a brief synopsis of the actual history of things that have happened since that time, following some of the historical themes that we have explored in the foregoing chapters.

I hope my story about the search of Zach and James has opened the eyes of my readers to the worldwide nature of the prophecies regarding the appearance of the Promised One. A search, in one form or another, was occurring in many places around the world during those days. The vast majority of seekers had preconceived notions regarding the manner in which the Promised One would appear based on attachments to a particular (often material, literal, or cultural) interpretation of their prophecies, which prevented them from finding Him at the time of His appearance.

However, for those who are willing to consider spiritual interpretations, the prophecies can be very helpful today, even though they are being viewed retrospectively. It was the same for early Jewish believers who converted to Christianity. They found the spiritual interpretation of Old Testament prophecies about Jesus' appearance to be a confirmation for them, while those religious leaders who clung to an overly literal interpretation of those prophecies remained blind to the truth of His teachings and His station.

At the time of Jesus' appearance, there were only a few (some say three) Wise Men who successfully followed the prophecies of their own religion—together with some assistance from the priests of Jerusalem—to locate God's Messenger prior to His actual ministry. More than 600 years later, in addition to the Jewish man who studied the Hebrew Bible, there were at least four Christians who were similarly able to find Muhammad based on their knowledge of Christian prophecies, which had been recorded in writings that were not included in the canonized books of the New Testament.

At the time of the Bab, 18 "Letters of the Living" (as the Bab called them)—one from as far away as India—were successful in their search for the Promised One immediately prior to His announcement of His mission. Alas, no one from the West was among them in those days.

Yet the benefit of the prophecies is not only for these few blessed souls who have found God's Messenger *beforehand*. It is also for the large majority of us who will find Him *after* His appearance. For all those who are searching, who are spiritually aware, and who are willing to consider a spiritual understanding of their scriptures, the fulfillment of the prophecies can play a major role in guiding sincere seekers, even when discovered retrospectively.

It was extremely difficult for the people of the early 1800s to fully unravel the meanings of their prophecies. But the present reader has the benefit of more than 175 years of history that have elapsed since then as well as a wealth of information that has become available through modern technological advances, many of which trace their earliest roots back to those days.

This epilogue is, therefore, a brief summary of some of the historical events that followed from the four main story lines that started in the early 1840s—lines that would converge 50 or 100 or more years later:

A. William Miller and religious movements of the West
B. The Jewish people and the return to the Holy Land
C. The new heaven and new earth and the ensuing technological revolution
D. The appearance of the Bab, followed by the coming of the One whom He had foretold as "Him Whom God shall make manifest," who was called "the Glory of God" or, in Arabic, Baha'u'llah, and the development of the Baha'i Faith, which together have fulfilled all three of the prophecies of Daniel 12 concerning the 1,260, 1,290, and 1,335 days.


## A) THE MILLERITES AND OTHER ADVENTIST DENOMINATIONS

Although William Miller was not inclined to start a new denomination, many of his followers who still expected an imminent advent of Christ were willing to do so. Thus the story of the Adventist churches began in April 1845 at the Albany Conference.[46] Differences in understandings as to why the clear prophecy was (seemingly) left unfulfilled led to the creation of different branches of Adventism. Some of them petered out, while some grew. The largest today is the Seventh Day Adventists, who maintain the original site of William Miller's farm in Low Hampton, NY. Some branches later merged and, through the work of Charles Taze Russell, started organizations that led to the present-day Jehovah's Witnesses, with new interpretations of the timing of Christ's return. By the 1920s and 1930s, some preachers combined versions of the Adventist message with the recently developed radio form of mass communication, which then developed into televangelism in the 1950s and beyond.

Some of the other leaders of the movement abandoned the idea that the time of Christ's return could be predicted at all. Some became preterists, choosing to interpret all of the Bible's prophecies including some sort of "return" as having occurred in the early centuries of the Christian era. Other denominations revised the predicted date, along with offering new theological explanations of why no fulfillment appeared on the earlier dates. This has continued to the present, generating inaccurate predictions of the end of the world.

Following the death of Joseph Smith, his followers similarly broke into dozens (by some counts as many as 90) branches, the largest of which today is known as the Church of Jesus Christ of Latter-day Saints.

Some people were inspired to go to the Holy Land in hopes of witnessing the great advent there. Corinda Minor, a Millerite from Philadelphia, moved to Palestine in 1849 and, together with German Adventists, established the Mount Hope Colony. In 1865–66, two Mormons, George J. Adams and Abraham McKenszie, traveled to the Holy Land, following the 1841–42 example of Orson Hyde, and attempted to establish the "American Colony" in Jaffa, with the aim of preparing for the return of Christ by encouraging Jewish resettlement in the Holy Land. Although the effort soon collapsed, it laid a foundation for the Adventist German Templers who, in 1869, purchased the land from the American Colony to establish their own Adventist colony in Jaffa. During the previous year, the Templers had established their first Adventist colony at the foot of Mt. Carmel in Haifa. One of the members of that colony had inscribed the reason for their presence by engraving on the lintel above the doorway to his home, "The Lord is Nigh." It remains there to this day.

The Adventist strand has remained part of, and in some cases central to, many Christian denominations to the present day. The evidence that we are living in a new age has continued to mount. The theme of the return of the Jewish people to the Holy Land is irrefutable. And yet a Messiah in the form of Christian or Jewish literal expectations has not appeared.

As to Mr. Miller himself, he did not live long beyond the end of our story. His eyesight and health started to decline in February 1848 and gradually worsened. On December 20, 1849, he departed from this world and undoubtedly ascended to a place from which he could see the whole story with an immensely greater level of awareness.

But perhaps the story of William Miller is not quite over. In 1847 he had a dream that he recounted to others and that lifted his spirits greatly even though he may not have entirely understood its whole meaning at that time. Since this is best understood in the context of the development of the Baha'i Faith, I will recount that story in the section entitled "The Promise Is Fulfilled" below.

## B) THE RETURN OF THE JEWS TO THE HOLY LAND

Although Theodore Herzl is regarded as the father of the modern Zionist movement, having formed the Zionist Organization in 1897, the roots of the return to the Holy Land go much further back.

The teachings of the Ga'on of Vilna in the late 1700s concerning an expectation from the Zohar that the Messiah might return in the Jewish year 5600 (1839–40 AD) sent a wave of Jewish immigrants to the Holy Land in the early 1800s. The Messiah of Jewish expectations did not appear during that year, but it was the year that the Ottoman Tanzimat reforms began— an effort to demonstrate to other European powers that the Ottomans were modernizing, much like their European counterparts. It included the principle that all people, regardless of their religion, were to be accorded equal rights. Within a year, the Ottomans had recaptured the Holy Land from its erstwhile Egyptian rulers. Thus, the right to own property in the Holy Land was, perhaps unwittingly, extended to the Jewish people, among others. This suggested to some that the return of the Jews could be accomplished not through conquest but rather through the gradual purchase of land, paid in part by contributions from the worldwide Jewish community. Most population records indicate that by the mid-1840s the Jewish people had already become the largest religious community in Jerusalem itself. It has remained so ever since.

Yehuda (or Judah) Alkalai taught that the year 5600 (1839–40) represented the start of a hundred-year period called "the days of the Messiah," during which Jews must make every effort to return to the Holy Land and after which "an outpouring of wrath will gather our dispersed." Given the events of World War II, which started at the end of this hundred-year period (i.e., in late 1939), it was a remarkable insight.

Alkalai also taught the principles of purchasing the land, the development of agriculture, and the promotion of the Hebrew language. Prior to 1880, the majority of the Jews in the Holy Land were there for religious reasons, often supported by outside donations. Religious persecution in Russia and Eastern Europe in the early 1880s fueled the "First Aliyah" (organized Jewish movement to the Holy Land), which focused on establishing self-sustaining farming colonies following Alkalai's principles. His teachings were also one of the inspirational forces for the later work of Theodore Herzl.

But it was not Jewish longing alone that brought about their return. It was also support for the idea from at least some Christian quarters that linked the return of the Jews with their own expectations of the return of Christ. It was persecution of Jewish communities in various trouble spots around the world. It was the rise of nationalism in Europe and nationalistic stresses that were bedeviling various parts of the Ottoman Empire while also encouraging thoughts of nationhood among the Jewish people. It was a curious and, yes, miraculous mix of forces that pulled together these "'dry bones" of "the whole house of Israel," just as Ezekiel had foretold, and set them on their feet.

The success of the British in their conquest of the Holy Land in World War I, and the attendant collapse of the Ottoman Empire, was an event of major historic significance. Not only was it the first time in over six centuries that the Holy Land was under Christian control but it was also the first time in 13 centuries that Sunni Islam had no caliph to lead it. And of even more significance, from the Jewish perspective at least, were the efforts of Chaim Weizmann, a British Zionist who worked with the British government to create that Balfour Declaration, recognizing that a "national home for the Jewish people" should be created in Palestine. The subsequent British victory in Palestine and the creation of the League of Nations, with its agreement to allow Britain to govern Palestine, converted that Declaration into a reality.

Continuing persecution in Russia and Europe motivated thousands, then tens of thousands, and, during the rise of the Nazi regime, hundreds of thousands, of Jews to move to the Holy Land. They turned large areas of swampland into productive farmland, planted trees to cover huge stretches of barren hills, organized large-scale irrigation projects, created schools and institutions of higher education, and generally provided the foundations for a modern economy.

Ultimately, the horrors of the Nazi Holocaust motivated the members of the newly created United Nations to grant statehood to the Jewish homeland after World War II. Thirty years after the Balfour Declaration, the control of parts of the Holy Land was given to the newborn government of the modern state of Israel as the British withdrew from the area. The new state organized efforts to bring persecuted Jewish populations from other countries into their new homeland, enlarging its population considerably.

Though born under the most difficult of circumstances, the new nation seemed to grow in strength with each test. Referring to the assembled bones, Ezekiel had written: *"And when I beheld, lo, the sinews and the flesh came up upon them, and skin covered them above..."* (Ezekiel 37:8).

Of course, struggles between the two branches of the family of Abraham in the Holy Land continue to this day. Nevertheless, it is undeniable that the ancient promise of the return of the Jewish people to that land has been most miraculously fulfilled. When we view the rapid advancement in the state of development in this country, it is hard to avoid the conclusion that the hand of Providence has somehow been involved.

*     *     *

THE RETURN HAS ALSO had a significant benefit to the Baha'i community. The teachings of the Bab and Baha'u'llah were scorned by Muslim religious orthodoxy in both the Shiah Persian land of its birth and the Sunni lands of the Ottoman Empire. In an effort to send its Founder to a remote prison city, they managed to exile Him to the one place in their entire realm that would soon be outside of Muslim control. Fifty years after Baha'u'llah's exile to the Holy Land, the World Center of the Baha'i Faith was placed beyond the reach of Muslim authorities when, in September 1918, forces under the command of the British General Allenby swiftly took the Haifa-Akka area from Ottoman rulership. It is said that some of the Arabs were reluctant to fight against him because, when they heard the general's last name, they heard the Arabic words 'Allah en Nabi'— God's prophet—and they were perhaps concerned that God might not be on their side.[47] His remarkable string of victories no doubt enhanced this concern. And thus the city of Akka itself surrendered without a fight.

## C) A NEW HEAVEN, A NEW EARTH, AND THE TECHNOLOGICAL REVOLUTION

In the midst of all of the theological discussions of Zach and James, one might have noted occasional reference to the technological revolution that had its beginnings in this same general timeframe. Although the discovery of several scientific principles had laid the foundation for this revolution in the 17th or 18th centuries and a few of the inventions (including early steam engines) were developed during those earliest years, the pace of technological development accelerated markedly in the early 19th century, aided considerably by the advent of usable electricity, which made its main debut with the telegraph on May 24, 1844—the day after the Bab's declaration.

Although much human effort has been needed to make these major advances, the rapidity with which they have rained down on us in this age forces one to ponder whether humanity has simply had a run of good fortune in its efforts to innovate or whether critical discoveries and inventions have been inspired, at least in part, by a divine Providence, which is driving us forward and revolutionizing our very conceptions of heaven and earth (as one might understand them in Revelation 21:1–2).

These developments have had a profound influence on the nature of the workplace as improvements in agricultural productivity enabled increasing numbers to move from farm fields into towns to do factory work. And thus it was known as the "Industrial Revolution."

Meanwhile, a less obvious but more profound revolution was taking place in the fields of transportation and communication. Ground transportation made the transition from horse-drawn carts to canals and later to rails and highways that cut through many physical barriers. And after many centuries of wind-powered ship transportation, the switch to steam-powered ships with subsurface propellers capable of crossing the oceans on reliable schedules revolutionized intercontinental transport. The Bab

216

had revealed a prayer for the improvement of sea travel in the winter of 1844–45[48]. The following summer, the SS Great Britain made the first such successful crossing. Today, huge diesel-powered cargo ships have become the foundation of the international aspect of the world's economy. Airplane and jet transportation have added yet another layer of speed and efficiency for human transportation. The field of communication has moved even faster, from telegraphy to radio communications, to television and satellite-based communications, and, finally, to the global fiber-optic/computer/cellphone communication system that now links billions of people across the globe daily, thus becoming the neural network for the body of humankind.

But as Zach could foresee, these changes do not come in a vacuum. Under such circumstances, people move and mix, and with them, their ideas and beliefs also move and mix. As new generations arise, they find that the belief systems of their ancestors are too constrained to accommodate the new reality in which they live. The "new wine," as Jesus explained in Luke 5:37–38, cannot be contained in the "old skins." A new belief system, "a new heaven"—one with a much wider perspective—is essential.

Thus, the "end of the age" and the beginning of a new age become synonymous with the coming of a new Messenger—a return of the Christ-spirit to guide us through all of the changes and to separate those changes that should be accepted and encouraged from those that would be destructive and must be avoided.

During such periods, God does not leave us without guidance. But *we* must be spiritually awake and open to new possibilities if we are to receive that guidance and benefit from it.


## D) THE PROMISE IS FULFILLED

In the physical world, Jesus had not descended from the sky as William Miller and his followers had hoped. Neither had the 12th Imam arisen from some fabled underground city, as many of the Shiites had expected. And yet, as we all now know, the spread of Jesus' message to all nations and the predicted return of the Jewish people to the Holy Land (inconceivable as

217

it seemed at the time) have actually happened. Because of this, our current age is indelibly marked as the *latter days* or the *last days* described in several places in the books of the Old Testament and as the *close of the eon* described by Jesus. And the return of the Messiah or the Lord of Hosts is inextricably linked to those prophecies. So the Western world—or at least all who accept the truth of either the Old or the New Testaments—remains faced with a vexing theological question: Where is the missing Messiah? Increasingly complex theological calculations and explanations have been offered. But as time goes by, they have become increasingly unsatisfactory to their hearers. The religions of Islam, Zoroastrianism, Buddhism, and Hinduism similarly suffer from such problems.

As to the story of the Bab, His teachings initiated a meteoric rise of followers, with approximately 100,000 conversions during the first four years.[49] While some initially thought that He was primarily a reformer of Islam, it became clear by 1848, with the revelation of new laws for a new age, that this was the dawn of a whole new Revelation. In July of that year, Qurratu'l-Ayn (who is known to history by the new title she had been given—"*Tahirih*" that is, the Pure One) made this stunningly clear by removing the veil that Muslim women had, for centuries, been required to wear over their faces. The Bab's support of this action signaled the abolition of ancient religious customs and Islamic laws, proclaiming the dawn of a new age. The Bab's teaching that men and women would be regarded henceforth as equals was so shocking that even many of the Bab's followers (let alone the general population) found it difficult to comprehend.[††††]

By this point, the Bab had been arrested for His "heretical" teachings and consigned to prison in the mountains of northwestern Iran. After four years of revealing new teachings, He was summoned to a trial, in which He, like Jesus, was asked who He claimed to be. His answer left no room for any doubt:

---

†††† Interestingly, the Seneca Falls Convention—the first convention on the rights of women—was convened in Upstate New York about a week after Tahirih's bold action in Persia. Indeed, the inspirational meeting that initiated that Convention took place on July 9, 1848, which quite possibly may have been on the same day as Tahirih's stunning proclamation. Yet none of the participants in either activity at that time had any conscious awareness of the other.

*I am, I am, I am the promised One!*
*I am the One whose name you have for a thousand years invoked,*
*at whose mention you have risen,*
*whose advent you have longed to witness,*
*and the hour of whose Revelation you have prayed God to hasten.*
*Verily I say, it is incumbent upon the peoples*
*of both the East and the West*
*to obey My word and to pledge allegiance to My person.*[50]

The story of the Bab reached a stunning conclusion with His execution two years later in northwestern Persia—about seven months after Mr. Miller's passing in Upstate New York. The Bab's martyrdom was similar in several respects to that which Jesus suffered. The news of His Revelation had spread rapidly throughout Persia among a population that was excited by an expectation of an imminent fulfillment, similar to the expectation that gripped the faithful in parts of America and Europe. Like the people of the West, the majority of Persians were expecting an outwardly miraculous return. They, too, hoped to see this with their physical eyes rather than to open their spiritual ones. In spite of the years of preparatory work by Shaykh Ahmad and Siyyid Kazim, many refused to acknowledge the possibility that a return or resurrection could occur without all manner of physical miracles. And so the return of the persecutors of a newly born faith had also appeared.

One of the earliest intersections of the Babi religion with Christianity occurred on the day of the Bab's execution. A Christian Armenian regiment of 750 men had been selected to carry out the execution. After witnessing the saintly demeanor of the Bab in contrast to the self-seeking behavior of the religious and civil authorities, the head of the regiment, Sam Khan, was seized with fear that this execution might bring down upon him the wrath of God. Were its similarities to the crucifixion of Jesus too clear for him to ignore?

"I profess the Christian Faith and entertain no ill will against you," he told the Bab. "If your Cause be the Cause of Truth, enable me to free myself from the obligation to shed your blood."

219

The Bab replied, "Follow your instructions, and if your intentions be sincere, the Almighty is surely able to relieve you from your perplexity."

Sam Khan did so. At the place of execution, all 750 men of his regiment, arranged in three rows, fired their rifles at the Bab. And yet not a single round succeeded in finding its mark. As the smoke cleared, the regiment, the officials, and the crowd of 10,000 witnesses were so dumbfounded by this incredible event that no one raised any objection when Sam Khan stood forth and ordered his men to leave the site and swore that he would never resume the task, even if his refusal were to cost him his own life.‡‡‡‡

A Muslim regiment was then brought in and the task was attempted again, this time successfully. Thus was fulfilled an Islamic prophecy that stated that the Islamic religion would, in the latter days, decline to such a degree that the Promised One would be killed at the hands of Muslims.

Like Jesus, the Bab's noble spirit ascended to heaven. Like Jesus also, His physical remains seemed to have mysteriously disappeared shortly after His execution.[51] Unlike the story of Jesus, however, the few followers who had recovered the sacred remains and knew the secret place where they had been carefully hidden were able to pass the knowledge forward. They quietly conveyed this knowledge to "Him Whom God will make manifest"— Baha'u'llah. A half century later, those precious remains were secretly brought to Akka and, in 1909, safely placed in a modest shrine, which 'Abdu'l-Baha, the son of Baha'u'llah and designated head of the Baha'i community, had completed on the slopes of Mount Carmel, as instructed by his Father almost twenty years earlier. And thus, the physical remains of the new Elijah came to rest on that very same mountain that was associated with so much of the life of the Elijah of the Old Testament and within a short distance of the place where the Elijah of the New Testament, John the Baptist, preached and baptized, preparing people for the advent of the great Messenger of that age.

*     *     *

ONE MIGHT WONDER WHY no one from the West actually traveled eastward in search of the Promised One in those days in the manner suggested in Zach's story. An answer can be found in the writings of the Bab Himself.

---

‡‡‡‡ This is just one of several miraculous events associated with the Bab's martyrdom. See Chapter 23 of The Dawn-Breakers for the full account.

He helped dispel some of our misconceptions about the "Day of Resurrection" when He wrote:

> *The Day of Resurrection is a day on which the sun riseth and setteth like unto any other day. How oft hath the Day of Resurrection dawned, and the people of the land where it occurred did not learn of the event. Had they heard, they would not have believed, and thus they were not told!*[52]

It is clear, then, that the Day of Resurrection occurs every time a new Messenger appears. It is not an outwardly miraculous day to most of the people of the time, who remain fast asleep. It will be seen as miraculous primarily by later generations, who will understand its spiritual import. The journey of Zach and James would have been to no avail, since no one from their home countries at that time would have been willing to consider such new ideas. Alas, we in the West were not ready.

However, had the leaders of Shiah Islam not arisen in opposition, it is easy to imagine how the teachings of the Bab could have spread in short order throughout not only Persia but through the Shiite communities in the rest of the Islamic world, including those the Holy Land itself. Had the Christian leaders been receptive to a spiritual understanding of Christian prophecies, they would have listened to the news of the Bab as it reached the Holy Land and would have recognized it as the fulfillment of the ancient prophecy from Daniel, whose timing Mr. Miller had so precisely explained.

The leaders of both religions would have acknowledged the prophetic right of the Jewish people to return to the Holy Land and would have facilitated a cooperative and peaceful migration. The Bab's teachings of universal brotherhood would have reached the West, and in recognizing His spiritual authority, Americans would have avoided the crisis of their great Civil War. Indeed, had there not been such religious opposition, a widespread understanding of the oneness of humankind would have dawned on the world at the same time as the widespread development of machinery, including the machinery of war. Such an understanding would have precluded the invention of the instruments of mass destruction that have, ever since that time, inflicted upon humanity an apocalyptic degree of suffering and death, the like of which the world has never known.

In retrospect, it comes as no surprise that Baha'u'llah should write:

> *My eyes rain down tears until My bed is drenched;*
> *But My sorrow is not for Myself...*
> *yea, because I see mankind going astray in their intoxication,*
> *and they know it not;*
> *they have exalted their lusts, and put aside their God,*
> *as though they took the command of God for a mockery,*
> *a sport, and a plaything;*
> *and they think that they do well,*
> *and that they are harbored in the citadel of security.*
> *The matter is not as they suppose:*
> *tomorrow they shall see what they now deny.* [53]

It seems that America in 1844 was still too young and inwardly focused to consider the possibility that the fulfillment of Jesus' promises could be just one part of a far larger story of the fulfillment of the promises of all religions. It would be 50 years before America would be ready. During that time, its ideals of equality would be tried in the crucible of a catastrophic civil war, and slavery would be abolished at the cost of vast and unimaginable suffering. The development of ocean-going steamships as well as transcontinental rail lines and both transoceanic and transcontinental communication lines would dramatically shorten the effective distance between the peoples of the world, making large-scale interactions between the people of distant lands inevitable.

An interest in foreign lands, their peoples, and their religions started to grow, fueled in part by the developments in the British Empire. During this period, most of the scriptures of the religions of the East would be translated into English through the pioneering efforts of Max Muller and his 50-volume project entitled *Sacred Books of the East*. Sponsored by Oxford University, this effort reflected the growing cultural interactions between East and West.

A high point of this trend was the holding of the World's Parliament of Religions, which occurred in 1893 as a part of the World's Columbian Exposition, held in Chicago. It included the first public mention of the Baha'i Faith in America. The following year—a half century after William Miller's prediction of Christ's return—the first Baha'i teacher would arrive on American soil, and the history of the Baha'i Faith in America would proceed from that point.

It is true that there have been others since the early 19th century who have advanced various claims to be the fulfillment of the promises of one or another of the religions of the past. However, it is also true that none of those attempts have had any substantial success beyond the bounds of their own original religion. Thus, they have not been able to become anything more than a new denomination within their original religion. The Baha'i Faith is the only modern example of a fulfillment claim that has been able to cite the prophetic expectations of each of the revealed religions of the past in a manner sufficient to attract a substantial number of the followers of those religions into its fold, thereby validating its claim to be an *independent* world religion rather than a new branch of an existing religion.

From the time of the Bab's declaration in 1844 to the present day, so many prophecies of the Bible, including Daniel's references to the 1,260, the 1,290, and the 1,335 days, have been fulfilled that I cannot hope to recount them all in a single book.

Most of the prophecies are clothed in allegory so that the spiritual eye may perceive while the physically oriented eye will not. But it seems that God, in His mercy, has granted a clear piece of the puzzle to each of the prophetic religions. To the Jewish community, He has granted the most clear *outward historical sign*: the return of their people into the land of their ancestors, as clearly foretold in their scriptures more than three millennia ago. The Christian world was given the clearest evidence of *the time* of the coming of the Promised One thanks to William Miller's elucidation of Daniel's prophecies. In the Hindu Bhagavad Gita, we find the clearest description of *the manner* of His return, as He builds a human body for Himself, suggesting that He comes forth into the world in a manner not too dissimilar from that of other people. The Buddhists were provided with a clear indication of *His name*—not the name of the Bab as the forerunner but the "new name" of

"Him Whom God will make manifest"—for in the name of the anticipated Amit-Abha Buddha, we have a variant of the same wording as found in the name Baha'u'llah, both referring to the Glory of God. The Zoroastrians were especially blessed in that He is a descendant of their royal lineage and thus comes from *their own land* and ethnic heritage. The Muslims have the great good fortune of having the Promised One appear within their *religious domain* and thus sharing a close spiritual heritage with Him as well as some similarity in religious laws due to the relatively recent date of Muhammad's revelation.

Thus it can be said that each of the major prophetic religions has at least one clear piece of the puzzle. But who could assemble this great puzzle as long as they confined their search by looking solely at their own religion?

\*     \*     \*

LET ME RETURN, NOW, to 1847 to recount a fascinating report of an event late in William Miller's life. The Great Disappointment had led to three years of ridicule and much heartache as well as division and disputations among his once-faithful followers. In the latter part of that year, Mr. Miller had a dream in which God gave him a "curiously wrought" chest of beautiful jewels and coins that "reflected a light and glory equaled only by the sun." Feeling that he should share the beauty of the jewels with others, he placed the open chest on a table so that everyone could see this wondrous gift and share in the joy of it. But the crowds that came to see it were not worthy. They heaped their own false jewelry and counterfeit coins on the gift. Crowding around it, they were pushing and shoving until they bumped into the chest, causing it to crash to the ground. The jewels were strewn about and the chest broken, with dirt and rubbish scattered all over them. Mr. Miller himself was heartbroken that this wonderful gift was now ruined, but he prayed to God to send him help. Then a man entered the room who opened the window and separated the dirt and false jewels so that the wind carried them away. He then gathered all of the true jewels and coins and gave the preacher a new larger and even more beautiful chest, filling it with jewels and coins that "shone with ten times their former glory." Mr. Miller was so happy that he was shouting with joy until he awoke from the dream.[54]

No doubt several have speculated on the meaning of this dream. From my own perspective, though, it seems clear. Mr. Miller was indeed given a great gift—the gift of the knowledge that the return of Christ was near at hand.§§§§

But the people of William Miller's time were too limited to appreciate the true value of that gift. Even the preacher himself seemed to be caught up in the prevailing literal expectations of the day. Had they come to pass, they surely would have been awe inspiring and would have compelled everyone to believe. But when this did not happen, those who came seeking a miracle had to leave, disappointed. "And He sighed deeply in His spirit, and saith, 'Why doth this generation seek after a sign? Verily I say unto you, 'There shall no sign be given unto this generation'" (Mark 8:12). So many had been seeking such a sign of their own imaginings, and when it did not happen, they cast their ridicule upon this great gift that Mr. Miller had been given and threw it down.

Yet a man entered the room to resolve the problem and to give Mr. Miller an even larger gift. We might understand this to be the Bab or Baha'u'llah, who fulfilled the biblical prophecies in unexpected ways and thus validated William Miller's conclusions regarding the year of the Return. But we might also take this to be 'Abdu'l-Baha, the son of Baha'u'llah— His appointed successor and interpreter. For if the "room" is taken to be this material world, it is interesting to note that 'Abdu'l-Baha "entered this room" (i.e., was born into this world) on that very same night that the Bab first announced His mission to Mulla Husayn in May 1844.

After Baha'u'llah's ascension in 1892, it was 'Abdu'l-Baha, following his Father's instructions, who began to spread the news to the West regarding

---

§§§§ With respect to the year 1844, Baha'is believe he was entirely correct. In one respect, he was even correct about one of the days he originally identified—March 21, 1843. The only thing of historical significance that happened on that day was the peaking of the appearance of the Great Comet of 1843. Yet it also represents "time zero" in the calendar that the Bab created. (Baha'u'llah continued its use.) For, unlike the way we mark the age of people, calendars mark time from "year 1," not "year 0." Since 1844 is "year 1," 1843 would be year 0 in the Babi/Baha'i calendar. Also, the Bab did not choose May 23 as the start of the year, even though it was the date of the historic event of His declaration. Rather, He maintained the ancient tradition of starting the year at the spring equinox—that same new beginning that the ancient Zoroastrians astronomers had used and that same day on which the Jewish people went forth, according to the proclamation of Artaxerxes to rebuild Jerusalem (as noted in Ezra 7:9)—the first day of spring 2300 years prior to the springtime of the Bab's declaration. Thus for Baha'is, the calendar "time zero" is March 21, 1843, which corresponds exactly with the earliest date that Mr. Miller had originally set.

the coming of the Promised One and the fulfillment of the prophecies of the Bible—sending out teachers to Europe and America and receiving early pilgrims from these countries. Many of these early Western followers knew the story of William Miller; indeed, some of the older ones had been young adults during that time. Others were children of Millerites, and at least one had been a follower of Mr. Miller himself.[55] The preacher's teachings were, in fact, a starting point for many of the early classes on the Baha'i Faith.[56] When early pilgrims from America came to visit 'Abdu'l-Baha in Akka, He explained to these new Baha'is how the visions of Daniel 8 and 9 concerning the "abomination of desolation" and the "cleansing of the sanctuary" after "2,300 days" pointed directly to the year 1844.[57] William Miller had followed similar reasoning and had reached a similar conclusion, with respect to the date of the fulfillment at least. Thus, Jesus' answer to the disciples' question in Matthew 24:3 concerning the time of His return was precisely correct if the reader made the effort to understand it, as Mr. Miller had done.

And so as the Baha'i Faith grows, the memory of Mr. Miller will grow too. But it will not be a sad memory of some historical oddity who caused the "Great Disappointment." Rather, it will be the memory of someone who successfully followed the instructions of Jesus to look at the prophecies of Daniel in order to determine the time of His return. And while it was perhaps too much to expect him, in that age, to seek the Promised One halfway across the world in the lands of Islam, yet his success in accurately predicting the time of the Return can be identified as one of the foundation stones upon which the early American Baha'i community was built. His teachings have also been an important confirmation to many Christians who have become Baha'is since that time (the current author included). They will continue to serve as a beacon for those who will travel this path in the future.

The wealth of spiritual gems brought by the Bab and Baha'u'llah was indeed "ten times their former glory," as Mr. Miller had seen in his dream. For They came not only as the fulfillment of the prophecies of Christianity but also as the fulfillment of the prophecies of all of the other revealed religions of mankind. These prophecies not only reiterated the gems of spiritual wisdom contained in each of the past religions but also brought additional spiritual truths that were too weighty for man to bear in past ages. Thus, Mr. Miller's new, larger box of jewels is very large indeed!

In retrospect, we can understand how very difficult it would have been for Mr. Miller, or anyone of that place and time, to make so profound a transition in his understanding of the manner in which Christ might return. The knowledge of other religions and their prophecies was extremely limited, hard to find, and largely untranslated in 1844. Their teachings were, understandably, considered "foreign" and something his followers could afford to ignore.

But we who are living two centuries after William Miller's time must acknowledge that we no longer have the excuse of ignorance or inaccessibility of information. The world has shrunk immeasurably as the flood of inventions has continued unabated. In particular, the revolution in the fields of communication and transportation, having some of their most important roots in the year 1844, have utterly transformed our world. It is certainly accurate to speak of that period as "the close of the age," as Jesus had done (Matt. 28:20, among others). No fair-minded observer can fail to acknowledge that a new age has surely dawned since the opening years of the 19th century, with its candles and oil lanterns, horse-drawn carriages, and wind-driven wooden ships.

Since that time, the world has opened up to us. Upheavals of all types have caused the migration and intermixing of peoples. Today, formerly unimaginable resources of information are available at our fingertips. So, yes, Mr. Miller, in 1844, may have had an acceptable reason for failing to understand the unified foundations underlying all of the revealed religions and what this implied regarding the manner in which the Promised One would appear. But given the information we now have available, *we simply have no such excuse today.*

The suggestion to wait—to see if God would provide a fulfillment that more closely matched our own limited expectations—might have made some sense in 1845. But with each passing year of un-fulfillment, it has made less and less sense. The Jewish people started to gather in the Holy Land, but the Messiah of Jewish expectation did not appear. All of the major monarchies—as keepers of the Lord's vineyard—either collapsed or witnessed their power being stripped from them, yet the Messiah of the

Christian expectations did not appear. The Caliphate of Islam, which had guided the Muslim community for 13 centuries, collapsed in 1924, but the Messiah of Muslim expectations did not appear. The Holy Land returned to Christian control during World War I and then to Jewish control after World War II, but still, the Messiah of traditional expectations did not appear. And ever since 1948, millennialists of all types have contorted their interpretations in an attempt to explain why so many signs have appeared, and yet the Promised One has not descended from the clouds nor arisen from a hiding place in the ground.

I ask, "How long will we cling to the interpretations of our own fancy? How much suffering must we endure before we are willing to consider an alternative understanding? How long can we afford to ignore the solutions to global problems—solutions that God has provided from the beginning of our modern age through the new teachings of the new Messengers?"

Baha'u'llah wrote:

> *The Revelation which, from time immemorial, hath been acclaimed as the Purpose and Promise of all the Prophets of God, and the most cherished Desire of His Messengers, hath now, by virtue of the pervasive Will of the Almighty and at His irresistible bidding, been revealed unto men. The advent of such a Revelation hath been heralded in all the sacred Scriptures. Behold how, notwithstanding such an announcement, mankind hath strayed from its path and shut out itself from its glory.*[58]

> *Followers of the Gospel, behold the gates of heaven are flung open. He that had ascended unto it is now come. Give ear to His voice calling aloud over land and sea, announcing to all mankind the advent of this Revelation—a Revelation through the agency of which the Tongue of Grandeur is now proclaiming: 'Lo, the sacred Pledge hath been fulfilled, for He, the Promised One, is come!'" "The voice of the Son of Man is calling aloud from the sacred vale: 'Here am I, here am I, O God my God!' ... whilst from the Burning Bush breaketh*

228

*forth the cry: 'Lo, the Desire of the world is made manifest in His tran-*
*scendent glory!' The Father hath come. That which ye were promised in*
*the Kingdom of God is fulfilled. This is the Word which the Son veiled*
*when He said to those around Him that at that time they could not bear*
*it... Verily the Spirit of Truth is come to guide you unto all truth... He is*
*the One Who glorified the Son and exalted His Cause... The Comforter*
*Whose advent all the scriptures have promised is now come that He*
*may reveal unto you all knowledge and wisdom. Seek Him over the*
*entire surface of the earth, haply ye may find Him."[59]*

And again:

*The time fore-ordained unto the peoples and kindreds of the earth*
*is now come. The promises of God, as recorded in the holy Scriptures,*
*have all been fulfilled. Out of Zion hath gone forth the Law of God,*
*and Jerusalem, and the hills and land thereof, are filled with the*
*glory of His Revelation. Happy is the man that pondereth in his heart*
*that which hath been revealed in the Books of God, the Help in Peril,*
*the Self-Subsisting. Meditate upon this, O ye beloved of God, and let*
*your ears be attentive unto His Word, so that ye may, by His grace*
*and mercy, drink your fill from the crystal waters of constancy, and*
*become as steadfast and immovable as the mountain in His Cause.*
*Verily I say, this is the Day in which mankind can behold the*
*Face, and hear the Voice, of the Promised One. The Call of God hath*
*been raised, and the light of His countenance hath been lifted up*
*upon men. It behoveth every man to blot out the trace of every idle*
*word from the tablet of his heart, and to gaze, with an open and*
*unbiased mind, on the signs of His Revelation, the proofs of His*
*Mission, and the tokens of His glory.*
*Great indeed is this Day! The allusions made to it in all the*
*sacred Scriptures as the Day of God attest its greatness. The soul*
*of every Prophet of God, of every Divine Messenger, hath thirsted*
*for this wondrous Day. All the diverse kindreds of the earth have,*
*likewise, yearned to attain it.[60]*

229

If we choose to ignore the evidence of all that has happened over the past two centuries, for what evidence shall we wait? Shall the community of Christ and the community of Muhammad follow in the footsteps of the Jewish and Zoroastrian communities that chose to ignore the evidence of Jesus' revelation and that have, as a result, spent two millennia waiting, looking for a fulfillment suited to fit their own imaginations?

If you have ever wondered why Christ's promise to return seems to be delayed, perhaps it has not been delayed. Perhaps it is only that the manner of its fulfillment has been contrary to one's expectations. If you have wondered why, in our modern age, it seems that God has not reached down to help mankind, perhaps it is because we have not stretched our thinking sufficiently to reach up to Him. Perhaps we have failed to consider the true implications of the teaching that the Good Shepherd will gather together all of His different flocks. Perhaps we have been thinking that we ourselves were the favored or central flock and that all others must deny their particular doctrines to become like us. Perhaps we have failed to consider that God's call for all humanity to come together to a common center implies that we ourselves must be willing to leave some details of manmade theology behind. Perhaps we have failed to meditate deeply on how the oneness of God necessarily implies the oneness of humankind and therefore the oneness of the religions.

In short, if we wonder whether God has forgotten us, perhaps we should ask instead whether we, in our unwillingness to cast aside centuries of manmade interpretations, have forgotten Him. Have we, like Jacob, after ages of waiting in sorrow while hoping for the return of the true Joseph, become blind? And if blind, are we at least able to inhale the fragrance of His presence as we hear His teachings, even when they are wafted over a vast distance, across numerous cultures and religions, from East to West? Herein lies the question for all those who seek Him to ponder deeply.

God has given unto each person the ability to listen with their own ears, to see with their own eyes, and to judge with their own heart. Thus, Jesus charged each of us to remain "awake" in order to find Him when He returned. The obligation to remain spiritually awake—to fulfill our part of

God's ancient Covenant—remains with each of us individually today. We cannot assign it to our religious leaders nor give it over to family or friends. Nor can we assume that an "alarm clock" of physical miracles has been set in order to awaken us at the right time.

Therefore, each one of us today is obligated to be a true seeker and to humbly look into the claim of the fulfillment with an open mind, detached from the limiting interpretations of the past, in order to make a judgment for himself or herself in this, the Day of Judgment.

I leave my readers now with a portion of Baha'u'llah's description of what a true seeker can, in this Day, achieve and how he can achieve it:

> *O My brother! When a true seeker determineth to take the step of search in the path leading unto the knowledge of the Ancient of Days, he must, before all else, cleanse his heart, which is the seat of the revelation of the inner mysteries of God, from the obscuring dust of all acquired knowledge, and the allusions of the embodiments of satanic fancy. He must purge his breast, which is the sanctuary of the abiding love of the Beloved, of every defilement, and sanctify his soul from all that pertaineth to water and clay, from all shadowy and ephemeral attachments. He must so cleanse his heart that no remnant of either love or hate may linger therein, lest that love blindly incline him to error, or that hate repel him away from the truth. Even as thou dost witness in this Day how most of the people, because of such love and hate, are bereft of the immortal Face, have strayed far from the Embodiments of the Divine mysteries, and, shepherdless, are roaming through the wilderness of oblivion and error.*

> *That seeker must, at all times, put his trust in God, must renounce the peoples of the earth, must detach himself from the world of dust, and cleave unto Him Who is the Lord of Lords. He must never seek to exalt himself above any one, must wash away from the tablet of his heart every trace of pride and vain-glory, must cling unto patience and resignation, observe silence and refrain*

# EPILOGUE

*from idle talk....*

    *Only when the lamp of search, of earnest striving, of longing desire, of passionate devotion, of fervid love, of rapture, and ecstasy, is kindled within the seeker's heart, and the breeze of His loving-kindness is wafted upon his soul, will the darkness of error be dispelled, the mists of doubts and misgivings be dissipated, and the lights of knowledge and certitude envelop his being. At that hour will the Mystic Herald, bearing the joyful tidings of the Spirit, shine forth from the City of God resplendent as the morn, and, through the trumpet-blast of knowledge, will awaken the heart, the soul, and the spirit from the slumber of heedlessness. Then will the manifold favors and outpouring grace of the holy and everlasting Spirit confer such new life upon the seeker that he will find himself endowed with a new eye, a new ear, a new heart, and a new mind. He will contemplate the manifest signs of the universe, and will penetrate the hidden mysteries of the soul. Gazing with the eye of God, he will perceive within every atom a door that leadeth him to the stations of absolute certitude. He will discover in all things the mysteries of Divine Revelation, and the evidences of an everlasting Manifestation.*

    *I swear by God! Were he that treadeth the path of guidance and seeketh to scale the heights of righteousness to attain unto this glorious and exalted station, he would inhale, at a distance of a thousand leagues, the fragrance of God, and would perceive the resplendent morn of a Divine guidance rising above the Day Spring of all things. Each and every thing, however small, would be to him a revelation, leading him to his Beloved, the Object of his quest. So great shall be the discernment of this seeker that he will discriminate between truth and falsehood, even as he doth distinguish the sun from shadow. If in the uttermost corners of the East the sweet savors of God be wafted, he will assuredly recognize and inhale their fragrance, even though he be dwelling in the uttermost ends of the West. He will, likewise, clearly distinguish all the signs of God—His wondrous utterances, His great works, and mighty deeds—from the doings, the words and ways of men, even as the jeweler who knoweth the gem from the stone, or the man who distinguisheth the spring from autumn, and heat from cold. When the channel of the human soul is cleansed of all worldly and impeding attachments, it will unfailingly perceive the breath of the Beloved across immeasurable distances, and will, led by its perfume, attain and enter the City of Certitude.*

*Therein he will discern the wonders of His ancient Wisdom, and will perceive all the hidden teachings from the rustling leaves of the Tree that flourisheth in that City. With both his inner and outer ear, he will hear from its dust the hymns of glory and praise ascending unto the Lord of Lords, and with his inner eye will he discover the mysteries of "return" and "revival."*

*How unspeakably glorious are the signs, the tokens, the revelations, and splendors which He, Who is the King of Names and Attributes, hath destined for that City! The attainment unto this City quencheth thirst without water, and kindleth the love of God without fire. Within every blade of grass are enshrined the mysteries of an inscrutable Wisdom, and upon every rosebush a myriad nightingales pour out, in blissful rapture, their melody. Its wondrous tulips unfold the mystery of the undying Fire in the Burning Bush, and its sweet savors of holiness breathe the perfume of the Messianic Spirit. It bestoweth wealth without gold, and conferreth immortality without death. In each one of its leaves ineffable delights are treasured, and within every chamber unnumbered mysteries lie hidden.*

*They that valiantly labor in quest of God, will, when once they have renounced all else but Him, be so attached and wedded unto that City, that a moment's separation from it would to them be unthinkable. They will hearken unto infallible proofs from the Hyacinth of that assembly, and will receive the surest testimonies from the beauty of its Rose, and the melody of its Nightingale. Once in about a thousand years shall this City be renewed and readorned.*

*Wherefore, O my friend, it behooveth Us to exert the highest endeavor to attain unto that City, and, by the grace of God and His loving-kindness, rend asunder the "veils of glory"; so that, with inflexible steadfastness, we may sacrifice our drooping souls in the path of the New Beloved. We should with tearful eyes, fervently and repeatedly, implore Him to grant us the favour of that grace. That city is none other than the Word of God revealed in every age and dispensation.*

Baha'u'llah, *The Book of Certitude*, p. 192–199

*...whoso readeth, let him understand.*
MATTHEW 24:15

# Endnotes

1. Genesis 21:13–21 & 25:12–16

2. *Muhammad: His Life Based on the Earliest Sources* by Martin Ling, chapters 39, 46, 57, and 61

3. *Muhammad: His Life Based on the Earliest Sources* by Martin Ling, pgs 301–3 & 330

4. *Muhammad: His Life Based on the Earliest Sources* by Martin Ling, pg 269

5. *The Qur'an* (Sales translation), 2:87

6. *The Euphrates Expedition*, by John S Guest, is an excellent account of this episode.

7. *The Dawn-Breakers—Nabil's Narrative*, pgs 40–42

8. *Dasam Granth* by Gobind Singh

9. *The Song of God—The Bhagavad-Gita* as translated by Swami Prabhavananda, pg 50 of 130

10. *Buddha Maitrya-Amitabha Hath Appeared*, pgs 236 to 279

11. *Buddha Maitrya-Amitabha Hath Appeared*, pg 288

12. *Buddha Maitrya-Amitabha Hath Appeared* pg 276. Additional information on Wikipedia can be found under "Surdas-Poet."

13. From the Buddha's farewell (Mahaparinirvana Sutra V, Verses 1:14) as translated in *Some Religious Weft and Warp* by Henry Warrum, pgs 54–55, Hollenbeck Press, 1915

14. *Buddhism and the Baha'i Faith*, Moojan Momen (1995) pgs 49–50

15. *Buddha Maitrya-Amitabha Hath Appeared*, pgs 282–284. See also Wikipedia article on "Pure Land Buddhism."

16. From the *Zand-i-Vohuman Yasn*, Chapter VII, verses 3 & 6, as translated by B.T. Anklesaria, Bombay, 1957. It should be noted that since the Zoroastrian scripture was memorized rather than written for about 13 centuries, the exact wording is not certain.

17. See *Journey of the Magi*, by Paul William Roberts pgs 30–38 for a non-fiction description of a modern-day visit to this site.

18. Matt.6:33

19. See, for example, *Fire on the Mountain-Top*, by Gloria Faizi, pgs 32–34 for the story of a Zoroastrian priest who was expecting their Promised One to return at this time.

20. *God Passes By*, by Shoghi Effendi, pages 58 & 95

21. See Note 17 for a non-fiction source of information on the Jameh Mosque and its presumed connections to the story of the Wise Men. The site is also visible on Google Earth.

22. *The Travels of Marco Polo*, from the Ronald Lantham translation; Harmondsworth, Middlesex; New York: Penguin Books, Penguin Classics, 1958, pg 58

23. From the Quran, as quoted in *The Dawn-Breakers—Nabil's Narrative*, pg 93

24. *The Dawn-Breakers—Nabil's Narrative*, pg 75–77

25. *TheDawn-Breakers—Nabil's Narrative*, pg 65

26. For a more detailed account of the historic story, see *The Dawn-Breakers—Nabil's Narrative*, Chapter 3.

27. This is more frequently known as *The Commentary on the Surih of Joseph*. The Surih of Joseph is the 12th chapter (aka surih) of the Qur'an and contains a more detailed version of the biblical story of Joseph in Egypt and his ultimate return to Jacob, his father. The Bab sees it as a metaphor for the return of the Promised One to mankind, who is suffering from His long absence.

28. *Selections from the Writings of the Bab*, Section 2:14, paragraph 3

29. *Selections from the Writings of the Bab*, Section 2:57

30. Qur'an 21:51–71

31. *Selections from the Writings of the Bab*, Section 2:12

32. *Selections from the Writings of the Bab*, Section 2:24

33. *Selections from the Writings of the Bab*, Section 2:3, paragraph 4

34. *The Dawn-Breakers—Nabil's Narrative*, pg 67

35. Qur'an 36:65

36. References are to Matt. 5:13–16 and 10:14

37. The five references to passages in these three paragraphs are from the Qur'an. They refer, respectively, to 89:22, 47:38, 35:10, 28:5, and 21:26–27

38. *The Dawn-Breakers—Nabil's Narrative*, pg 92

39. *Summer on the Lakes, in 1843*, by Margaret Fuller pg 128

40. Qur'an 10:47

41. *A Week on the Concord and Merrimack Rivers*, by Henry David Thoreau, pg 59

42. Psalm 46:4–5 and Chapters 56 and 108 of the Qur'an, among others

43. From Chapter XXIX of the Qayyumu'l-Asma in *Selections from the Writings of the Bab*, page 69

44. This passage can now be found in The Hidden Words, #19 (Persian). The book was revealed in the year 1274 A.H., partly in Persian, partly in Arabic, but according to Shoghi Effendi, "it was originally designated the Hidden Book of Fatimih and was identified by its author with the book of that same name, believed by Shí'ah Islam to be in the possession of the promised Qá'im and to consist of words of consolation addressed by the angel Gabriel, at God's command, to Fatimih and dictated to the Imam Ali for the sole purpose of comforting her in her hour of bitter anguish after the death of her illustrious Father." (God Passes By, p. 139)

45. *God Passes By*, by Shoghi Effendi, pg 94

46. See *1844: Convergence in Prophecy*, pgs 123–144 for more details on the evolution of the various Adventist denominations in the years after 1844.

47. *The Servant, the General and Armageddon*, pg 71

48. *The Dawn-Breakers—Nabil's Narrative*, pg 131

49. "A Note on Babi and Baha'i Numbers in Iran" by Peter Smith, published in *Iranian Studies*, Vol 17, No 2–3 (Spring–Summer 1984). The figure was given by the Bab in late 1848, according to Denis

MacEoin in an article from 1982. Stable URL: http://www.jstor.org/stable/4310446

50. *The Dawn-Breakers—Nabil's Narrative*, pg 315-6

51. *Robe of Light*, pgs 117–118

52. *Selections from the Writings of the Bab*, pg 78

53. *A Traveler's Narrative*, pg 79

54. See *God's Strange Work—William Miller and the End of the World*, pg 222. Also, *1844—Convergence in Prophecy*, pgs 146–149 for the text of Miller's story about the dream.

55. See *Memories of Nine Years in Akka*, by Younis Afroukhteh, pg 267, regarding a 108-year-old man who had been a Millerite in the 1840s and continued to search for the Promised One until the early years of the 20th century, when he discovered the teachings of the Baha'i Faith and became a member.

56. See *The Baha'i Faith in America—Origins 1892 to 1900, Vol.1*, by Robert Stockman, pg 75-77

57. *Some Answered Questions*, by 'Abdu'l-Baha, Chapter 10, paragraphs 10 to 22

58. *Gleanings from the Writings of Baha'u'llah*, Selection # III

59. Baha'u'llah, as quoted by Shoghi Effendi in *The World Order of Baha'u'llah*, pg. 102

60. *The Proclamation of Baha'u'llah*, pgs 111-112

# Bibliography

CHRISTIAN TOPICS:

*The Bible* (King James Version)—Note that this was the main English version of the Bible in use during the time period in which the story takes place.

*The Apocryphal Books of the New Testament* edited by William Hone, 1890. (Note that the *Syriac Infancy Gospel* can also be found in *The Suppressed Gospels and Epistles of the Original New Testament of Jesus Christ, Vol. 3, Infancy of Jesus Christ,* by William Wake, Aeterna Publishing, 2010)

*God's Strange Work: William Miller and the End of the World,* by David L. Rowe, William B. Eerdmans Publishing, 2008

*Evidence from Scripture and History of the Second Coming of Christ,* by William Miller, 1840, reprinted by Isha Books, New Delhi, 2013

*The Prophecies of Jesus* by Michael Sours, One World Publications, Ltd, Oxford, England, 1991

# BIBLIOGRAPHY

## ZOROASTRIANISM/MAGI:

*The Magi: From Zoroaster to the "Three Wise Men"* by Ken R. Vincent, BIBAL Press/D&F Scott Publishing, North Richland Hills, Texas, 1999

*The Man Who Sent the Magi*, by Douglas Roper Krotz, Intermedia Publishing Group, Peoria, AZ, 2011

*The Journey of the Magi*, by Paul William Roberts, Tauris Parke Paperbacks, New York, NY, 2006

*Fire on the Mountain-top*, by Gloria Faizi, Baha'i Publishing Trust, New Delhi, 2003

*In Search of Zarathustra*, by Paul Kriwaczek, Vintage Books, New York, 2002

*The Death of Ahriman* a dissertation by Susan Maneck, K.R. Cama Oriental Institute, 1997

*History of Iran: An Empire of the Mind*, by Michael Axworthy, Basic Books, New York, NY, 2008

*Zand-i-Vohuman Yasn*, Chapter VII, verses 3 & 6, as translated by B.T. Anklesaria, Bombay, 1957. Also from www.avesta.org/mp/vohuman.html

*The Travels of Marco Polo*, Ronald Lantham translation, New York, NY: Penguin Books, 1958

## ISLAM:

*The Qur'an* as translated by George Sales in 1734—Note that this version was generally used because it was the main English version of the Qur'an available during the time period in which the story takes place. Occasionally, the Picktall translation was used.

*Muhammad: His Life Based on the Earliest Sources* by Martin Lings, Inner Traditions, Rochester, Vermont 2006

*Salman al Farsi* by Muhammad 'Ali-Qutb, Ta-Ha Publishers Ltd, London, 1994

*The Last Day* by Wahlied Jassat, George Ronald Publishers, Oxford, 2012

*An Introduction to Shi'i Islam* by Moojan Momen, George Ronald Publishers, Oxford, 1985

*Islam and the Baha'i Faith* by Moojan Momen, George Ronald Publisher, Oxford, 2000.

*Muhammad and the Course of Islam* by H. M. Balyuzi, George Ronald Publisher, Oxford, 1976

*The House of Wisdom—How Arabic Science Saved Ancient Knowledge and Gave Us the Renaissance* by Jim al-Khalili, Penguin Press, NY 2011

## JUDAISM:

*Hastening Redemption: Messianism and the Resettlement of the Land of Israel* 1st Edition by Arie Morgenstern (Author), Joel A. Linsider (Translator), Oxford Univ Press 2006

*Zohar*, the book of Jewish mysticism, is available from many sources.

# BIBLIOGRAPHY

## SIKHISM:

*Dasam Granth* by Gobind Singh (Various English translations are available.)

## HINDUISM:

*The Song of God: Bhagavad-Gita* translated be Swami Prabhavananda and Christopher Isherwood, 1952

*Hinduism and the Baha'i Faith* by Moojan Momen, George Ronald Publisher, Oxford, 1990

## BUDDHISM:

*Buddha Maitrya-Amitabha has Appeared* by Jamshed Fozdar (1ˢᵗ edition primarily; the 2ⁿᵈ edition also)

*Buddhism and the Baha'i Faith* by Moojan Momen, George Ronald Publisher, Oxford, 1995

*Some Religious Weft and Warp* by Henry Warrum, Hollenbeck Press, 1915

## BABI / BAHA'I (HISTORY):

*The Dawn-Breakers—Nabil's Narrative* Baha'i Publishing Trust, Wilmette, IL, 1932

*The Bab* by H. M. Balyuzi, George Ronald Publisher, Oxford 1973

*God Passes By* by Shoghi Effendi, Baha'i Publishing Trust, Wilmette, IL, 1970

*The Chosen Highway* by Lady Bloomfield, Baha'i Publishing Trust, Wilmette, IL, 1970

*Studies in Babi & Baha'i History, Vol. 1* edited by Moojan Momen, Kalimat Press, Los Angeles, 1982

*The Baha'i Faith in America, Vol. 1* by Robert Stockman, Baha'i Publishing Trust, Wilmette IL, 1985

*The Baha'i Faith in America, Vol. 2* by Robert Stockman, George Ronald Publisher, Oxford, 1995

*The 1844 Ottoman "Edict of Toleration" in Baha'i Secondary Literature* by Michael W. Sours, Journal of Baha'i Studies, Vol 8. No. 3.1998, pgs 5–80

*Mulla Husayn—Disciple at Dawn* by R. Mehrabkhani, Kalimat Press, Los Angeles, 1987

*'Alí Bastámí, Mullá*—Article in the Baha'i Encyclopedia, by Moojan Momen, 2009 (http://bahai- library.com/bahai_encyclopedia_ali_ bastami )

*Rejoice in My Gladness—The Life of Tahirih* by Janet Ruhe Schoen, Baha'i Publishing Trust, Wilmette IL, 2011

*Robe of Light* by David S. Ruhe, George Ronald Publisher, Oxford 1994

*Gate of the Heart* by Nader Saiedi, Wilfrid Laurier University Press, 2008

*Resurrection and Renewal* by Abbas Amanat, Kalimat Press, Los Angeles, 1989

# BIBLIOGRAPHY

*The Servant, the General and Armageddon*, by Roderic Maude & Derwent Maude, George Ronald Publisher, Oxford 1998

*Memories of Nine Years in Akka*, by Younis Afroukhteh, George Ronald Publisher, Oxford, 2005

*Iranian Studies*, "A Note on Babi and Baha'i Numbers in Iran," Vol 17, No. 2–3 (Spring–Summer 1984)


## BABI / BAHA'I (GENERAL):


*Selections from the Writings of the Bab*, Baha'i Publications of Australia, 2011

*The Book of Certitude (Kitab-i-Iqan)* by Baha'u'llah, Baha'i Publishing Trust, Wilmette, IL 1950

*The Proclamation of Baha'u'llah*, (a compilation of quotations), Baha'i World Centre, Haifa, 1972

*Epistle to the Son of the Wolf*, by Baha'u'llah, Baha'i Publishing Trust, Wilmette, IL 1969

*Gleanings from the Writings of Baha'u'llah*, Baha'i Publishing Trust, Wilmette, IL 1952

*The Hidden Words* by Baha'u'llah, Baha'i Publishing Trust, Wilmette, IL 2012

*The Seven Valleys*, by Baha'u'llah, Baha'i Publishing Trust, Wilmette, IL 1978

*Some Answered Questions*, by 'Abdu'l-Baha, Baha'i World Centre, 2014

*A Traveler's Narrative* by 'Abdu'l-Baha, Baha'i Publishing Trust, Wilmette, IL, 1980 edition

*Baha'i Scriptures,* (a compilation, edited by Horace Holley), Brentano's Publisher, 1923

*The World Order of Baha'u'llah* by Shoghi Effendi, Baha'i Publishing Trust, Wilmette, IL 1955


RELIGIOUS HISTORY (MULTIPLE RELIGIONS):


*Persia and the Bible* by Edwin M. Yamauchi, Baker Book House, Grand Rapids, MI 1990

*Evolution of Human Spirituality*, a lecture series by Dr. Ron Hershel, Menucha, Oregon, 2002

*Founders of Faith* by Harold Rosen, Baha'i Publishing Trust, Wilmette, IL 2010

*The War of the Three Gods* by Peter Crawford, Skyhorse Publishing, 2014

*1844–Convergence in Prophecy for Judaism, Christianity, Islam and the Baha'i Faith* by Eileen Maddocks, Jewel Press, Burlington, Vermont, 2018


GENERAL (TO PROVIDE HISTORICAL CONTEXT):


*The Euphrates Expedition* by John S Guest, Kegan Paul International Ltd, London (1992)

*The Year Without Summer—1816 and the Volcano That Darkened the World and Changed History* by William K. Klingaman & Nicholas P. Klingaman, St Martin's Press, NY, 2013

*Summer on the Lakes, in 1843,* by Margaret Fuller, University of Illinois Press, 1991

# BIBLIOGRAPHY

*A Week on the Concord and Merrimack Rivers* by Henry David Thoreau, Blackmask Online (Blackmask.com), 2001

*Embraced by the Light* by Betty J. Eadie, Gold Leaf Press, Placerville, CA (1992)


## WEBSITES:


Wikipedia, for checking all sorts of miscellaneous historical items

Google Earth—It is virtually as good as being there.

The Wilmette Institute provided several short courses that provided much helpful background material.

Prophecy Fulfilled (prophecies from all religions that point to the coming of the Bab and Baha'u'llah)—http://prophecy-fulfilled.com

Adventist Digital Library—https://adventistdigitallibrary.org/ADL-14800/advent-herald . (Select 1844 from the "Year of publication" drop down menu.)


## AUDIO LECTURES:


*The Apocalypse: Controversies and Meaning in Western History* by Craig R. Koester of Luther Seminary, The Great Courses, Chantilly, Virginia, 2011

*Turning Points in Middle Eastern History* by Eamonn Gearon of Johns Hopkins University, The Great Courses, Chantilly, Virginia, 2016

*The Ottoman Empire* by Kenneth W. Harl of Tulane University, The Great Courses, Chantilly, Virginia, 2017

*The World's Great Religions: Buddhism* by Malcom David Eckel of Boston University, The Great Courses, Chantilly, Virginia, 2003

*The Persian Empire* by John W. I. Lee, University of California at Santa Barbara, The Great Courses, Chantilly, Virginia, 2012

*Sacred Text of the World* by Grant Hardy, University of North Carolina at Asheville, 2014

*The Barbarian Empires of the Steppes* by Kenneth W. Harl of Tulane University, The Great Courses, Chantilly, Virginia, 2014

# About the Author

JAY TYSON grew up outside of Detroit, Michigan, and graduated from Princeton University with a degree in civil engineering in 1976. Shortly thereafter, he married Eileen Cregge. They spent four years in Liberia, where Jay worked on road construction projects. They also spent seven years in Haifa, Israel, where he assisted with historic restoration at the Baha'i World Center. They returned to New Jersey in 1989, where they raised two daughters and Jay continued his career in civil engineering.

Raised in a Presbyterian household, Jay was apt from an early age to deeply ponder spiritual matters. The suicides of three men in his upper-middle-class neighborhood over the course of a few years caused him to question the idea that material success holds the key to fulfillment and happiness.

He became a member of the Baha'i Faith in 1970 and has long observed a daily regime of reading scriptures or books on religion and religious history. *The Wise Men of the West* is his first novel and reflects his commitment to studying religion, history, and geography. Jay may be reached at Jay.Tyson@SOOPLLC.com.

www.ingramcontent.com/pod-product-compliance
Lightning Source LLC
Chambersburg PA
CBHW072033090426
42733CB00032B/1288